On the Currency of Egalitarian Justice, and Other Essays in Political Philosophy

On the Currency of Egalitarian Justice, and Other Essays in Political Philosophy

G. A. COHEN

Edited by Michael Otsuka

PRINCETON UNIVERSITY PRESS
PRINCETON AND OXFORD

Published by Princeton University Press, 41 William Street, Princeton, New Jersey 08540
In the United Kingdom: Princeton University Press, 6 Oxford Street, Woodstock, Oxfordshire OX20 1TW

press.princeton.edu

Library of Congress Cataloging-in-Publication Data

Cohen, G. A. (Gerald Allan), 1941–2009.
On the currency of egalitarian justice, and other essays in political philosophy / G. A. Cohen ; edited by Michael Otsuka.
p. cm.
Includes bibliographical references and index.
ISBN 978-0-691-14870-0 (hardcover : alk. paper) — ISBN 978-0-691-14871-7 (pbk. : alk. paper) 1. Equality. 2. Capitalism. 3. Distributive justice. 4. Social justice. 5. Communism. 6. Political science—Philosophy. I. Otsuka, Michael. II. Title.
HM821.C645 2011
306.3′42—dc22 2010020742

British Library Cataloging-in-Publication Data is available

This book has been composed in Sabon

Printed on acid-free paper. ∞

Printed in the United States of America

1 3 5 7 9 10 8 6 4 2

CONTENTS

EDITOR'S PREFACE

AT THE TIME OF HIS DEATH IN AUGUST 2009, G. A. Cohen had plans to bring together a number of his previously uncollected papers but had not yet chosen which ones to collect. This volume is an attempt to fulfill those plans. Cohen's selections were to have been informed by a list of "prime articles" that he had compiled in 2005 while preparing a collection to be published in Chinese translation.[1] Although most of the listed articles have already appeared in one or another of Cohen's six books published in English, nine of them have not. This volume publishes five of these nine articles, either in whole or in part, and the other four will be published, along with other writings, in one or another of two forthcoming volumes of Cohen's work.[2]

The five that are published here are "On the Currency of Egalitarian Justice," "Capitalism, Freedom, and the Proletariat," "Illusions about Private Property and Freedom," "Freedom and Money," and "Back to Socialist Basics." This volume brings together those and other publications, plus some unpublished material, that fall squarely within the category of contemporary political philosophy. Three of Cohen's six books mentioned above have already brought together previously published papers in contemporary political philosophy.[3] Although the papers reprinted in this volume were originally published as long ago as 1981, none of them had been excluded from any of those three collections on grounds of quality. Rather, as I shall explain below, they were uncollected because they fell outside the organizing concepts of any of the previous collections. Cohen left us with thematically distinct and coherent bodies of outstanding work in contemporary political philosophy for collection here. The major theme of this book is "luck egalitarianism," which is the name Cohen borrowed to describe his view that "accidental inequality is

[1] This collection was published as *Between Marx and Nozick* in 2007.

[2] One of these books will collect Cohen's writings on the history of moral and political philosophy, and another will collect various philosophical reflections along with some memoirs.

[3] These three books are *Self-Ownership, Freedom, and Equality* (1995), *If You're an Egalitarian, How Come You're So Rich?* (2000), and *Rescuing Justice and Equality* (2008). The reprinted papers were often extensively revised for these volumes, which also included previously unpublished papers. (Cohen's other three books are *Karl Marx's Theory of History* [1978, rev. ed. 2000], *History, Labour, and Freedom* [1988], and *Why Not Socialism?* [2009].)

unjust."[4] Two minor themes are the relation between property and freedom and between ideal theory and political practice. These three themes form the three parts of this book.

"On the Currency," which has been reprinted as the first chapter of this book, is Cohen's best-known and most widely cited article. This was the paper in which Cohen first advanced and defended his luck egalitarian thesis that "the right reading of egalitarianism" is "that its purpose is to eliminate *involuntary disadvantage*." By 'disadvantage' he meant an individual's shortfall in resources, capacities, or welfare. Such a shortfall was involuntary, on Cohen's account, when it did not appropriately reflect the choices of the sufferer.

"On the Currency" traces its origin to a paper that Cohen prepared for a World Institute for Development Economics Research (WIDER) symposium, "The Quality of Life," in Helsinki in July 1988. The symposium paper was too long for publication as an article or book chapter, and Cohen therefore divided it into two partially overlapping parts. The larger part was published as "On the Currency" in 1989, and the rest of it was published as "Equality of What?" in the following year. The views of Ronald Dworkin and T. M. Scanlon provided the distinctive critical focus of "Currency," whereas "Equality of What?" was oriented around the views of Amartya Sen. In bringing these two papers back together as Chapters 1 and 2 of this volume, I have eliminated most of the overlap between them through an abridgment of "Equality of What?"

I have also included a previously unpublished Afterword to these two chapters that Cohen wrote in the early nineties when he intended to reprint this pair of articles as the concluding chapters of his 1995 collection *Self-Ownership, Freedom, and Equality*. Cohen ultimately decided against publication there on grounds that these two papers detracted from that book's focus on Nozick, self-ownership, and world-ownership and would be better placed in a later collection around the theme of egalitarian justice. The ideal of equality figured prominently in Cohen's next two books—*If You're an Egalitarian* and *Rescuing Justice and Equality*. But since these works were an unanticipated flowering of a critique of Rawls that was rooted in Cohen's Tanner Lectures from the early nineties,[5] it turned out once again that inclusion of "Currency" and "Equality of What?" would have been out of place.

During his extended period of reflection on Rawls, Cohen continued to be engaged by the debate over luck egalitarianism that "On the Cur-

[4] See *Rescuing Justice and Equality*, p. 8. Elizabeth Anderson coined the term 'luck egalitarianism' in her "What Is the Point of Equality?"

[5] See "Incentives, Inequality, and Community."

rency" and "Equality of What?" had played a major role in shaping. He published work consisting of defenses, clarifications, and refinements of his earlier arguments and conclusions. Part I (Chapters 1–6) of this book collects most of these subsequent articles along with the original pair.

Chapter 3 ("Sen on Capability, Freedom, and Control") consists of excerpts from a review of Amartya Sen's *Inequality Reexamined*. I have chosen to reprint those passages which provide an illuminatingly clear and simple statement of Sen's notion of 'capability' and which expand upon Cohen's critique of Sen on freedom in "Equality of What?"

Chapters 4 and 5 arose as responses to criticisms of "Currency" by Ronald Dworkin and Susan Hurley, respectively.

Cohen's was a more comprehensively luck egalitarian position than Dworkin's insofar as it was opposed to unchosen disadvantage in the denomination of welfare. Chapter 4 ("Expensive Taste Rides Again") offers a robust and extended defense of the welfarist component of Cohen's egalitarian principle of distribution against Dworkin's objections to the subsidy of expensive tastes that the equalization of people's opportunities for welfare requires.[6]

Chapter 5 ("Luck and Equality") defends Cohen's claim, in "Currency," that "a large part of the fundamental egalitarian aim is to extinguish the effect of brute luck on distribution," where brute luck consists of differences in fortune that are not a reflection of choice.

'Brute luck' is to be contrasted with 'option luck,' where the latter consists of differences in fortune that are the upshot of chosen gambles.[7] Whereas Cohen had previously endorsed Dworkin's view that egalitarian justice does not call for the compensation of those whose misfortune is purely down to bad option luck,[8] in Chapter 6 ("Fairness and Legitimacy in Justice") he voices sympathy for the conflicting position that option luck never preserves the justice of the prior distribution. Cohen's skepticism regarding the justice of option luck, as voiced in this, his last

[6] I should explain why I have not collected an earlier and related piece by Cohen entitled "Expensive Tastes and Multiculturalism." His claim in that paper that state support for minority cultures is analogous to the subsidy of an "expensive taste" has left a mark on the literature on multiculturalism. Moreover, this paper was published in a book that is hard to obtain. Nevertheless, I believe that Cohen would not have wanted to reprint it in a collection of his work, as he came to believe that his discussion of multiculturalism rested upon a misrepresentation of the work of Will Kymlicka. In an email of June 2009, he wrote: "I should warn that I don't think the article is very good. Its best bits were extracted and developed in my later article 'Expensive Taste Rides Again' [i.e., Chapter 4 of this volume—Ed.]. They are the bits that aren't about multiculturalism in particular."

[7] The terminology is Dworkin's. See his "Equality of Resources," p. 293, and p. 131 of this volume below.

[8] See, for examples, the first paragraph, including n. 3, of Section 2 of Chapter 1 and Cohen's remarks on "Shirley" in Section 10 of Chapter 4 of this volume.

published word on the subject, was another respect in which his version of luck egalitarianism was more thoroughly opposed than Dworkin's to differences in advantage that are a matter of good or bad fortune.

The relation between freedom and property is the theme of Part II (Chapters 7 and 8) of this book.

In the concluding sentence of "Robert Nozick and Wilt Chamberlain" (1977), which was Cohen's debut publication in normative political philosophy, he wrote that "it should now be clear that 'libertarian' capitalism sacrifices liberty to capitalism, a truth its advocates are able to deny only because they are prepared to abuse the language of freedom."[9] Cohen's subsequent writings on freedom can be seen as developments and further vindication of that early charge.

This case against libertarianism achieved refined form in the revised version of "Capitalism, Freedom, and the Proletariat" (1991), which is reprinted as Chapter 7. The "principal contention" of this paper "is that, while liberals and libertarians see the freedom which is intrinsic to capitalism, they overlook the unfreedom which necessarily accompanies capitalist freedom." Moreover, the socialist communalization of capitalist private property would often be "in the interest of liberty itself."

Cohen had published an earlier version of this paper in 1979, and his revised version drew heavily on two papers published during the intervening period: "Illusions about Private Property and Freedom" (1981) and "The Structure of Proletarian Unfreedom" (1983, and, in revised form, 1988). Although "Illusions" appeared along with "Capitalism, Freedom, and the Proletariat" on Cohen's list of "prime articles," this volume does not reprint the former in full, since most of that article, and everything that was central to its main lines of argument, was incorporated in revised and more tightly focused form into the revised version of "Capitalism, Freedom, and the Proletariat" included here. The volume does, however, include an Appendix to Chapter 7 that consists of a section of "Illusions" to which Cohen referred in a footnote to "Capitalism, Freedom, and the Proletariat." I have also added a footnote of my own that reproduces a passage from "Illusions" which extends some remarks on communal versus private property in "Capitalism, Freedom, and the Proletariat."

The above articles showed the ways in which the property holdings of *others* constrain a person's freedom. Cohen noted, for example, that another's title deed to his back garden restricts my freedom to pitch my tent on that stretch of land. When he returned to this topic in "Freedom and Money" (2001), which is reprinted as Chapter 8, Cohen showed how a

[9] P. 21.

person's *own* holdings—his money, to be more precise—confer freedom upon him, and how his "lack of money, poverty, carries with it lack of freedom." I have also included two previously unpublished Addenda to "Freedom and Money": one on the relation between freedom and ability, which rejects Cohen's earlier stance on this topic, and another on goods, services, and interference.

Part III (Chapters 9–12) consists, among other things, of reflections on the relation between ideal theory and political practice.

In Chapter 9 ("Mind the Gap"), which is an abridged version of a review of Nagel's *Equality and Partiality*, Cohen argues that Nagel misapplies moral theory in defense of existing practice when he appeals to the "distinction between the impersonal and personal standpoints" in a manner that privileges the status quo and the inequalities it contains.

In Chapter 10 ("Back to Socialist Basics"), Cohen argues that "[f]undamental socialist values which point to a form of society a hundred miles from the horizon of present possibility are needed to defend every half-mile of territory gained and to mount an attempt to regain each bit that has been lost."

Chapter 11 ("How to Do Political Philosophy") is a previously unpublished paper that Cohen presented at the first session of a standing Oxford M.Phil. Seminar on Contemporary Political Philosophy. In the original version of this paper, the material included in this volume was followed by a critique of Rawlsian constructivism that drew on a distinction between fundamental normative principles of justice and optimal rules of social regulation that Cohen was honing as he completed his book *Rescuing Justice and Equality*. This critique later took the expanded form of a paper—published here as Chapter 12 ("Rescuing Justice")—that Cohen delivered as an academic talk while that book was in press.

I'm grateful to my editor, Ian Malcolm, for taking a special interest in this project and moving things along so swiftly and smoothly, to Lauren Lepow, for acutely observant copyediting, and to Kimberley Johnson, for her editorial assistance. Hillel Steiner and Andrew Williams served as readers for Princeton University Press, and I've benefited from their excellent judgment at several points. I'm grateful to Patrick Tomlin and Juri Viehoff for their assistance in preparing the index and checking the page proofs, and to All Souls College for funding their efforts. Special thanks to Jerry Cohen's wife, Michèle, and his three children, Gideon, Miriam, and Sarah, for all their support.

ACKNOWLEDGMENTS

The following works, which constitute all or part of the chapters numbered below, have been reprinted, with gratefully acknowledged permission where appropriate:

1. "On the Currency of Egalitarian Justice." *Ethics* 99 (1989): 906–44.
2. "Equality of What? On Welfare, Goods, and Capabilities." In Martha C. Nussbaum and Amartya Sen, eds. *The Quality of Life*. Oxford: Oxford University Press, 1993. Reprinted in part.
3. "Amartya Sen's Unequal World." *New Left Review*, No. 203, January–February 1994, pp. 117–29. Reprinted in part. The complete version can be found online at www.newleftreview.org.
4. "Expensive Taste Rides Again." In Justine Burley, ed. *Dworkin and His Critics*. Oxford: Blackwell, 2004.
5. "Luck and Equality: A Reply to Hurley." *Philosophy and Phenomenological Research* 72 (2006): 439–46.
6. "Fairness and Legitimacy in Justice, And: Does Option Luck Ever Preserve Justice?" In S. de Wijze, M. H. Kramer, and I. Carter, eds. *Hillel Steiner and the Anatomy of Justice*. New York: Routledge, 2009.
7. (i) "Capitalism, Freedom, and the Proletariat." In David Miller, ed. *The Liberty Reader*. Edinburgh: Edinburgh University Press, 2006.
   (ii) "Illusions about Private Property and Freedom." In Steven Cahn, ed. *Philosophy for the 21st Century: A Comprehensive Reader*. Oxford: Oxford University Press, 2002. Reprinted in part.
8. "Freedom and Money." *Revista Argentina de Teoria Juridica* 2 (2001): 1–32.
9. "Mind the Gap." *London Review of Books*, Vol. 14, No. 9, May 14, 1992, pp. 15–17. Reprinted in part. The complete version can be found online at www.lrb.co.uk.
10. "Back to Socialist Basics." *New Left Review*, No. 207, September–October 1994, pp. 3–16. Reprinted in part. The complete version can be found online at www.newleftreview.org.
12. *Rescuing Justice and Equality*. Cambridge, Mass.: Harvard University Press, 2008. Reprinted in part.

The Afterword to Chapters 1 and 2, Addenda to Chapter 8, all of Chapter 11, and part of Chapter 12 are previously unpublished.

PART ONE

Luck Egalitarianism

Chapter One

ON THE CURRENCY OF EGALITARIAN JUSTICE

1. Introduction

In his Tanner Lecture of 1979 called "Equality of What?" Amartya Sen asked what metric egalitarians should use to establish the extent to which their ideal is realized in a given society. What aspect(s) of a person's condition should count in a *fundamental* way for egalitarians, and not merely as cause of or evidence of or proxy for what they regard as fundamental?

In this study I examine answers to that question, and discussions bearing on that question, in recent philosophical literature. I take for granted that there is something which justice requires people to have equal amounts of, not no matter what, but to whatever extent is allowed by values which compete with distributive equality; and I study what a number of authors who share that egalitarian view have said about the dimension(s) or respect(s) in which people should be made more equal, when the price in other values of moving toward greater equality is not intolerable.

I also advance an answer of my own to Sen's question. My answer is the product of an immanent critique of Ronald Dworkin, one, that is, which rejects Dworkin's declared position because it is not congruent with its own underlying motivation. My response to Dworkin has been influenced by Richard Arneson's work in advocacy of "equality of opportunity for welfare," but my answer to Sen's question is not that Arnesonian one, nor is my answer as well formulated as Arneson's is.[1] It needs much further refinement, but I nevertheless present it here, in a rough-and-ready form, because of its association with relatively finished criticisms of others which I think are telling. If this study contributes to understanding, it does so more because of those criticisms than because of the positive doctrine it affirms.

"On the Currency of Egalitarian Justice." *Ethics* 99 (1989): 906–44. By permission of The University of Chicago Press.

[1] See Arneson, "Equality and Equal Opportunity for Welfare." My criticisms of Dworkin were conceived without knowledge of Arneson's partly parallel ones, but it was reading Arneson which caused me to see what positive view my criticisms implied, even though that view is not the same as Arneson's.

In Section 2 of the article I distinguish between egalitarian theses of different strengths, and I indicate that certain (not all) counterexamples to stronger sorts of theses fail to disturb correlative weaker ones.

Section 3 scrutinizes two Rawlsian criticisms of equality of welfare. The first says that an uncorrected welfare metric wrongly equates pleasures and preferences which differ in moral character. It puts the pleasure of domination, for example, on a par with pleasure from an innocent pastime, where the two are equal in intensity. And the second criticism says that the welfare metric caters unjustifiably to expensive tastes which are generated by, for example, their bearer's lack of self-discipline. Those criticisms defeat equality of welfare, but, so I claim, they do not, as Rawls thinks, also induce support for a primary goods metric, and the second criticism is, moreover, hard to reconcile with Rawls's views on effort and desert.

Ronald Dworkin refines and extends both Rawlsian criticisms of equality of welfare, although primary goods are replaced by resources in the Dworkinian development of the Rawlsian view. In Section 4 I show that much of Dworkin's critique of equality of welfare will be met if egalitarians allow deviations from equality of welfare which reflect people's choices: that is, Arneson's *equal opportunity for welfare* theory. But some of Dworkin's objections to equality of welfare cannot be handled in Arneson's way, and the right response to them is to affirm what I call *equal access to advantage*, where "advantage" is understood to include, but to be wider than, welfare. Under equal access to advantage, the fundamental distinction for an egalitarian is between choice and luck in the shaping of people's fates. I argue that Dworkin's different master distinction, between preferences and resources, is less true to the motivation of his own philosophy than the one I favor is.

Thomas Scanlon argues, however, that the fact that a person chose to develop a certain taste is only superficially significant for distributive justice. The reason, he says, why egalitarians do not compensate people for chosen expensive tastes is that those tastes, being chosen, are ones which they might not have had. According to Scanlon, it is not their chosen but their peripheral or idiosyncratic character which explains why expensive tastes have no claim to be satisfied. In Section 5 I defend my emphasis on choice against Scanlon's skepticism, but I also significantly amend the choice-centered egalitarian proposal to cater to what seems undeniable in Scanlon's case against it.

Finally, in Section 6, I claim that Amartya Sen's writings on "capability" introduce two answers to his "Equality of what?" question, each of which has its attractions but which differ substantially in content, as I shall show at length elsewhere.[2]

[2] See my "Equality of What?" [reprinted as Chapter 2 of this volume—Ed.].

2. Methodological Preliminaries

A person is *exploited* when unfair advantage is taken of him, and he suffers from (bad) *brute luck* when his bad luck is not the result of a gamble or risk which he could have avoided.[3] I believe that the primary egalitarian impulse is to extinguish the influence on distribution of both exploitation and brute luck. To be sure, principled non- and antiegalitarians also condemn (what they consider to be) exploitation, but they do not have the same view of exploitation as egalitarians have, partly because they are less disturbed by brute-luck-derived asset differences which skew distributive outcomes.

On the foregoing sketch of the primary egalitarian impulse, a statement which purports to express and assert it is exposed to two kinds of challenge. First, such a statement might be criticized for misidentifying what should, in the light of the fundamental egalitarian aim, be equalized. I shall myself so criticize Dworkin's equality of resources proposal, since I think that (among other things) it penalizes people who have tastes for which they cannot be held responsible but which, unluckily for them, cost a lot to satisfy. But one might also reject equality of resources on the quite different ground that it conflicts with some important nonegalitarian values. One might say, for example, that while it is indeed brute luck which distributes children into rich and poor families, it would be wrong to seek rectification of the results of that luck, since that would undermine the institution of the family.

In this article I shall not discuss problems for egalitarian proposals of that second kind, problems, that is, of trade-off between equality and other values. That is because I shall treat the various egalitarian proposals to be reviewed below as *weak equalisandum claims*.

An *equalisandum* claim specifies that which ought to be equalized, what, that is, people should be rendered equal in. An unqualified or *strong equalisandum* claim, which is the sort that an uncompromising egalitarian asserts, says that people should be as equal as possible in the dimension it specifies. A qualified or *weak equalisandum* claim says that they should be as equal as possible in some dimension but subject to whatever limitations need to be imposed in deference to other values: those limitations are not specified by the claim in question.

Now, strong *equalisandum* claims face objections of the two kinds distinguished above, and which I shall now call *egalitarian* and *nonegalitarian* objections. An egalitarian objection rests on a view about the right way to treat people equally which differs from the one embodied in the

[3] The latter kind of luck is *option luck*. The distinction between brute and option luck comes from Dworkin, "Equality of Resources," p. 293.

strong *equalisandum* claim it challenges. The egalitarian objector thinks that people should be equal, to some or other extent, in something other than what the claim he opposes specifies, but he does not, qua egalitarian objector, object to the *strength* of that claim as such. By contrast, a nonegalitarian objection to a strong *equalisandum* claim says that, while the claim might (and might not) correctly identify what should be equalized, it wrongly fails to defer to nonegalitarian values which restrict the extent to which the form of equality it proposes should be pursued: because of those values, so the objection says, the *equalisandum* proposal is unacceptable (at least) in its strong form. An egalitarian objection to a strong *equalisandum* claim also applies to the weak one correlative to it, whereas a nonegalitarian objection challenges strong proposals only. Since mine will be a weak proposal, objections of a nonegalitarian kind will not detain me.

Taking welfare as a sample *equalisandum* proposal, I shall presently illustrate the distinction I have tried to draw by describing supposed objections to the welfare *equalisandum* which are (*i*) plainly not egalitarian, (*ii*) arguably, and so I believe, egalitarian, and (*iii*) problematic with respect to how they should be classified. But, before embarking on that exercise in differentiation, a word about what I shall mean by 'welfare' here, and throughout this study. Of the many readings of 'welfare' alive (if not well) in economics and philosophy, I am interested in two: welfare as enjoyment, or, more broadly, as a desirable or agreeable state of consciousness, which I shall call *hedonic welfare*; and welfare as *preference satisfaction*, where preferences order states of the world, and where a person's preference is satisfied if a state of the world that he prefers obtains, whether or not he knows that it does[4] and, *a fortiori*, whatever hedonic welfare he does or does not get as a result of its obtaining. A person's hedonic welfare increases as he gets more enjoyment, and his preference satisfaction increases as more of his preferences, or his stronger

[4] These two readings of welfare correspond to Sen's "happiness" and "desire fulfillment" readings and exclude his "choice" reading (see Sen, "Well-Being, Agency and Freedom," pp. 187ff.). It is reasonable to ignore the "choice" reading, since, as Sen shows, it comes from confusion about the relationship between preference and choice. My two readings also correspond to Dworkin's "conscious state" and "relative success" conceptions (see Dworkin, "Equality of Welfare," pp. 191–94, 204–9, 220–21). I do not consider welfare as "overall success" (ibid., pp. 209ff.) because it is very hard to handle, and in any case it is, arguably, undermotivated (see n. 34 below). I also set aside so-called objective theories of welfare (ibid., pp. 224–26), since most philosophers would consider them alternatives to any sort of welfare theory: Scanlon, for whom welfare is preference satisfaction, would describe his theory as antiwelfarist, yet it is an objective theory of welfare in Dworkin's sense. Finally, to complete the review of the five thinkers whose work is salient in this study, Arneson has the same understanding of welfare as Scanlon does, and Rawls has not specified a particular conception, which is not to say that he should have done.

preferences, are fulfilled. Note that one way to achieve more preference satisfaction is to cultivate, if you can, preferences that are easier to satisfy than those which you currently have.

It will sometimes be necessary to say which of those two ideas I mean by 'welfare,' but not always. For very often the debates on which I comment have a similar shape under either interpretation of welfare, so that I shall have each in mind (by which I do not mean some amalgam of the two) at once. Unless I indicate otherwise, my contentions are meant to hold under either of the two readings of welfare which I just distinguished, and the rest of the present section is a case in point.

(i) Many people think that a policy of equalizing welfare is inconsistent with the maintenance of family values, because, so they say, those values endorse practices of benefiting loved ones which generate welfare inequalities.

Now, however penetrating that point may be, it does not represent an egalitarian objection to equality of welfare. Unregulated kinship generosity may be precious on other grounds, but it could not be thought to promote the result that people get an equal amount of something that they should have equal amounts of. Accordingly, if the family values objection indeed has force against equality of welfare, it is a reason for restricting the writ of that particular *equalisandum*, or form of equality, and not a reason for proposing another *equalisandum* in its stead. Family values do not challenge equality of welfare when the latter is construed as a qualified *equalisandum* proposal.

Another objection to unqualified equality of welfare which is not egalitarian is that implementing it would involve intolerably intrusive state surveillance.[5] ("Hi! I'm from the Ministry of Equality. Are you, by any chance, unusually happy today?") Gathering the information needed to apply unqualified equality of resources might well involve less intrusion, and that would be *a* reason for preferring unqualified equality of resources to unqualified equality of welfare, but not one which impugned the egalitarian character of equality of welfare.[6]

Still another nonegalitarian objection to equality of welfare is that, if priority were always given to relieving misery, then no resources could be devoted to maintaining cathedrals and other creations of inestimable

[5] I do not have in mind the objection that the level of welfare a person enjoys is none of the state's business. I mean the objection that, whether or not welfare levels are any business of the state, the procedures necessary to find out what they are would be unacceptably invasive.

[6] Recall that "an egalitarian objection *rests* on a view about the right way to treat people equally" (see p. 5 above). Hence, even if the "intrusion" objection to unqualified equality of welfare *issued in* support for unqualified equality of resources, it would not therefore be an egalitarian objection.

value. That powerful objection to uncompromising equality of welfare does not challenge the claim that, to the extent that equalization is defensible, welfare is the right thing to equalize.

(ii) Consider people who convert resources into welfare inefficiently, so that, if welfare is to be equalized, they must be given twice the resources that ordinary converters get. These bad converters divide into various subsets. Some of them are inefficient because they are negligent or feckless in a morally culpable way: they buy their food at Fortnum's because they cannot be bothered to walk up to the Berwick Street market. Others are blamelessly inefficient, because they are in some way disabled. They need twice the normal ration because half of such a double-share is required to overcome the illfare effects of a handicap from which they suffer. That half could be the cost of their renal dialysis.

Now there seems to me to be an egalitarian objection to a policy of ensuring that the Fortnum's customer's welfare level is as high as everybody else's. It seems to me that, when other people pay for his readily avoidable wastefulness, there is, *pro tanto*, an exploitative distribution of burden which egalitarians should condemn. Equality of welfare should here be rejected not because of other values but because it is inegalitarian.

But there could also be an objection to servicing kidney failure (and similar) sufferers to the extent required to equalize welfare: the policy could be said—*is* often said—to have too depressive an effect on the welfare of everybody else in society. Yet, while that may be right, it hardly represents an *egalitarian* objection to equality of welfare. Keeping aggregate welfare high at the expense of kidney sufferers is not a way of distributing something more equally.[7]

(iii) There are people whose inefficiency at turning resources into welfare is clearly their own fault, and others whose inefficiency is clearly bad luck. But, between these extreme types, there is a vast range of cases where it is unclear whether or not fault applies. It is very hard to say, with respect to many grumpy people, for example, whether they can be held to account for their grumpiness, whether, as we say, they are more to be pitied than blamed. Now grumpy people are bad converters, and, if we feel reluctant to service them with the extra resources they need to become a bit cheerful, then it is unclear whether the objection to equality of welfare associated with that reluctance is (at least in part) egalitarian, since it is unclear whether or not their conversion inefficiency is their own fault.

So much in illustration of different bases on which egalitarian claims might be challenged. Let us now take equality of welfare as a proposed solution to the *equalisandum* problem—it seems to me the most naive

[7] I believe that I here display disagreement with what Dworkin says in "Equality of Welfare," p. 242, which I find obscure.

one, and therefore a natural one with which to start—and let us see how it must be modified in the light of egalitarian objections to it which have been raised in recent philosophical literature.

3. Rawlsian Criticism of Equality of Welfare

A good way to begin is by examining two objections to equality of welfare, in both its hedonic and its preference interpretations,[8] which derive from the work of John Rawls, and which I shall call the *offensive tastes* and *expensive tastes* criticisms. I believe that each criticism can be accommodated by a welfare egalitarian through a natural modification of his original view. In the case of the offensive tastes criticism, that would probably be conceded by Rawls (and by Ronald Dworkin, who develops the criticism more systematically and at some length). But the second criticism is supposed by Rawls and Dworkin to justify an abandonment of the terrain of welfare altogether, and, as I shall indicate, I do not think that it does. The second criticism also creates a problem for Rawls's system, which I shall describe in a brief digression.

Rawls adverts to offensive tastes in the course of his critique of utilitarianism, but, as Amartya Sen notes, he is at that point really criticizing welfarism as such, where welfarism is the view that just distribution is some or other function of nothing but the welfares of individuals.[9] It follows logically that the offensive tastes criticism also applies against a conception of justice in which equality of welfare is the only principle. And although a "weak" (see Section 2 above) egalitarian of welfare need not be a welfarist (save, of course, with respect to the metric of equality in particular), it is extremely unlikely that a good criticism of welfarism proper will not also apply to that restricted welfarism which acknowledges the relevance of no information but welfare in the context of equality, even if its proponent admits nonwelfare information elsewhere. In any case, the offensive tastes criticism strikes me as powerful against even a weak welfare-egalitarian claim.

The offensive tastes criticism of welfarism is that the pleasure a person takes in discriminating against other people or in subjecting others to a lesser liberty should not count equally with other satisfactions in the calculus of justice.[10] From the point of view of justice, such pleasures deserve condemnation, and the corresponding preferences have no claim to be satisfied, even if they would have to be satisfied for welfare equality to

[8] For the difference between these interpretations, see above.

[9] Sen, "Equality of What?" p. 211.

[10] Rawls, *A Theory of Justice*, pp. 30–31.

prevail. I believe that this objection defeats welfarism, and, hence, equality of welfare. But the natural course for a welfare egalitarian to take in response to the offensive tastes criticism is to shift his favor to something like equality of *inoffensive* welfare. The criticism does not seem to necessitate abandoning equality of welfare in a more fundamental way.[11]

The *expensive tastes* criticism is thought to necessitate such an abandonment. It occurs in the context of Rawls's advocacy of primary goods as the appropriate *equalisandum*: "Imagine two persons, one satisfied with a diet of milk, bread and beans, while the other is distraught without expensive wines and exotic dishes. In short one has expensive tastes, the other does not." A welfare egalitarian must, *ceteris paribus*, provide the epicure with a higher income than the person of modest taste, since otherwise the latter might be satisfied while the former is distraught. But Rawls argues powerfully against this implication of the welfare egalitarian principle:

> As moral persons citizens have some part in forming and cultivating their final ends and preferences. It is not by itself an objection to the use of primary goods that it does not accommodate those with expensive tastes. One must argue in addition that it is unreasonable, if not unjust, to hold such persons responsible for their preferences and to require them to make out as best they can. But to argue this seems to presuppose that citizens' preferences are beyond their control as propensities or cravings which simply happen. Citizens seem to be regarded as passive carriers of desires. The use of primary goods . . . relies on a capacity to assume responsibility for our ends.

People with expensive tastes could have chosen otherwise, and if and when they press for compensation, others are entitled to insist that they themselves bear the cost "of their lack of foresight or self-discipline."[12]

[11] In fairness to Rawls, one should recall that he presented the offensive tastes criticism as an objection not to equality of welfare but to utilitarianism, and for utilitarians a move to "inoffensive welfare" no doubt constitutes a pretty fundamental shift. From the fact that the same criticism applies against both views, and that each should be revised in the same way in the face of it, it does not follow that the distance between the original and the revised view is the same in both cases.

[12] Rawls, "Social Unity and Primary Goods," pp. 168–69. Compare Rawls, "Fairness to Goodness," p. 553; "Justice as Fairness," pp. 243–44. For a somewhat different explanation of why justice ignores expensive tastes, with less (not no) emphasis on the idea that they are subject to the agent's control and more on the idea that it is appropriate to hold him accountable for them, see the reply to Arrow's "Some Ordinalist-Utilitarian Notes," in Rawls's "Citizens' Needs and Primary Goods." For interesting comment on and sympathetic development of Rawls's views on responsibility for preference, see Landesman, "Egalitarianism," p. 37.

I believe that this objection defeats welfare egalitarianism but that it does not, as Rawls supposes, also vindicate the claims of the primary goods metric. The right way for an erstwhile welfare egalitarian to respond to the objection seems to me to be the following: "To the extent that people are indeed responsible for their tastes, the relevant welfare deficits do not command the attention of justice. We should therefore compensate only for those welfare deficits which are not in some way traceable to the individual's choices. We should replace equality of welfare by equality of opportunity for welfare. It would be utterly unjustified to adopt a primary goods metric because of the expensive tastes counterexample."

I shall pursue that response further in the next section, in confrontation with Dworkin's extensive development of the theme of expensive taste. But, before turning to Dworkin, I want to indicate a serious problem for Rawls's system which his remarks about expensive tastes raise.

The problem is that the picture of the individual as responsibly guiding his own taste formation is hard to reconcile with claims Rawls elsewhere uses in a fundamental way to support his egalitarianism. I have in mind the skepticism which he expresses about extra reward for extra effort: "The effort a person is willing to make is influenced by his natural abilities and skills and the alternatives open to him. The better endowed are more likely, other things equal, to strive conscientiously, and there seems to be no way to discount for their greater good fortune. The idea of rewarding desert is impracticable."[13]

Now there are two ways of taking this passage. One way is as I think Rawls intended it, and the other is as Robert Nozick took it, and on the basis of which he entered strong criticism of Rawls. Nozick, I am sure, misread the passage, but his misreading of it constitutes a correct reading of what many socialists and egalitarians say about effort, so it will be worth our while to pause, digressively, to attend to Nozick's criticism. On either reading of the passage, it is hard to reconcile with what Rawls says about foresight, self-discipline, and expensive tastes. But I shall come to that point in a moment, for the passage can also be criticized independently, and I want to do that first.

The two readings of the passage divide with respect to how they take the word 'influenced' in Rawls's use of it here. In my reading of it, it means "influenced." In Nozick's, it means something like "wholly determined." There is difficulty for Rawls whichever way we take it, but not the same difficulty in each case.

In my reading of Rawls, in which he means "influenced" by 'influenced,' he does not say that the more effortful have no control over,

[13] Rawls, *A Theory of Justice*, p. 312.

and therefore deserve no credit for, the amount of effort they put in. His different point is that we cannot reckon the extent to which their above-par effort is attributable not to admirable striving but to "greater good fortune": there is "no way to discount" for the latter. That is a practical objection to trying to reward effort that deserves reward, not a claim that there is no such effort—see the final sentence of the passage.

If Rawls is right that not all effort is deserving, then, we might agree, not all effort deserves reward. But why should it follow that effort deserves no reward at all? The practical difficulty of telling how much of it merits reward hardly justifies rewarding it at a rate of 0 percent, as opposed to at a rate somewhere between 0 percent and 100 percent, for example, through a taxation scheme whose shape and justification escapes, because of its deference to effort, the writ of the difference principle.

But that criticism of Rawls is mild by comparison with the one to which he is exposed on Nozick's reading of his remarks. The plausibility of that reading is enhanced by Nozick's careless or mischievous omission of what follows "conscientiously" when he exhibits the *Theory of Justice* passage quoted above. Thereby, Nozick creates the impression that Rawls is presenting a familiar egalitarian determinist doctrine. Nozick's response to that doctrine is very powerful. He says that "denigrating a person's autonomy and prime responsibility for his actions is a risky line to take for a theory that otherwise wishes to buttress the dignity and self-respect of autonomous beings. . . . One doubts that the unexalted picture of human beings Rawls' theory presupposes and rests upon can be made to fit together with the view of human dignity it is designed to lead to and embody."[14] Nozick is pressing a dilemma: either people have real freedom of choice, in which case they may be credited (at least to some extent) with the fruits of their labors; or, there is no such thing as free choice, in which case liberals should take the purple out of the passages in which they set forth their conception of humanity, and—we can add—socialists should stop painting inspiring pictures of the human future (unless they believe that people lack free will under capitalism but that they will get it after the revolution).

On Nozick's reading of the "effort" passage, it is clearly inconsistent with the responsibility for taste formation with which Rawls credits citizens. That does not matter so much, since Nozick's reading is a misreading. But it is not easy to reconcile what Rawls says about effort with what he says about tastes even on my less creative reading of his text. On my reading of it, effort is partly praiseworthy and partly not, but we cannot separate the parts, and the indicated policy consequence is to

[14] Nozick, *Anarchy, State, and Utopia*, p. 214.

ignore effort as a claim to reward. Now, the passage about tastes begins with the thought that "citizens have *some* part in forming and cultivating their final ends and preferences," though it ends by assigning a more wholesale responsibility for them to citizens. If we stay with the opening thought, then we can wonder why partial responsibility for effort attracts no reward at all while (merely) partial responsibility for expensive taste formation attracts a full penalty (and those who keep their tastes modest reap a welfare reward). And if we shift to the wholesale responsibility motif, then we can wonder why beings who are only in a limited way responsible for the effort they put in may be held wholly responsible for how their tastes develop.

4. Relocating Dworkin's Cut

a. Ronald Dworkin denies that equality of welfare provides the right reading of the egalitarian aim, and I agree with him about that. But I do not share his view that the demise of equality of welfare should prompt egalitarians to embrace equality of resources instead. Part of my reason for disagreeing with Dworkin on that score is my belief, to be defended in a moment, that one of his major objections to equality of welfare can be met by a revised form of that principle. The revised welfare principle, unlike equality of welfare, permits and indeed enjoins departures from welfare equality when they reflect choices of relevant agents, as opposed to deficient *opportunity* for welfare. If a person's welfare is low because he freely risked a welfare loss in gambling for a welfare gain, then, under the opportunity form of the principle, he has no claim to compensation. Nor does a person who frittered away welfare opportunities which others seized. Nor, to take a different kind of example, does a person who chose to forgo welfare out of devotion to an ideal which (expressly, or merely as it happened) required self-denial.

The revised principle can be called equality of opportunity for welfare.[15] It is not a principle that I shall endorse. Equality of opportunity for welfare is a better reading of egalitarianism than equality of welfare itself is, but it is not as good as what currently strikes me as the right reading of egalitarianism, namely, that its purpose is to eliminate *involuntary disadvantage*, by which I (stipulatively) mean disadvantage for which the sufferer cannot be held responsible, since it does not appropriately reflect choices that he has made or is making or would make.[16]

[15] For a clear articulation and persuasive defense of it, in its preference satisfaction interpretation, see Arneson's "Equality and Equal Opportunity for Welfare."

[16] The need to add that third disjunct is explained in Section 5*a* below.

Equality of opportunity for welfare eliminates involuntary welfare deficiencies, and welfare deficiencies are forms of disadvantage. Hence the principle I endorse responds to inequalities in people's welfare opportunities. But, as will be illustrated below, advantage is a broader notion than welfare. Anything which enhances my welfare is *pro tanto* to my advantage, but the converse is not true. And disadvantage is correspondingly broader than welfare deficiency, so the view I favor, which can be called *equal opportunity for advantage*, or, preferably, equal *access* to advantage, corrects for inequalities to which equal opportunity for welfare is insensitive.

Why is "equal *access* to advantage" a better name for the view than "equal *opportunity* for advantage" is? We would not normally regard meager personal capacity as detracting from opportunity. Your opportunities are the same whether you are strong and clever or weak and stupid: if you are weak and stupid, you may not use them well—but that implies that you have them. But shortfalls on the side of personal capacity nevertheless engage egalitarian concern, and they do so because they detract from access to valuable things, even if they do not diminish the opportunity to get them. Hence my preference for "access,"[17] but I still require this possibly unnatural stipulation: I shall treat anything which a person actually has as something to which he has access.[18]

Some of Dworkin's counterexamples to equality of welfare fail to challenge equality of opportunity for welfare, and they fail, *a fortiori*, to challenge the wider disadvantage principle. The Dworkin examples I here have in mind, which are to do with expensive tastes, not only do not challenge equality of opportunity for welfare: one can say the stronger thing that they bring its claims to the fore as a candidate reading of the egalitarian aim. But other counterexamples to equality of welfare presented by Dworkin necessitate movement beyond equality of opportunity for welfare to the broader conception of equality of access to advantage. One sort of counterexample that has that effect concerns handicaps, in the literal sense of the word, and I shall be presenting a handicap counterexample to equality of opportunity for welfare at the beginning of the next subsection.

[17] For analogous reasons, Arneson would have been better advised to call his theory "equality of access to welfare."

[18] I am not entirely happy with the word "advantage" in the title of the view I am espousing; I use the word only because I have been unable to find a better one. Its infelicity relates to the fact that it is so frequently used to denote competitive advantage, advantage, that is, *over* somebody else. But here "advantage" must be understood shorn of that implication, which it does not always have. Something can add to someone's advantage without him, as a result, being better placed, or less worse placed, than somebody else, and the word will here be used in that noncompetitive sense.

In my view, however, equality of resources is subject to objections which are just as strong as those which defeat equality of welfare (and equality of opportunity for welfare). I shall now defend that conclusion, by describing the case of a doubly unfortunate person. I believe that egalitarians will be moved to compensate him for both of his misfortunes, but the fact that the first calls for egalitarian compensation challenges equality of welfare and the fact that the second does challenges equality of resources.

b. My unfortunate person's legs are paralyzed. To get around, he needs an expensive wheelchair. Egalitarians will be disposed to recommend that he be given one. And they will be so disposed before they have asked about the welfare level to which the man's paralysis reduces him. When compensating for disability, egalitarians do not immediately distinguish between the different amounts of misery induced by similar disabilities in people who have different (dis)utility functions. They propose compensation for the disability *as such*, and not, or not only, for its deleterious welfare effects. Insofar as we can distinguish compensation for resource deficiency from compensation for welfare deficiency, the first appears to enjoy independent egalitarian favor.

The egalitarian response to disability seems to defeat not only equality of welfare but also equality of opportunity for welfare. Tiny Tim is not only *actually* happy, by any standard. He is also, because of his fortunate disposition, blessed with abundant *opportunity* for happiness: he need not do much to get a lot of it. But egalitarians would not on that account strike him off the list of free wheelchair receivers. They do not think that wheelchair distribution should be controlled exclusively by the welfare opportunity requirements of those who need them. Lame people need them to be adequately resourced, whether or not they also need them to be, or to be capable of being, happy.

Note that I do not say that, whatever other demands they face, egalitarians will always service people like Tiny Tim. One could imagine him surrounded by curably miserable sound-limbed people whose welfare was so low that their requirements were judged to precede his. The essential point is that his abundant happiness is not as such decisive against compensating him for his disability.

In face of (what I say are) the intuitive phenomena, the only way of sustaining the view that equality of welfare is the right reading of the egalitarian aim is to claim that egalitarians propose assistance for disability without gathering welfare information because of a general correlation between disability and illfare which it is impossible or too costly to confirm in individual cases. Like Sen and Dworkin, I find that defense unpersuasive, and I consequently conclude that the egalitarian response to disability defeats equality of welfare.[19] And, as I argued, it also defeats equality of opportunity for welfare, since the response to disability is shaped by something other than the different costs in lost opportunity for welfare which disability causes in different people.

I have not completed my description of the man's misfortune. There is also something wrong with his arms. He is not less able to move them than most people are: I shall even assume, to make my point more vivid, that he is especially good at moving them. But there is, nevertheless, something seriously wrong with them, and it is this: after he moves them, he suffers severe pain in his arm muscles.

In the terms of a distinction which I once had occasion to make in a different context, it is not *difficult* for the man to move his arms, but it is very *costly* for him to do so.[20] What I call 'difficulty' and 'cost' are two widely conflated but importantly distinct ways in which it can be *hard* for a person to do something. (It is costly, but not difficult, for me to supply you with a check for £500, or for me to tell you some secret the revelation of which will damage me. It is extremely difficult for me to transport you to Heathrow on the back of my bicycle, but it is not costly, since I love that kind of challenge, and I have nothing else to do today. At the far end of the difficulty continuum lies the *impossible*, but it is the *unbearable* which occupies that position in the case of costliness.)[21]

Now there is an expensive medicine which, taken regularly, suppresses the pain that otherwise follows the man's arm movement, and this medicine is so expensive that it has no adverse side effects. Egalitarians would, I am sure, favor supplying our man with the medicine, even if it costs what a wheelchair does. But providing the medicine cannot be represented as compensating for a resource incapacity. The man's capacity to move his arms is, *in the relevant sense*, better (so I stipulated) than that of most people.

"In the relevant sense" does a lot of work here, so let me explain it. Someone might insist, and I do not have to deny, that there is *a* sense in which a typical normal person has a capacity which this man lacks. I need not deny that he lacks the capacity to move his arms without pain, or, if you prefer, to move his arms without pain without taking medicine.

[19] Dworkin, "Equality of Welfare," pp. 241–42, following Sen, "Equality of What?" pp. 217–18. Sen is surely right that it is his deficient capability as such which explains the claim to assistance of a contented crippled person who requires expensive prosthesis and who is not particularly poor. Compare Sen, "Well-Being, Agency and Freedom," pp. 195–97.

[20] Cohen, *Karl Marx's Theory of History*, p. 238.

[21] A man otherwise like the one I described might find it difficult to move his arms for the psychological reason that he could not face the thought of what would follow their movement. But my man is psychologically robust: he can easily move his arms, though he often (coolly) decides not to on occasions when other people would move theirs.

I can even agree that it is his lack of *that* capacity which is the egalitarian ground for compensating him. *But compensating for a lack of capacity which needs to be described in that way for the ground of the compensation to be revealed cannot be represented as compensating for incapacity when that is opposed to compensating for welfare opportunity deficiency.* A would-be resource egalitarian who said, "Compensation is in order here because the man lacks the resource of being able to avoid pain" would be invoking the idea of equality of opportunity for welfare even if he would be using resourcist language to describe it.

My example was medically fanciful, but a medically more ordinary example makes the same point, though you have to exercise slightly sharper perception to see it. It was fanciful in the foregoing case that the pain should wholly succeed and not also accompany the pain-inducing movement. Think now of a more ordinary case, in which arthritic pain accompanies movement, and suppose, what is likely, that the movement is not only painful but, consequently and/or otherwise, *also* difficult. That difficulty introduces a resource deficiency into the case, but the example nevertheless stands as a challenge to equality of resources. For it seems not coherently egalitarian to cater only to the difficulty of moving and not independently to the pain which moving occasions. So there is an irreducible welfare aspect in the case for egalitarian compensation in real-life disability examples.

Or just think of poor people in Britain who suffer discomfort in the winter cold. The egalitarian case for helping them with their electricity bills is partly founded on that discomfort itself. It does not rest entirely on the disenablement which the cold, both through discomfort and independently, also causes.

People vary in the amount of discomfort which given low temperatures cause them, and, consequently, in the volume of resources which they need to alleviate their discomfort. Some people need costly heavy sweaters and a great deal of fuel to achieve an average level of thermal well-being. With respect to warmth, they have what Dworkin calls *expensive tastes*: they need unusually large doses of resources to achieve an ordinary level of welfare. They are losers under Dworkin's equality of resources, because, as we shall see, it sets itself against compensation for expensive tastes.

The two grounds of egalitarian compensation which apply in the case of the disabled man have something in common. The man's straightforward inability to move his legs and his liability to pain when moving his arms are both disadvantages for which (I tacitly assumed) he cannot be held responsible, and, I suggest, that is why an egalitarian would compensate him for them. Both aspects of his plight represent unavoidable disadvantages, which he was unable to forestall and which he cannot now rectify. On my understanding of egalitarianism, it does not enjoin redress of or compensation for disadvantage as such. It attends, rather, to "involuntary" disadvantage, which is the sort that does not reflect the subject's choice. People's advantages are unjustly unequal (or unjustly equal) when the inequality (or equality) reflects unequal access to advantage, as opposed to patterns of choice against a background of equality of access. Severe actual disadvantage is a fairly reliable sign of inequality of access to advantage, but the prescribed equality is not of advantage per se but of access, all things considered, to it.

When deciding whether or not justice (as opposed to charity) requires redistribution, the egalitarian asks if someone with a disadvantage could have avoided it or could now overcome it.[22] If he could have avoided it, he has no claim to compensation, from an egalitarian point of view. If he could not have avoided it but could now overcome it, then he can ask that his effort to overcome it be subsidized, but, unless it costs more to overcome it than to compensate for it without overcoming it, he cannot expect society to compensate for his disadvantage.

I affirm equality of access to advantage, whatever advantage is rightly considered to be, but I cannot say, in a pleasingly systematic way, exactly what should count as an advantage, partly because I have not thought hard enough about this question, which is surely one of the deepest in normative philosophy.[23] What does appear clear is that resource deficiencies and welfare deficiencies are distinct types of disadvantage and that each of them covers pretty distinct subtypes: poverty and physical weakness are very different kinds of resource limitation, and despondency and failure to achieve aims are very different kinds of illfare. Whatever the boundaries and types of welfare may be,[24] lack of pain is surely a form of it, and lack of disability, considered just as such, is not, *if* there is to be a contrast between equality of resources and equality of welfare. Those two classificatory judgments are reasonably uncontentious, and they are the ones I need to sustain the criticism of Dworkin which arises from reflection on the case of involuntary pain.

(I warned at the outset that my positive proposal would be crude. One thing that makes it so and makes me wish that it will be superseded is

[22] The answers to those questions will not always be as simple as the sample answers that follow, but they are always the right questions to ask.

[23] Another matter about which I cannot say anything systematic is the problem of how to compare the net advantage positions of different people. The right place to begin would be with Amartya Sen's perspicacious discussion of the (at least) structurally analogous problem of how to order different capability-sets (see his *Commodities and Capabilities*, chapter 5). (I say "[at least] structurally analogous" because it may turn out to be the same problem [see Section 6 below].)

[24] Dworkin's "Equality of Welfare" is a masterful exposé of ambiguities in the concept of welfare, even if it does not prove that egalitarian justice should ignore welfare comparisons.

the unlovely heterogeneity of the components of the vector of advantage. One hopes that there is a currency more fundamental than either resources or welfare in which the various egalitarian responses which motivated my proposal can be expressed. But I certainly have not discovered it, so, at least for now, I stay with the appearances, which contradict welfare, resources, and opportunity for welfare readings of the egalitarian demand, and which point, in the first instance, to the theory [or semi-theory: it is perhaps too close to the intuitive phenomena to merit the name "theory"] I have affirmed.)

c. Whatever number of dimensions the space of disadvantage may have, egalitarianism, on my reading, cuts through each of its dimensions, judging certain inequalities of advantage as acceptable and others as not, its touchstone being a set of questions about the responsibility or lack of it of the disadvantaged agent.

In Ronald Dworkin's different reading of egalitarianism, people are to be compensated for shortfalls in their powers, that is, their material resources and mental and physical capacities, but not for shortfalls traceable to their tastes and preferences. What they get should reflect differences in what they want and seek, but not in their *ability* to get things.

Dworkin's "cut" contrasts with mine in two ways. First, it calls for compensation for resource deficiencies only, and not also for pain and other illfare considered as such. "There is no place in [Dworkin's] theory . . . for comparisons of the welfare levels of different people," nor, I infer, for catering to people whose pains do not diminish their capacity, since that service reflects a judgment about how their welfare, in one relevant sense, compares with that of others.[25] My cut awards redress for both resource and welfare disadvantages, but, in Dworkin's theory, there is not even "some small room for equality of welfare," alongside other considerations.[26]

So, for purposes of egalitarian intervention, Dworkin-style, only one dimension of disadvantage is recognized. And the second difference between our cuts is that, within that single resource dimension, Dworkin does not put absence of responsibility in the foreground as a necessary condition of just compensation.

I say that the question of responsibility is not *foregrounded* in Dworkin's presentation, because I shall argue that, insofar as he succeeds in making his cut plausible, it is by obscuring both of the differences between it and the different cut that I have recommended. I shall also argue that the grounding idea of Dworkin's egalitarianism is that no one should suffer because of bad brute luck and that, since the relevant

[25] The quoted material is from Dworkin, "Equality of Resources," p. 335.

[26] Dworkin, "Equality of Welfare," p. 240.

opposite of an unlucky fate is a fate traceable to its victim's control, my cut is more faithful to Dworkin's grounding idea than the one he ostensibly favors is.

For Dworkin, it is not choice but preference which excuses what would otherwise be an unjustly unequal distribution. He proposes compensation for power deficiencies, but not for expensive tastes,[27] whereas I believe that we should compensate for disadvantage beyond a person's control, as such, and that we should not, accordingly, draw a line between unfortunate resource endowment and unfortunate utility function.[28] A person with *wantonly* expensive tastes has no claim on us, but neither does a person whose powers are feeble because he recklessly failed to develop them. There is no moral difference, from an egalitarian point of view, between a person who irresponsibly acquires (or blamelessly chooses to develop) an expensive taste and a person who irresponsibly loses (or blamelessly chooses to consume) a valuable resource. The right cut is between responsibility and bad luck, not between preferences and resources.

The difference between those two cuts will have policy significance in the case of those expensive tastes which cannot be represented as reflecting choice. There will be no policy difference with respect to Dworkin's leading example of a person with expensive tastes. I refer to Louis, who requires ancient claret and plovers' eggs in order to reach an ordinary level of welfare. I treat Louis in practice the way Dworkin does, because, as Dworkin describes him, he did not just get stuck with his taste: he schooled himself into it. But, while Dworkin and I both refuse Louis's request for a special allowance, we ground our refusals differently. Dworkin says: sorry, Louis, we egalitarians do not finance expensive tastes; whereas I say: sorry Louis, we egalitarians do not finance expensive tastes which people choose to develop.

Now consider a case of expensive taste where there will be a policy difference. Paul loves photography, while Fred loves fishing.[29] Prices are such that Fred pursues his pastime with ease while Paul cannot afford to. Paul's life is a lot less pleasant as a result: it might even be true that it has less meaning than Fred's does. I think the egalitarian thing to do is to subsidize Paul's photography. But Dworkin cannot think that. His envy

[27] On the hedonic conception of welfare, *X*'s taste is *pro tanto* more expensive than *Y*'s if more resources are needed to raise *X* to a given level of enjoyment. On the preference satisfaction conception of welfare, levels of preference satisfaction replace levels of enjoyment in the characterization of what makes a taste expensive. The discussion below of expensive tastes may be interpreted along either hedonic or preference lines.

[28] An unfortunate utility function could itself be regarded as a resource deficiency, but not by someone concerned to contrast equality of resources and equality of welfare.

[29] I thank Alice Knight for this example.

test for equality of resources is satisfied: Paul can afford to go fishing as readily as Fred can. Paul's problem is that he hates fishing and, so I am permissibly assuming, could not have helped hating it—it does not suit his natural inclinations. He has a genuinely involuntary expensive taste, and I think that a commitment to equality implies that he should be helped in the way that people like Paul are indeed helped by subsidized community leisure facilities. As this example suggests, there is between Dworkin's account of egalitarian justice and mine the difference that my account mandates less market pricing than his does.

I distinguish among expensive tastes according to whether or not their bearer can reasonably be held responsible for them. There are those which he could not have helped forming and/or could not now unform, and then there are those for which, by contrast, he can be held responsible, because he could have forestalled them and/or because he could now unlearn them. Notice that I do not say that a person who deliberately develops an expensive taste deserves criticism. I say no such severe thing because there are all kinds of reasons why a person might want to develop an expensive taste, and it is each person's business whether he does so or not. But it is also nobody else's business to pick up the tab for him if he does. Egalitarians have good reason not to minister to deliberately cultivated expensive tastes, and equality of welfare must, therefore, be rejected. But we should not embrace equality of resources instead, since that doctrine wrongly refuses compensation for involuntary expensive tastes, and it does not refuse compensation for voluntary ones for the right reason.

In Dworkin's view, only the principle of equality of resources can explain why Louis's expensive tastes should not be indulged by egalitarians. But his long discussion of Louis rejects the most obvious reason the egalitarian has for denying Louis the resources needed to service his taste: that he "sets out deliberately to cultivate" it.[30] It is crucial that, as Dworkin acknowledges, "Louis has a choice": the taste is not instilled in him by a process which circumvents his volition.[31]

Instead of foregrounding the fact of Louis's choice, Dworkin asserts that he can be denied extra resources only if we think that, were Louis to demand them, he would be asking for more than his fair share of resources, where "fair share" is defined in welfare-independent terms. For Dworkin, it requires great "ingenuity" to "produce some explanation or interpretation of the argument in question—that Louis does not deserve more resources just because he has chosen a more expensive life—which does not use the idea of fair shares or any similar ideas."[32]

[30] Dworkin, "Equality of Welfare," p. 229.

[31] The quoted material is from ibid., p. 237.

[32] Ibid., p. 239.

Now, it is certainly, because trivially, true that if we think that Louis should be denied the resources he demands, then we must believe that he would have more than his fair share if we gave them to him. But we could use equality of opportunity for welfare to define fair shares here: we could say that shares are fair when they equalize welfare opportunities. It is therefore false, and it scarcely takes ingenuity to show it, that only if we move toward equality of resources, toward fair shares in Dworkin's special sense, can we explain egalitarianism's lack of sympathy for Louis.

I conclude that while it is indeed true that "expensive tastes are embarrassing for the theory that equality means equality of welfare precisely because we believe that equality . . . condemns rather than recommends compensating for deliberately cultivated expensive tastes," the proposal that equality means equality of opportunity for welfare[33] glides by the Louis counterexample.[34]

d. While a proponent of equality of opportunity for welfare can readily deal with Louis, the case of Jude is much harder for him to handle.[35] I shall argue that Jude's case reflects credit on equality of access to advantage, by comparison with both equality of resources and equality of opportunity for welfare.

[33] Which must, on other grounds, be broadened into equality of access to advantage (see Sections 4*b* and 4*d*). The quoted material is from Dworkin, "Equality of Welfare," p. 235.

[34] Equality of opportunity for welfare and, *a fortiori*, equality of access to advantage also supply what seems to me to be an adequate response to a complicated argument which Dworkin thinks contributes a great deal to this drive to subvert equality of welfare in favor of equality of resources. The argument first appears in the context of Dworkin's exploration of the hypothesis that equality of welfare be understood as equality of overall success—that hypothesis surfaces after the supposed wreckage of several previous ones. The argument has two premises, each of which I find hard to assess, but neither of which I shall here contest. The first premise is that "equality of overall success cannot be stated as an attractive ideal at all without making the idea of reasonable regret central" (ibid., p. 217): equality of overall success will seem defensible only if it promises to make people "equal in what they have reasonably to regret" (ibid., pp. 217, 218). And the second premise is that the idea of reasonable regret "requires an independent theory of fair shares of social resources . . . which would contradict equality of overall success" (ibid., p. 217). But if both premises are true, so that such a theory is indeed required, why can it not be a theory which says that shares are fair when they induce equality of opportunity for welfare, or equality of access to advantage? I do not find anything in Dworkin's dense ratiocination which appears to rule that out. It follows that the supposed self-destruction of equality of welfare on the altar of reasonable regret is much less of an argument for equality of resources than Dworkin appears to think it is. (For criticism of Dworkin's second premise, see Griffin, "Modern Utilitarianism," pp. 365–66; and for an argument that the idea of overall success should never have been floated in the first place, see Arneson's "Liberalism, Distributive Subjectivism and Equal Opportunity for Welfare," [pp. 180–81, n. 28—Ed.].)

[35] Dworkin, "Equality of Welfare," pp. 239–40.

Jude has what might be called *cheap expensive tastes*. They are cheap in that he needs fewer resources to attain the same welfare level as others. But they are expensive in that he could have achieved that welfare level with fewer resources still, had he not cultivated tastes more expensive than those with which he began. Jude began with very modest desires, but then he read Hemingway and cultivated a desire to watch bullfights, and, once he had it, he needed more money than before to achieve an average level of welfare, though still less than what others needed.

A believer in equality of opportunity for welfare has to keep Jude poor, since he did not have to become a bullfight-lover (it is reasonable to suppose that he could have suppressed, at no great cost, his desire to cultivate that taste). A believer in Dworkin-style equality of resources ignores Jude's tastes, and their history, and finds no reason, in anything said so far, to grant him less income than anyone else. I reject both views. *Pace* equality of opportunity for welfare, I see no manifest injustice in Jude's getting the funds he needs to travel to Spain. He then still has fewer resources than others, and only the same welfare, so equality of access to advantage cannot say, on that basis, that he is overpaid. But, *pace* equality of resources, it seems not unreasonable to expect Jude to accept some deduction from the normal resource stipend because of his fortunate high ability to get welfare out of resources. Unlike either Dworkin's theory or Arneson's, mine explains why both gross underresourcing and gross "underwelfaring" (despite, respectively, a decent welfare level and a decent resource bundle) look wrong.[36]

e. There are some expensive tastes which Dworkin regards as "obsessions" or "cravings" and which he is prepared to assimilate to resource deficiency, for the purposes of distributive justice. This kind of taste is one that its bearer "wishes he did not have, because it interferes with what he wants to do with his life and offers him frustration or even pain if it is not satisfied."[37] Dworkin concludes that "these tastes are handicaps," and, since equality of resources redistributes for handicap, it will presumably do so (within the bounds of practicality) in the case of tastes which meet the quoted description.

Now, Dworkin's description of them assigns (at least) two features to "handicap" tastes, and he fails to say which feature makes them handicaps, or, equivalently, endows their owner with a claim to compensation. Is the crucial feature of the taste the fact that the person wishes he did not

[36] I do not feel comfortable about this victory, since, in achieving it, I exploit to the hilt a feature of my theory which I regard as suspect: the heterogeneity of its conception of advantage (see latter part of Section 4*b* above).

[37] Dworkin, "Equality of Resources," p. 302.

have it? Or is it his reason for wishing he did not have it, namely, that, among other things, it threatens to cause him frustration and pain?[38]

The latter proposal is unavailable to Dworkin. An involuntary liability to frustration and pain does indeed command compensation, but, as I urged in Section 4*b* above, that thought reflects egalitarian sensitivity to people's welfare, rather than to their resources position. Since Dworkin defends intervention in response to handicaps but not in response to shortfalls in welfare, he is not entitled to classify a taste as a handicap *because* it causes pain.

But perhaps the crucial feature of the tastes we are considering is that the individual whose tastes they are "wishes he did not have" them. He disidentifies with them, so that—we can attribute this thought to Dworkin—they are not inalienable aspects of his person (see Section 4*f* below), but more like unfortunate environing circumstances. They form no part of his *ambition*, in the special sense in which Dworkin uses that word, and that is why equality of resources can regard them as handicaps. I believe that this is indeed Dworkin's position, that the following regimented statement of it is not unfair: tastes are (subsidy-warranting) handicaps if and only if they represent obsessions, which they do if and only if the individual whose tastes they are disidentifies with them.

I have four comments on the thesis that it is the individual's alienation from his taste which makes it an obsession and therefore allows us to regard it as a handicap.

1. Some people in the grip of cravings are too unreflective to form the second-order preference-repudiating preference by reference to which Dworkin justifies the "handicap" epithet. But it would seem unfair to deny to them the assistance to be extended to others, just because of their deficient reflectiveness. So the misidentification criterion does not cover all compensation-worthy cravings.

2. Not all tastes which hamper the individual's life and therefore raise a case for compensation qualify either as obsessions or as tastes whose bearers, even if highly reflective, would repudiate. Paul (see Section 4*c* above) might not want not to want to take pictures, and a person whose unhappy taste is "for music of a sort difficult to obtain" might well not disidentify with his desire for that music.[39] He has *a* reason to regret his musical preference, since it causes him frustration, but that is not a conclusive reason for wishing he did not have it. What he most likely

[38] This is one of several key places at which there is reason to regret that, in expounding his views, Dworkin abjures the device of canonical statement. Other cases in point are passages quoted at Section 4*f* below (on choosing tastes and choosing pursuits) and passages quoted at Sections 4*f* and 4*g*, which give three materially different renderings of Dworkin's "master cut."

[39] The quote comes from Dworkin, "Equality of Resources," p. 302.

regrets is not (as Dworkin stipulates) his musical preference as such, but the impossibility or expense of satisfying it. His taste is involuntary and unfortunate, but it is probably not an "obsession" or "craving": addiction is not the right model here.

A typical unrich bearer of an expensive musical taste would regard it as a piece of bad luck *not that he has the taste itself but that it happens to be expensive* (I emphasize those words because, simple as the distinction they formulate may be, it is one that undermines a lot of Dworkin's rhetoric about expensive tastes). He might say that in a perfect world he would have chosen to have his actual musical taste, but he would also have chosen that it not be expensive. He can take responsibility for the taste, for his personality being that way, while reasonably denying responsibility for needing a lot of resources to satisfy it.

3. By contrast with the more representative person described above, Dworkin's music craver prefers not to have his unfortunate preference yet, by hypothesis, persists in having it. That rather suggests that he cannot help having it, and that in turn raises the suspicion that it is its unchosen and uncontrolled, rather than its dispreferred, character which renders compensation for it appropriate. Would not Dworkin's attitude to the music craver be less solicitous if he learned that he had been warned not to cultivate his particular musical interest by a sapient teacher who knew it would cause frustration?

4. Suppose that there was no such warning, that our unfortunate contracted his expensive taste innocently, and that we now offer him, *gratis*, an inexpensive unrepugnant therapy which would school him out of it. If he agrees to the free therapy, then, so I believe, the ideal of equality says that he should get it, regardless of whether he says farewell to his taste with unmixed relief or, instead, with a regret which reflects some degree of identification. This suggests that identification and disidentification matter for egalitarian justice only if and insofar as they indicate presence and absence of choice.[40]

f. The foregoing reflection brings me to the claim which I ventured in Section 4*c*, to wit, that, insofar as we find Dworkin's cut plausible, it is because we are apt to suppose that it separates presence and absence of choice. Choice is in the background, doing a good deal of unacknowledged work. Here is a passage which supports this allegation: "It is true that [my] argument produces a certain view of the distinction between a person and his circumstances, and assigns his tastes and ambitions to his

[40] For an amendment to that suggestion, see Section 5*a* below, where, *inter alia*, I comment on the case, which is not addressed above, of a person who would refuse the offer of therapy because of his musical convictions.

person, and his physical and mental powers to his circumstances. That is the view of the person I sketched in the introductory section, of someone who *forms* his ambitions with a sense of their cost to others against some presumed initial equality of economic power, and though this is different from the picture assumed by equality of welfare, it is a picture at the center of equality of resources."[41]

This passage offers two characterizations of "tastes and ambitions" in putative justification of placing them outside the ambit of redistributive compensation. The first says that, by contrast with mental and physical powers, they belong to the person rather than to his circumstances. But, in the usual senses of those words, that classification cannot be sustained. Using language in the ordinary way, my mental powers are as integral to what I am as my tastes and ambitions are. The person/circumstances distinction must therefore be a technical one, which means that there must be another way of expressing it, and a possible different way emerges in the second sentence of the passage. That different way has to do with the suggestion that people *form* their preferences but not, presumably, their powers. But there are difficulties with this suggestion.

The first is that it proposes a false alignment. People certainly form some of their ambitions, but they arguably do not form all of them, and they certainly do not form all of their tastes, which are also supposed to belong to the person.[42] Dworkin emphasizes that people "decide what sort of lives to pursue," but they do not decide what in all pertinent respects their utility functions will be: *pace* Dworkin, they are extensively unable to "decide what sorts of lives they *want*."[43] So being "formed" by the person cannot be a necessary condition of being part of the person, if tastes and ambitions make up the person.

It confirms my claim that Dworkin's cut looks plausible because it seems to separate presence and absence of choice that he uses the two phrases "decide what sort of life to pursue" and "decide what sort of life one wants" interchangeably, thus assimilating two very different kinds of process, only the first of which straightforwardly embodies choice, in

[41] Dworkin, "Equality of Resources," p. 302, my emphasis. The word 'produces' in the first sentence of the passage should, Dworkin confirms, be 'presupposes': note the contrast with the picture "assumed" by equality of welfare. (But the question whether Dworkin has argued for, as opposed to from, his distinction does not matter here.) Dworkin does not describe the different picture which he thinks is assumed by equality of welfare. If it is a picture of the person as passive and unchoosing, that would help to justify my immanent critique of his view. For that picture, see Rawls, "Social Unity and Primary Goods," p. 169.

[42] Dworkin does not actually say in the passage under scrutiny that people form their *tastes*: "tastes and ambitions" have shrunk to "ambitions" by the time that we get to the motif of self-formation. But unless Dworkin claims that tastes, too, are in general formed, on what basis is he here assigning them to a person's person?

[43] The quotes are from Dworkin, "Equality of Resources," p. 288, my emphasis.

the general case. Elsewhere, and similarly, "the choice between expensive and less expensive *tastes*" is put on the same level as "choosing a more [or a less] expensive *life*."[44] And we are also told, in another place, that, when "people choose plans or schemes for their lives," "their choices define a set of [resultant] preferences."[45] That formulation sweeps away the (often unchosen)[46] preferences which lie in the determining background of choice. A person in possession of his faculties always chooses (within the constraints he faces) what career to pursue, but he does not always choose what career to prefer, and the latter fact may reasonably restrict his responsibility for choosing to pursue an expensive one.

Being "formed" is not only not a necessary condition of belonging to what Dworkin calls the person: it is also not a sufficient one. For mental and physical powers fall outside the person, in his circumstances, and some of those powers are, unquestionably, formed. On either side of the preference/circumstance line people both find things and form things. Hence appeal to formedness does not show that distributive justice should ignore variations in preference and taste.

If, moreover, the false alignment (formed/not formed = person/circumstances) indeed worked, it would, surely, constitute a reduction of the person/circumstances distinction to the distinction between what is and what is not subject to choice. To repeat one of my main claims: it is only because Dworkin's preference/resource distinction *looks* alignable with the one it cannot in the end match that it commands appeal.

The idea that we *form* our ambitions is absent from a different formulation of the person/circumstances distinction, which comes soon after the one we have just studied: "The distinction required by equality of resources is the distinction between those beliefs and attitudes that define what a successful life would be like, which the ideal assigns to the person, and those features of body or mind or personality that provide means or impediments to that success, which the ideal assigns to the person's circumstances."[47] This proposal has different implications from the one (see above) which counterposes *tastes and ambitions* to circumstances,

[44] Dworkin, "Liberalism," p. 193, my emphases.

[45] Dworkin, "Equality of Welfare," p. 206. I introduce 'resultant' to forestall the misinterpretation that Dworkin means that the choices *reflect* preferences.

[46] "Many of a person's desires are indeed voluntary, since they derive simply from his own decisions. Someone typically acquires the desire to see a certain movie, for example, just by making up his mind what movie to see. Desires of this sort are not aroused in us; they are formed or constructed by acts of will that we ourselves perform, often quite apart from any emotional or affective state. However, there are also occasions when what a person wants is not up to him at all, but is rather a matter of feelings or inclinations that arise and persist independently of any choice of his own" (Frankfurt, *The Importance of What We Care About*, p. 107).

[47] Dworkin, "Equality of Resources," p. 303.

since not all ambitions, and few tastes, are informed by beliefs and attitudes: plenty of tastes and ambitions arise without being drawn forth by any sort of doxastic pull.[48] But I shall here set aside the problem of discrepancy between the "belief" cut and the "preference" one, in order to assess the belief cut in its own terms, in the light of Dworkin's larger purposes.

Within those purposes, the person/circumstances distinction is meant to be not only exclusive but (relevantly) exhaustive: we do not have to review anything beyond people's persons and circumstances to know how to treat them from an egalitarian point of view.[49] But, if that is so, then where are we to place the life-enhancing feature of cheerfulness, from the point of view of egalitarian justice? Cheerfulness raises two difficulties, one small and one big.

First, the small difficulty. Cheerfulness is not something that "defines what a successful life would be like." It should therefore count as a circumstance. But circumstances are elsewhere characterized as powers and incapacities, and cheerfulness is neither of those. It is not a power but a fortunate disposition which, for given inputs, generates higher than ordinary utility outputs. It is not something a person *exercises* when pursuing his goals, even if it tends often to improve his pursuit of them. Since it does the latter, the fact that it is not, strictly, a power is perhaps not a very important point. But there is another point which is certainly important.

The important point is that the value of cheerfulness is not merely, or mainly, that it raises the probability of a person's achieving what, by his lights, is "a successful life." Cheerfulness is a marvelous thing quite apart from that, and one different thing that it does is diminish the sadness of failure. It is a welfare-enhancer independently of being a goal-promoter. This makes it difficult for Dworkin to compensate cheerless people fully for their gloominess. But then there is an inconsistency between the criterion for determining what lies outside the person and the principle that disadvantages not deriving from the character of the person require compensation. Cheerlessness lies outside the person, but it is difficult to see how Dworkin can award appropriate compensation for it.

[48] Frankfurt's sensitive distinction (see n. 46 above) between desires which do and desires which do not reflect decisions could be matched by a similar one between those which do and those which do not display attitude and commitment. For more on that differentiation within desire, see Section *5a* below.

[49] At an Oxford seminar on economic justice of February 22, 1988, Dworkin was explicitly exhaustive. He spoke of his proposal requiring "a sharp distinction between personality (equals attachments, projects, etc.) and circumstances (equals everything else, the material with and against which people labor to achieve what their personality favors)."

When I discussed gloominess with Dworkin he suggested that it was a borderline case with respect to the person/circumstances dichotomy and that the best way to cope with it would be to ask whether an individual would have insured against turning out to be gloomy, and to compensate him for his gloom if we think that the answer is "yes."

I think that the insurance device does have some appeal as a method of deciding whether or not to compensate for gloom. But its appeal seems to me to have nothing to do with the person/circumstances distinction: the individual who chooses to, or not to, insure against gloom is not thereby making *that* distinction. And if we suppose that he is indeed making it, then another problem arises. For in Dworkin's main use of the insurance device the individual *knows* what belongs to his person when he decides whether or not to insure: Dworkin's veil of ignorance is, in that important way, thinner than Rawls's.[50] But an individual who decides not to insure against gloominess remains, *ex hypothesi*, ignorant of whether or not he is gloomy.

The insurance device seems, then, unable to solve Dworkin's gloom problem. It is, nevertheless, independently attractive, especially when the veil of ignorance is indeed thickened, and that, I opine, is because it seems to sort out a big difference that really matters for egalitarian justice: between disadvantages that are and disadvantages that are not due to bad brute luck.[51] It is in the essential nature of insurance that luck is what we insure against, and genuine choice contrasts with luck. So anyone who, like Dworkin, is strongly drawn to the insurance test should consider accepting the choice/luck cut and giving up the attempt to defend the different cut of preferences/resources.

g. In my view, a large part of the fundamental egalitarian aim is to extinguish the influence of brute luck on distribution (see Section 2 above). Brute luck is an enemy of just equality, and, since effects of genuine choice contrast with brute luck, genuine choice excuses otherwise unacceptable inequalities.

Curiously enough, Dworkin advocates something very like the foregoing point of view in sketchy statements in "Why Liberals Should Care about Equality," but he is not faithful to it in "What Is Equality?" He says, in "Why Liberals Should Care about Equality," that we should

[50] Dworkin's main use of the insurance device is to deal with handicaps and talents: see "Equality of Resources," sections 3, 5, and 6 and see p. 296, and esp. p. 345 for the particular point that Dworkin insurers know what they think "is valuable in life."

[51] If it is relevant that, given the chance, a person might have insured against cheerlessness, why is it not relevant that he might have insured against ending up with tastes that happen to be expensive? Compare Alexander and Schwarzschild, "Liberalism, Neutrality, and Equality of Welfare versus Equality of Resources," pp. 99ff.

attend to "which aspects of any person's economic position flow from his choices and which from advantages and disadvantages that were not matters of choice."[52] That is the compelling core idea, but it is misrendered in the cut between preferences and resources. Elsewhere in "Why Liberals Should Care about Equality," Dworkin also comes close to adopting genuine-choice/*luck* as the basic distinction. He says that the liberal "accepts two principles":

> The first requires that people have, at any point in their lives, different amounts of wealth insofar as the genuine choices they have made have been more or less expensive or beneficial to the community, measured by what other people want for their lives. The market seems indispensable to this principle. The second requires that people not have different amounts of wealth just because they have different inherent capacities to produce what others want, or are differently favored by chance. This means that market allocations must be corrected in order to bring some people closer to the share of resources they would have had but for these various differences of initial advantage, luck and inherent capacity.[53]

I say that Dworkin comes close to the basic distinction I favor here, but he does not quite get there, partly because luck (or chance) appears in his text as only one element in a set of unjust distributors, others being differences in initial advantage and in inherent capacity. And I find Dworkin's disjunctions of unjust distributors strange. For anyone who thinks that initial advantage and inherent capacity are unjust distributors thinks so because he believes that they make a person's fate depend too much on sheer luck: the taxa in Dworkin's disjunctions belong to different levels, and one of them subsumes the others.

Now, once we see the central role that luck should play in a broadly Dworkinian theory of distributive justice, Dworkin's own propensity to compensate for resource misfortune but not for utility function misfortune comes to seem entirely groundless. For people can be unlucky not only in their unchosen resource endowments but also in their unchosen liabilities to pain and suffering and in their unchosen expensive preferences. A willingness to compensate for deficiencies in productive capacity but not in capacity to draw welfare from consumption consequently leads to absurd contrasts.

Consider lucky Adrian and unlucky Claude.[54] "The desires and needs of other people" mean that unlike Claude, Adrian can pursue "a satis-

[52] Dworkin, "Why Liberals Should Care about Equality," p. 208. ("What Is Equality?" is the joint title of "Equality of Welfare" and "Equality of Resources.")

[53] Dworkin, "Why Liberals Should Care about Equality," p. 207.

[54] Dworkin, "Equality of Resources," p. 308.

fying [gainful] occupation." People are happy to buy what Adrian, but not Claude, can enjoy producing, and that, for Dworkin, gives Claude a claim to redress quite separate from the one arising from the income difference between him and Adrian. But now suppose that, with respect to their leisure preferences, Adrian is like fisherman Fred, and Claude is like would-be photographer Paul,[55] and that the reason why fishing is cheap and photography is expensive is that many want to fish and few want to take pictures, so that economies of scale are realized in the production of fishing, but not of photographic, equipment. It would follow that "the desires and needs of other people" mean that, unlike Claude, Adrian can pursue "a satisfying [leisure] occupation." Yet Dworkin will not redistribute for that luck-derived discrepancy, since it lies in the domain of consumption and not that of production.[56] But that is not a good basis for redistributive reluctance. It is quite absurd to regard Adrian's opportunity to pursue a satisfying profession as an enviable "circumstance," justifying redistribution,[57] without extending the same treatment to his opportunity for satisfying leisure.[58]

We must eschew Dworkin's preferences/resources distinction in favor of a wider access-oriented egalitarianism. We can agree with him that "it is perhaps the final evil of a genuinely unequal distribution of resources that some people have reason for regret just in the fact that they have been cheated of the chances others have had to make something valuable of their lives."[59] But equalizing those chances requires a discriminating attention to what is and is not chosen, not to what belongs to preference as opposed to endowment. In a brilliant exposition of how Dworkin's theory corrects deficiencies in Rawls's, Will Kymlicka remarks that "it is unjust if people are disadvantaged by inequalities of their circumstances, but it is equally unjust for me to demand that someone else pay for the costs of my choices."[60] That expresses Dworkin's fundamental insight very well, but a proper insistence on the centrality of choice leads to a

[55] See Section 4*c* above.

[56] Dworkin's refusal to redistribute for the discrepancy is explicit at "Equality of Resources," p. 288.

[57] Ibid., p. 308.

[58] The foregoing criticism depends on Dworkin's classification (ibid., p. 304) of a satisfying occupation as, so described, a resource. In "Justice and Alienation," Michael Otsuka argues that that was a superficial error on Dworkin's part. But I do not think that Dworkin can declassify occupation as a resource—and thereby escape my argument in the text—except at the severe cost of losing his argument against throwing people's powers to produce into his island auction, since that argument rests on the idea that, with people's powers to produce up for auction, the talented would end up envying the package of occupation and income enjoyed by the ungifted (see Dworkin, "Equality of Resources," pp. 311–12).

[59] Dworkin, "Equality of Welfare," p. 219.

[60] Kymlicka, "Subsidizing People's Choices," p. 5.

different development of the insight from Dworkin's own. Dworkin has, in effect, performed for egalitarianism the considerable service of incorporating within it the most powerful idea in the arsenal of the antiegalitarian Right: the idea of choice and responsibility.[61] But that supreme effect of his contribution needs to be rendered more explicit.

Someone might say that to make choice central to distributive justice lands political philosophy in the morass of the free will problem. The distinction between preferences and resources is not metaphysically deep, but it is, by contrast, awesomely difficult to identify what represents *genuine* choice. Replacing Dworkin's cut by the one I have recommended subordinates political philosophy to metaphysical questions that may be impossible to answer.

To that expression of anxiety I have one unreassuring and one reassuring thing to say. The unreassuring thing is that we may indeed be up to our necks in the free will problem, but that is just tough luck. It is not a reason for not following the argument where it goes.

Now for the reassuring point. We are not looking for an absolute distinction between presence and absence of genuine choice. The amount of genuineness that there is in a choice is a matter of degree,[62] and egalitarian redress is indicated to the *extent* that a disadvantage does not reflect genuine choice. That extent is a function of several things, and there is no aspect of a person's situation which is wholly due to genuine choice.

Let me illustrate this point. One of the things that affects how genuine a choice was is the amount of relevant information that the chooser had. But we do not have to ask, Exactly what sort and amount of information must a person have to count as having genuinely chosen his fate? All that we need say, from the point of view of egalitarian justice, is: the more relevant information he had, the less cause for complaint he now has.

It seems to me that this plausible nuancing approach reduces the dependence of political philosophy on the metaphysics of mind.[63]

h. In a theory of distributive justice whose axis is the distinction between luck and choice, the positive injunction is to equalize advantage, save where inequality of advantage reflects choice. Now that sounds rather

[61] It is an idea much less deniable than the different idea of self-ownership, which is also central to right-wing thought. See the closing pages of Cohen, "Are Freedom and Equality Compatible?"

[62] This point corresponds to Dworkin's point that there is a continuum between brute and option luck (see "Equality of Resources," p. 293).

[63] Scanlon's recent Tanner Lectures entitled "The Significance of Choice" present a liberatingly nonmetaphysical approach to choice in the context of, among other things, distributive justice. I have not yet had the time to determine to what extent what he offers can be used to improve the statement of a broadly Dworkinian theory of distributive justice.

like equalizing the scope of genuine choice, of what, one might perhaps equivalently say, people are capable of doing. But, if those assimilations are correct, then the position latent in Dworkin looks close to the "capability equality" espoused by Amartya Sen, to which I shall turn after first facing a challenge to the emphasis I have placed on choice in articulating my conception of egalitarianism. The challenge will induce a needed revision of that conception.

5. Scanlon's Doubts about Voluntariness

a. According to Thomas Scanlon, when we examine a person's condition with a view to determining what distributive justice owes him, we treat some of his interests as commanding more attention than others on a basis which is independent of his own ranking of those interests. It follows that we do not pursue a policy of equality of welfare, where welfare is understood as preference satisfaction (and it will be so understood throughout this section).

Scanlon does not address the view that justice should concern itself with opportunity for welfare, as opposed to welfare *tout court*. But the fact that he rejects the sovereignty, from the point of view of justice, of the subject's own preference ordering means that he would also reject an opportunity form of egalitarian welfarism.

Now, the features of Scanlon's position described above produce no conflict with the view I have espoused, since equality of access to advantage is not identical with equality of opportunity for welfare; and, in deciding both what qualifies as an advantage and the relative sizes of advantages, it is necessary to engage in objective assessment of the kind that Scanlon emphasizes. I nevertheless find two challenges to the view I have adopted in Scanlon's writings.[64]

As thus far developed, that view favors compensation for *all* deficits in ("inoffensive")[65] welfare which do not reflect the subject's *choice*. On this reading of the egalitarian attitude, it recommends a two-stage procedure. First, any deficit in welfare is treated as a possible case for compensation; then, whether it actually constitutes such a case is decided by facts about choice.[66] I discover in Scanlon's writings an objection to each stage of that procedure. First, he adduces examples of welfare deficit

[64] There are further challenges in his "The Significance of Choice," which I have not yet been able to study with care. See, in particular, the second lecture's critique of the "Forfeiture View," with which my own has affinities.

[65] See Section 3 above. I shall henceforth take the parenthesized qualification as read.

[66] I do not here mean a *conclusive* case: not only the distribution of nonwelfare advantages but also nonegalitarian considerations might defeat the welfare deficit claim.

where the idea of compensation seems excluded from the start. Second, he offers a train of reasoning whose conclusion is that choice lacks the importance for distributive justice which it initially appears to have. If Scanlon is right, choice is just a surface indicator of something different and deeper.

According to Scanlon, (certain?) welfare deficits which reflect the subject's adherence to a religion raise no *prima facie* case for compensation:

> Differences in religious belief are one thing that can produce differences in utility level, and someone who regarded equality of welfare as the standard of interpersonal justification would have to regard these differences as being grounds for compensation: compensation for having acquired a particularly onerous or guilt-inducing religion or one particularly unsuited to one's own personal strengths and weaknesses. This strikes me as distinctly odd. Quite apart from the fact that it might destroy the point of religious burdens to have them lightened by social compensation, the idea that these burdens are grounds for such compensation (a form of bad luck) is incompatible with regarding them as matters of belief and conviction which one values and adheres to because one thinks them right.[67]

Scanlon's powerful example forces me to choose among the following strategies: (1) to argue that it is because the burdens of religion so manifestly reflect choice that compensation for them is out of the question; (2) to argue that it is not as odd as Scanlon maintains to compensate a person for those burdens; (3) to revise my view that all burdens which do not reflect choice raise a case for compensation.

Before exploring these alternatives, I want to remark on a difference between the two kinds of religiously derived burdens mentioned by Scanlon in the passage quoted above. First, there is the burden of religiously induced guilt. And then there is the burden of one's religion being unsuited to one's strengths and weaknesses. Those two burdens seem to me to be relevantly different. It does seem, at least at first, "distinctly odd" to compensate for religiously induced guilt, but there are *some* discrepancies between a person's religion and his repertoire of capacity for which it is not similarly peculiar to offer compensation. I do not think that it is strange for a lame or poor person to request the cost of transport for a pilgrimage mandated by his religious convictions. And even if Scanlon means "strengths and weaknesses" of an intimately psychological kind only, there would still, I think, be cases falling under that description where compensation did not look so odd. I shall, however, focus on the particularly powerful guilt example.

[67] Scanlon, "Equality of Resources and Equality of Welfare," pp. 116–17.

Strategy 1 for dealing with that example is to represent the person's guilt as due to his choice of religion and as not raising a case for compensation for that reason. But people often no more choose to acquire a particular religion than they do to speak a particular language: in most cases, both come with upbringing. And when upbringing instills a religion which, like the one Scanlon describes, has a doxastic character (it is not just a way of life but, centrally, a set of beliefs), then we cannot regard its convinced adherent as choosing to retain it, any more than we can regard him as choosing to retain his belief that the world is round.

Strategy 2 says that compensating a person for religious guilt is not as strange as Scanlon maintains. To be sure, it would be strange for the subject himself to request compensation for his painful guilt feelings, since he believes that he *should* feel guilty: although he has in no sense chosen to have the feelings, *he would not choose not to have them if he could.*[68] It is, however, far less clear that those of us who reject his religion should have no inclination to compensate him for his guilt. If a person suffers because of (what we think is) a *plainly* false belief that God has commanded him to suffer, and we cannot persuade him that he is under an illusion, should we do nothing for him because he believes that he is owed nothing? If his belief is sapping his life, might we not give him priority when we distribute scarce recreational facilities? Why should *his* belief be sovereign here?[69]

When our own convictions match those of the believer there is no purchase for the main claim of strategy 2, which is that the demands of justice may exceed the demands a person could intelligibly make on his own behalf. Strategy 3 does not employ that claim. This final strategy is to revise the view I have defended, as follows. Instead of saying, "compensate for disadvantages which are not traceable to the subject's choice," say, "compensate for disadvantages which are not traceable to the subject's choice *and* which the subject would choose not to suffer from." The revisionary element is the second clause. In the revised view, choice appears at two levels, actual and counterfactual. The revision seems to me not *ad hoc* but a natural development of the original view in the face of Scanlon's example.

The amendment is natural because it is true to the grounding idea that disadvantage is to be redressed when it reflects either exploitation or bad

[68] I do not mean that if, contrary to fact, he could choose not to have them, he would not so choose: ". . . if he could" is within the scope of the description of what he would not (now) choose. In saying "I would not give it up if I could" he is not making a prediction.

[69] One might say: because it would destroy the point for him of his religious commitment to compensate him for the burdens associated with it. But that answer is here out of place; I am responding to the part of Scanlon's case which he represents as "quite apart" (see the last sentence of the passage quoted at n. 67 above) from the foregoing consideration.

luck. Up to now, I have treated choice as the only relevant opposite of luck, but the Scanlon example shows that some of the costs of unchosen commitments (and they are commitments because one would not choose not to have them) are also not bad luck: they are not bad luck when they are so *intrinsically connected* with his commitments that their bearer would not choose to be without them.

The strong requirement of intrinsic connection establishes a contrast between Scanlon's believer and people whose expensive preferences engage my concern but not Dworkin's. The believer differs from a person whose preferences are not governed by belief at all and which *a fortiori* represent no commitment, such as someone who prefers plovers' eggs to hens' because the former were household fare in childhood. And the costs the believer incurs also differ relevantly from those sustained by the committed lover of expensive esoteric music (see Section 4*e* above), since the high price of satisfying the latter's preference is not integral to the commitment mandating that preference: that Berg is more expensive than bebop is no part of what makes Berg better for most Berg lovers. It is just an unfortunate fact, and Berg lovers consequently do not break faith with their commitment to what they think is good music when they campaign for a Lincoln Center in which to hear it. Most would not choose to lack their esoteric taste, but they would certainly choose not to sustain the frustration that happens to accompany it, and that produces a relevant disanalogy with the case of the guilty religious believer. It means that we might think it right to provide a Lincoln Center even for those who forgo an offer to be schooled out of their highbrow musical tastes (see comment 4 in Section 4*e* above).

It follows from those contrasts that the Scanlon-inspired amendment enforces no retreat from anything ventured above in critique of Dworkin's view. I do not, however, want to understate the amendment's significance. Its policy implications are entirely negligible, but it does introduce a conceptual element very different from anything required to resist Dworkin. For counterfactual choice is *not* a kind of choice, even though, like choice, it is strictly inconsistent with luck. It is neither because of his choice nor because of bad luck that Scanlon's believer suffers.

Since the Scanlon amendment charges only for the intrinsic costs of commitments, it is not engaged by the pilgrimage case introduced earlier in this section. That case is similar to the example of the monument, which Scanlon uses in prosecution of his opposition to welfarism:

> The strength of a stranger's claim on us for aid in the fulfillment of some interest depends upon what that interest is and need not be proportional to the importance he attaches to it. The fact that someone would be willing to forgo a decent diet in order to build a monu-

> ment to his god does not mean that his claim on others for aid in his project has the same strength as a claim for aid in obtaining enough to eat (even assuming that the sacrifices required of others would be the same). Perhaps a person does have some claim on others for assistance in a project to which he attaches such great importance. All I need maintain is that it does not have the weight of a claim to aid in the satisfaction of a truly urgent interest even if the person in question assigns these interests equal weight.[70]

I see no glaring oddity in a believer's claim that, since all should be equally able to worship as they will, his own worship, because it requires what happens to be expensive, warrants public subsidy.[71] Note that even Scanlon allows that, unlike the man burdened with a sense of sin, the monument builder might well have *a* claim on us. But, under the suggested amendment to my view, and as I am sure Scanlon would agree, the man's claim would lapse if his religion required him to build a monument *because* it was expensive, and therefore onerous to supply, for its cost to him would not then be a disadvantage which he would choose to have removed: it would be intrinsic to his religious commitment.

b. I turn to Scanlon's second challenge to the position I have espoused. I have in mind his argument against the importance of beliefs about choice in the explanation of our unwillingness to cater to expensive preferences.

Citing Rawls's suggestion that distributive justice does not attend to desire as such because desires are subject to our control, Scanlon provisionally hypothesizes that it is because preferences are "too nearly voluntary" that they are not "an appropriate basis for the adjudication of competing claims."[72]

Scanlon then asks in what way or sense preferences could be considered voluntary. He notes that they are not voluntary in the sense of being immediately subject to the will but allows that there is scope for volition "in the malleability of preferences over time."[73] So "perhaps the force of the voluntariness objection[74] lies in that it is possible for unusually strong

[70] Scanlon, "Preference and Urgency," pp. 659–60. Since Scanlon later (p. 666) assigns a special urgency to religious concern, one must charitably read the suggestion above that the need for a monument is not a "truly urgent interest" as a too strong way of saying that it is less urgent than a person's interest in a decent diet.

[71] Compare Arneson, "Equality and Equal Opportunity for Welfare."

[72] Scanlon, "Preference and Urgency," pp. 663–64. Scanlon cites Rawls, "A Kantian Conception of Equality," p. 97. See, too, the passage from Rawls, "Social Unity and Primary Goods," quoted in Section 3 above.

[73] Scanlon, "Preference and Urgency," p. 664.

[74] To, i.e., the idea that distributive justice should track preference strength as such.

or unusually expensive preferences" not, indeed, to be chosen at will, but "to be 'manufactured' by the person who has them."[75] But Scanlon proceeds to reject this account of the matter:

> But if this were the whole basis for the voluntariness objection one would expect that, at least in principle, the actual genesis of a person's preferences would be relevant to the strength of their claim to be satisfied. The very same intense interest might have arisen out of a conscious decision to "take up" a certain activity, or it might have grown almost unnoticed as the result of a series of chance encounters. Which of these is the case does not, however, seem to matter for the purposes of determining the strength of the person's claim on others for aid in the satisfaction of this interest. (Although it may be relevant to the assessment of his claim to aid in getting rid of the interest should he come to regard it as an obsession which cripples him in the pursuit of his normal activities.)[76]

I do not agree with Scanlon's contention that "the actual genesis of a person's preferences" is irrelevant to the strength of his claim to have them satisfied. Suppose that each of two people have developed an expensive interest, and it is of a kind which, once contracted, cannot be extinguished, so that there is no question of any claim for assistance in getting rid of it. One of them, however, made a "conscious decision" to develop the interest, with full foreknowledge of the cost of satisfying it, while the other just happened to come by it, unawares, or developed it before it became expensive for wholly unforeseeable reasons. Then, so I believe, we should extend more sympathy and favor to the second person. We might say of the first, "we must, in all charity, help him"; but it would be much harder to say in his case than in the case of the other, "we must, in all justice, help him." I therefore dissent from Scanlon's reasoning at this point. But it will nevertheless prove instructive to see how it continues.

Scanlon holds that there is something quite different from voluntariness underlying the reference to voluntariness. It is the very "fact that an interest, given its content, *could* have arisen" either voluntarily or not which is crucial, for that fact shows that the interest in question might not have arisen at all.[77] And, since it might not have arisen, Scanlon concludes that, from an objective point of view, it is of "peripheral importance," whatever may be the importance it has to the individual himself.[78] Hence, by a roundabout route, the suggestion that expensive tastes have

[75] Scanlon, "Preference and Urgency," p. 664.
[76] Ibid., pp. 664–65.
[77] Quoted material from ibid., p. 665, my emphasis.
[78] Ibid.

no claim on us because they are deliberately cultivated is transmuted into the idea that they are of objectively secondary significance, however high the person himself may rank them: in a word, justice should not cater to *idiosyncrasy*, whatever its genesis may be.

One may say that, according to Scanlon, the liaison between interest and volition has implications for justice because of the following argument:

(1) Sometimes people choose to develop a certain interest.
∴ (2) It is the sort of interest that a person could develop as a matter of choice.
∴ (3) It is an interest that might not develop: it is objectively peripheral.
∴ (4) It is an interest not commanding the urgent attention of justice (whether or not it was developed as a result of choice).

The final inference in this argument appears to me to be questionable. Scanlon himself raises a question about it: "Could there be an interest which . . . people might or might not happen to have—but which, if a person had it, would be the basis for urgent claims? . . . I cannot come up with an example. . . . Religion might seem to be an example. In our society some people are concerned with religion, others are not. Yet the claims of one's religious preferences not to be interfered with are thought to have a special urgency. But would this be so if it were not thought that religion *or something like it* has a central place in anyone's life?"[79]

In assessing Scanlon's claim that there is no urgent interest which is not universally shared, we have to be careful about the level of generality at which interests are individuated. Faced with the putative counterexample of religion, Scanlon regresses to a higher level of generality: he says that we think religion merits certain forms of protection because "religion *or something like it* has a central place in anyone's life." But now one has to ask: like religion in what way? And the answer cannot be: like it in mattering so much to the person in question, for that would return us to the subjective welfare ordering which Scanlon is seeking to eschew: "central place," at the end of the foregoing passage, has to be taken objectively. But then I cannot see what thing relevantly similar to religion appears in every normal person's life. And I therefore disagree with Scanlon's suggestion that religion fails to provide a counterexample of the required kind.

I do not, in conclusion, disacknowledge the need for objective assessment in arriving at distributive decisions: I recognized its inescapability at the beginning of this section. It is necessary for the purpose of deciding

[79] Ibid., pp. 665–66.

what an advantage is. My more limited conclusion is that the apparent importance for justice of facts about volition with respect to the genesis of a disadvantage deriving from preference is not a confused surface reflection of the priority of objective assessment.

6. Sen on Capability

How does *equality of access to advantage* relate to what Amartya Sen has called *capability equality*?

As I am using 'access,' a person enjoys access to something which he does not have only if he has both the *opportunity* and the *capacity* to obtain it, in the ordinary senses of those words, under which they name distinct requirements, neither of which entails the other. Now, even if 'capability,' in its ordinary meaning, differs from "capacity," it, too, nevertheless fails to entail "opportunity" (one might be capable of swimming without having the opportunity to swim), and from that one might conclude that my access is more demanding than Sen's capability and that our readings of equality consequently differ. But Sen's capability is not ordinary capability. It requires possession of external wherewithal, and it covers opportunity too: sometimes, indeed, Sen uses the very word 'opportunity,' in an extended sense, to mean what he more usually uses the word 'capability' to mean.[80] Hence the ordinary meanings of the words 'access' and 'capability' do not establish that our two readings of equality are distinct.

It would, however, be premature to conclude that they are identical, for several reasons. One of them is that there is a substantial ambiguity in Sen's use of the term 'capability,' which makes it hard to be sure exactly what his conception of equality implies. For in his seminal "Equality of What?" Sen identified two ways of assessing a person's condition under the single name "capability," and the unnoticed and confusing duality has persisted in his subsequent writings. Both dimensions of assessment should attract egalitarian interest, but at most one of them merits the name "capability." The identification of the other dimension constitutes a striking contribution to normative understanding, but just that dimension is hard to perceive in Sen's exposition, because it is not felicitously described in the language (of "functioning" and "capability") which Sen uses to characterize it.

[80] Immediately after introducing the notion of "*capability* to function" in his Dewey Lectures, Sen shifts to the alternative language of "opportunity" to express the same idea (see "Well-Being, Agency and Freedom," pp. 200–201). Compare Sen, *Commodities and Capabilities*, p. 59; *The Standard of Living*, p. 36.

Sen arrived at what he called "capability" through reflection on the main candidates for assessment of well-being which were in the field when he gave his 1979 lecture, to wit, utility, or welfare, and Rawlsian primary goods.[81] Sen pleaded for a metric of well-being which measured something falling *between* primary goods and utility, in a sense that will presently be explained, a something which had, amazingly, been largely neglected in previous literature. He called that something 'capability.'

Right from the start, however, 'capability' was used to denote two things, one of which was larger than the other, and 'capability' was not a felicitously chosen name for the larger one.

Sen said that "what is missing in all this framework[82] is some notion of 'basic capabilities': a person being able to do certain basic things."[83] But that relatively narrow characterization of the missing dimension was different from another which he offered in the same text, and which was more in keeping with his *argument* for the new perspective.

Sen's argument against the primary goods metric was that differently constructed and situated people require different amounts of primary goods to satisfy the same needs, so that "judging advantage purely in terms of primary goods leads to a partially blind morality."[84] It is, Sen rightly said, a "fetishist handicap" to be concerned with goods as such to the exclusion of what goods "*do* to human beings."[85] Both hedonic and preference satisfaction welfarists are free of that particular fetishism, since they are concerned "with what these things do to human beings, but they use a metric [utility] that focuses not on the person's capabilities

[81] A notable further candidate not yet then in print was Dworkin's equality of resources. Dworkinian resources differ from Rawlsian primary goods in a number of ways. One is that they include a person's mental and physical powers. It would be a worthwhile—and difficult—exercise to distinguish each of the two Sen dimensions I shall describe from the Dworkin resources dimension. (For pertinent remarks, see Sen's excellent rebuttal, all of which strikes me as correct, of Dworkin's criticism of Sen's view, at pp. 321–23 of "Rights and Capabilities.")

[82] That is, the framework of discussion restricted to the rival claims of primary goods and utility as measures of well-being, and, within "primary goods," to goods in the ordinary sense. That is the relevant subset of primary goods here, and also in Rawls's discussion of expensive tastes.

[83] Sen, "Equality of What?" p. 218.

[84] Ibid., p. 216.

[85] Ibid., p. 218. Compare this statement: "What people get out of goods depends on a variety of factors, and judging personal advantage just by the size of personal ownership of goods and services can be very misleading. . . . It seems reasonable to move away from a focus on goods as such to what goods do to human beings" (Sen, introduction to *Choice, Welfare and Measurement*, pp. 29–30). Compare Sen, "Ethical Issues in Income Distribution," p. 294; *Commodities and Capabilities*, p. 23; and *The Standard of Living*, pp. 15–16, 22.

but on his mental reaction."[86] And that mental reaction is an unsuitable guide to policy, if only because people adjust their expectations to their conditions. The fact that a person has learned to live with adversity, and to smile courageously in the face of it, should not nullify his claim to compensation.[87]

Capabilities were thereby identified with what goods do to (or for) human beings, in abstraction from the utility they confer on them. But that identification was a mistake. For, even when utility has been set aside, it remains untrue that all that goods do for people is confer capability[88] on them, or that the uniquely important thing they do for them is that, or that that is the only thing they do for them which matters from an egalitarian point of view. In naming his view "Capability Equality" Sen failed to recognize the true shape and size of one of the dimensions he had uncovered.

It is indeed false that the normatively relevant effect on a person of his bundle of primary goods depends entirely on his mental reaction to what they do for him. There is also what welfarists ignore: what they do for him, what he gets out of them, apart from his mental reaction to or personal evaluation of that service. Consequently, Sen was right that, in the enterprise of assessing a person's well-being, we must consider his condition or state in abstraction from its utility for him. We must look at something which is "posterior" to "having goods" and "prior" to "having utility."[89] We must look, for example, at his nutrition level, and not just, as Rawlsians do, at his food supply, or, as welfarists do, at the utility he derives from eating food.[90]

But this significant and illuminating reorientation is not equivalent to focusing on a person's capability, where that is what he is able, all things considered, to do. Capability, and exercises of capability, form only part of the neglected intermediate (between primary goods and utility) state. *What goods do to or for people is not identical with what people are able to do with them*, nor even with what they actually do with them. To be sure, it is usually true that a person must do something with a good (take it in, put it on, go inside it, etc.) in order to be benefited by it, but that is

[86] Sen, "Equality of What?" p. 218. "Mental reaction" must here cover not only a kind of experience but also a subjective valuation, to cater for the preference form of welfarism.

[87] This argument against the utility metric was not fully explicit in Sen, "Equality of What?" It appears at *Commodities and Capabilities*, pp. 21–22, 29; "Rights and Capabilities," pp. 308–9; introduction to *Resources, Values and Development*, p. 34; "Goods and People," in *Resources, Values and Development*, p. 512, *The Standard of Living*, pp. 8–11.

[88] Even in Sen's acceptably extended sense of the term—see earlier in this section—which is the sense in which I use it here.

[89] Sen, *Commodities and Capabilities*, p. 11.

[90] Sen, introduction to *Choice, Welfare and Measurement*, p. 30.

not always true, and, even when it is true, one must distinguish what the good does for the person from what he does with it.

Not all that matters and is not utility is capability or an exercise of capability or a result of exercising capability. And many states which are indeed a result of exercising capability have a (nonutility) value which is unconnected with their status as effects of capability exercise, and which is not clearly exhibited in its true independence of capability (properly so-called) by Sen. A further development and defense of these critical contentions will appear elsewhere.[91, 92]

[91] [See Chapter 2 of this volume.—Ed.]

[92] I thank Jerry Barnes and Tim Scanlon for their generously extended and very incisive criticism of a draft of this article. And, for their many helpful comments, I also thank Richard Arneson, John Baker, Tim Besley, Ronald Dworkin, John Gardner, David Knott, Will Kymlicka, David Lloyd-Thomas, Grahame Lock, John McMurtry, Michael Otsuka, Derek Parfit, Joseph Raz, Amartya Sen, and Philippe Van Parijs.

Chapter Two

EQUALITY OF WHAT? ON WELFARE, GOODS, AND CAPABILITIES

1. Introduction

The publication of John Rawls's *A Theory of Justice* in 1971 was a watershed in discussion bearing on the question, derived from Sen, which forms my title. Before *A Theory of Justice* appeared, political philosophy was dominated by utilitarianism, the theory that sound social policy aims at the maximization of welfare. Rawls found two features of utilitarianism repugnant. He objected, first, to its aggregative character, its unconcern about the pattern of distribution of welfare, which means that inequality in its distribution calls for no justification. But, more pertinently to the present exercise, Rawls also objected to the utilitarian assumption that welfare is the aspect of a person's condition which commands normative attention. Rawls replaced aggregation by equality and welfare by primary goods. He recommended normative evaluation with new arguments (goods instead of welfare quanta) and a new function (equality[1] instead of aggregation) from those arguments to values.

Rawls's critique of the welfare metric was undoubtedly powerful, but his motivation for replacing it by attention to primary goods was not correspondingly cogent. He did not consider, as an alternative to equality of welfare, the claims of equality of opportunity for welfare, which his criticisms of equality of welfare do not touch. What is more, those criticisms positively favor equality of opportunity for welfare as a remedy for the defects in the rejected doctrine.[2]

Reprinted in part from *The Quality of Life*, ed. Martha C. Nussbaum and Amartya Sen, 1993. Chapter: "Equality of What? On Welfare, Goods, and Capabilities," by Cohen, pp. 9–29. By permission of Oxford University Press.

Editor's note: This chapter is an abridgment of Cohen's "Equality of What?" The first two paragraphs of the Introduction and the section entitled "Rawlsian Criticism of Equality of Welfare" have been eliminated because they overlap with material in "On the Currency," which has been reprinted in full as Chapter 1 of this volume.

[1] Or, strictly, the maximin function, which enjoins departures from equality when the worst off benefit as a result. But that complication is of no significance here.

[2] [Here Cohen sketches a critique of Rawls that receives its full statement in Section 3 of "On the Currency."—Ed.]

But while equality of opportunity for welfare survives Rawls's criticisms of equality of welfare, arguments against the welfare metric which were later advanced by Sen also apply against its opportunity-defined cousin. Sen called for attention to something like opportunity (under the title "capability"),[3] but it was not welfare, or not, at any rate, welfare alone, which Sen thought people should have the opportunity to achieve. Instead, he drew attention to the condition of a person (e.g., his level of nutrition) in a central sense captured neither by his stock of goods (e.g., his food supply) nor by his welfare level (e.g., the pleasure or desire satisfaction he obtains from consuming food). In advancing beyond Rawls, Sen therefore proposed two large changes of view: from actual state to opportunity, and from goods (and welfare) to what he sometimes called "functionings."

In my view, Sen's answer to his own question was a great leap forward in contemporary reflection on the subject. But often a thinker who achieves a revolution misdescribes his own achievement, and I shall argue, at some length, that Sen's work is a case in point. He moved away from Rawlsian and other views in two directions which were orthogonal to each other. If Rawls and welfarists fixed on what a person gets in welfare or goods, Sen fixed on what he gets in a space between welfare and goods (nutrition is delivered by goods supply and it generates welfare), but he also emphasized what a person *can* get, as opposed to (just) what he *does*. Sen's misdescription of his achievement lay in his appropriation of the word 'capability' to describe both of his moves, so that his position, as he presented it, is disfigured by ambiguity. I shall here expose the ambiguity in Sen's use of 'capability' (and cognate terms), and I shall also propose an answer to his (my title) question which departs from his own in a modest way.

2. Sen and Capability

a. The foregoing critique of Rawls [that was sketched in the second paragraph of the previous section—Ed.] does not prove that quantity of primary goods is the wrong metric for egalitarian evaluation; it just proves that a major reason Rawls offered for favoring primary goods points, instead, to equality of opportunity for welfare. For a more thorough refutation of the primary goods proposal, I turn to Sen's "Equality of What?" That seminal article also argues persuasively against the welfare metric,

[3] Immediately after introducing the notion of "*capability* to function" in the Dewey Lectures, Sen shifts to the alternative language of "opportunity" to express the same idea. See "Well-Being, Agency and Freedom," pp. 200–201. Cf. *Commodities and Capabilities*, p. 59; *The Standard of Living*, p. 36.

and, while Sen did not address equality of opportunity for welfare, his argument against equality of welfare readily extends itself to the former view. After presenting and endorsing Sen's negative arguments, I shall argue that his positive replacing proposal, capability equality, suffers from a severe expositional obscurity.

Sen's argument against the primary goods metric was simple but powerful. It was that differently constructed and situated people require different amounts of primary goods to satisfy the same needs, so that "judging advantage in terms of primary goods leads to a partially blind morality."[4] It is, Sen rightly said, a "fetishist handicap" to be concerned with goods as such, to the exclusion of what goods "*do* to human beings."[5] Or, as Sen later expressed the point: "what people get out of goods depends on a variety of factors, and judging personal advantage just by the size of personal ownership of goods and services can be very misleading . . . It seems reasonable to move away from a focus on goods as such to what goods do to human beings."[6] The principle of equality condemns equal goods provision to a sound-limbed person and a paraplegic, because greater resources are necessary to enable the latter to achieve mobility, a desideratum to which a metric of stock of wealth is blind.[7]

Sen also used the example of the needy cripple to good effect against the welfare alternative to primary goods. For the egalitarian response to his plight is not determined by a judgment that he suffers a welfare deficiency. Perhaps, indeed, he suffers no such thing, "because he has a jolly disposition. Or because he has a low aspiration level and his heart leaps up whenever he sees a rainbow in the sky."[8] So while both hedonic and preference satisfaction welfarists are free of the goods theorist's fetishistic neglect of what goods do to human beings, Sen criticized them for their too-narrow view of what people get from goods, for focusing "not on the person's capabilities but on his mental reaction," not, for example, on how much nourishment a person gets from food, but on how much utility, which is a matter of mental reaction or attitude, he derives from such nourishment.[9] Utility is an unsuitable guide to policy, if only because a person may adjust his expectations to his condition. The fact that a

[4] "Equality of What?" p. 216.

[5] Ibid., p. 218; see also "Ethical Issues in Income Distribution," p. 294; *Commodities and Capabilities*, p. 23; *The Standard of Living*, pp. 15–16, 22.

[6] Introduction to *Choice, Welfare and Measurement*, pp. 29–30.

[7] "Equality of What?" p. 218.

[8] Ibid., p. 217.

[9] Ibid., p. 218. "Mental reaction" must here cover not only a kind of experience but also a subjective valuation, to cater for the preference form of welfarism.

person has learned to live with adversity, and to smile courageously in the face of it, should not nullify his claim to compensation.[10]

His high welfare score is thus not a decisive reason for not assisting someone who labors under a severe disadvantage, which is recognizable as such from an objective point of view. His equanimity may, after all, reflect admirable and reward-worthy striving to overcome a natural reaction of misery. But even if no such striving is necessary, because the person is blessed from birth with an extra-sunny disposition, the requirement of compensation retains intuitive force. And that means that not only equality of welfare but also equality of opportunity for welfare falls before the case of the cripple. Consider the poor and lame but sunny-spirited Tiny Tim. Tiny Tim is *actually* happy, by any welfarist standard. And we may also suppose that, because of a fortunate innate disposition, he is blessed with abundant *opportunity* for happiness, that he need not do much to get a lot of it. Yet egalitarians would not on that account strike him off the list of free wheelchair receivers. Hence they do not think that wheelchair distribution should be controlled exclusively by the welfare opportunity requirements of those who need them. They need wheelchairs to be adequately resourced, whether or not they also need them to be, or to be capable of being, happy.

b. In the course of making the critical points reported and endorsed above, Sen used the term 'capability,' and he appropriated that term to denote his own positive counterproposal. I shall now argue that, in "Equality of What?," Sen brought two distinct aspects of a person's condition under that single name, and that this unnoticed duality has persisted in his subsequent writings. Both aspects, or dimensions of assessment, should attract egalitarian interest, but one of them is not felicitously described as "capability." The identification of that latter dimension constitutes a particularly striking contribution to normative understanding, but just that dimension is hard to perceive in Sen's exposition, because of the unfortunate and ambiguous nomenclature.

As we have seen, Sen arrived at what he called "capability" through reflection on the main candidates for assessment of well-being that were in the field when he gave his 1979 lecture [entitled "Equality of What?" —Ed.], to wit, utility, or welfare, and Rawlsian primary goods.[11] Sen pleaded for a metric of well-being which measured something falling

[10] See, for further development of this point, *Commodities and Capabilities*, pp. 21–22, 29; introduction to *Resources, Values and Development*, p. 34; "Rights and Capabilities," pp. 308–9; "Goods and People," p. 512; *The Standard of Living*, pp. 8–11.

[11] A notable further candidate not yet then in print is Dworkin's equality of resources. It would be a worthwhile—and difficult—exercise to distinguish each of the two Sen

between primary goods and utility, in a sense that will presently be explained—a something which had, amazingly, been largely neglected in previous literature. He called that something "capability": "what is missing in all this framework[12] is some notion of 'basic capabilities': a person being able to do certain basic things."[13] But that characterization of the missing dimension was different from another which Sen offered in the same text, and which was more in keeping with his *argument* for the new perspective.

According to that argument, as we have seen, it is necessary to attend to what goods do to (or for) human beings, in abstraction from the utility they confer on them. But to call what goods supply to human beings "capability" was a mistake. For even when utility has been set aside, it is not true that all that goods do for people is confer capability on them—provide them, that is, with the capacity to do things—or that that is the uniquely important thing they do for them, or that that is the one thing they do for them that matters from an egalitarian point of view. In naming his view "Basic Capability Equality" Sen failed to delineate the true shape and size of one of the dimensions he had uncovered, and which I shall now try to describe.

It is indeed false that the whole relevant effect on a person of his bundle of primary goods is on, or in virtue of, his mental reaction to what they do for him. There is also what welfarists ignore: what they do for him, what he gets out of them, apart from his mental reaction to or personal evaluation of that service. I shall call that nonutility effect of goods *midfare*, because it is in a certain sense midway between goods and utility. Midfare is constituted of states of the person produced by goods, states in virtue of which utility levels take the values they do. It is "posterior" to "having goods" and "prior" to "having utility."[14]

Midfare is a heterogeneous collocation, because goods do categorially various things for people: (1) they endow them with capabilities properly so called, which they may or may not use; (2) through people's exercise of those capabilities, goods contribute to the performance of valuable activities *and* the achievement of desirable states; and (3) goods cause further desirable states directly, without any exercise of capability on the part of

---

dimensions I shall describe from the Dworkin resources dimension. (For pertinent remarks, see Sen's excellent rebuttal, all of which strikes me as correct, of Dworkin's criticism of Sen's view: "Rights and Capabilities," pp. 321–23.)

[12] That is, the framework of discussion restricted to the rival claims of primary goods and utility as measures of well-being, and, within "primary goods," to goods in the ordinary sense. It is that subset of primary goods which is pertinent here.

[13] "Equality of What?" p. 218.

[14] *Commodities and Capabilities*, p. 11. Midfare is the "*state* of a person" in the sense of ibid., p. 23.

their beneficiary: an example would be the goods which destroy the insects that cause malaria. Capability (properly so called) is, then, a part of midfare, for it certainly cannot be excluded from the range of things that goods confer on people, yet, equally certainly, it does not exhaust that range.

Each terminus of the goods–midfare–utility sequence has seemed to some the right focus for assessment of a person's situation from an egalitarian point of view. Rawlsians look at the beginning of the sequence and welfarists look at its end. Welfarists think that the Rawlsian measure is too objective, that it takes too little account of distinguishing facts about individuals. Rawlsians think that the welfare measure is too subjective, that it takes too much account of just such facts. The reasons each side gives for disparaging its opponent's dimension suggest that each should prefer midfare to the dimension favored by its opponent. Welfarists draw attention to utility because, so they say, people do not care about goods as such but about the utility they provide. But, since people also care more about midfare than about goods as such (save where they are *themselves* being fetishistic), the welfarist reason for preferring welfare to goods is also a reason for preferring midfare to the latter. Advocates of goods oppose the welfare metric because, they say, the welfare consequences of goods consumption are (1) too subject to volition (Rawls, sometimes[15]), (2) too much a matter of people's (not necessarily chosen) identifications (Rawls at other times,[16] Dworkin[17]), or (3) too idiosyncratic (Scanlon[18]). On all three grounds midfare arguably scores better than utility does.

Given that each side in the foregoing division has reason to prefer the midfare dimension to the one favored by its opponents, it is extraordinary that midfare had not been uncovered, and Sen's reorienting proposal was consequently profound and liberating, albeit remarkably simple. For it simply says that, in the enterprise of assessing a person's well-being, we must look to her condition in abstraction from its utility for her. We must look, for example, at her nutrition level, and not just, as Rawlsians do, at her food supply, or, as welfarists do, at the utility she gets out of eating food.[19]

But this significant and illuminating reorientation is not equivalent to focusing on a person's capability, in any ordinary sense. Capability, and

[15] See [the paragraph in the main text of "On the Currency" to which n. 12 is appended—Ed.].

[16] See the reference to "Citizens' Needs and Primary Goods" in [n. 12 of "On the Currency"—Ed.].

[17] See "Equality of Welfare," pp. 228–40; "Equality of Resources," pp. 302–3; and, for criticism of the latter, see Section 3*c* of my "On the Currency."

[18] See his "Preference and Urgency," pp. 659–66, and see Section 5*b* of my "On the Currency" for criticism of Scanlon's idiosyncrasy claim.

[19] Introduction to *Choice, Welfare and Measurement*, p. 30.

exercises of capability, form only one part of the intermediate midfare state. *What goods do to people is identical neither with what people are able to do with them nor with what they actually do with them* (and it is also not identical with all or part of the combination of these two things). To be sure, it is usually true that a person must do something with a good (take it in, put it on, go inside it, etc.) in order to be benefited by it, but that is not always true, and, even where it is true, one must distinguish what the good does *for* the person from what he does *with* it. The colloquial question "How are you doing?" can be used to ask after a person's midfare (especially when this pedantic rider is attached to it: "by which I do not mean how do you feel about how you are doing"), but the usual answer will not be (just) a list of capacities, activities, and results of activities, because not all midfare is capability or an exercise of capability or a result of exercising capability. And many midfare states which are indeed a result of exercising capability have a (nonutility) value which is unconnected with their status as effects of exercising capability, and which is not clearly exhibited in its true independence of capability by Sen.

The case of food, which has, of course, exercised Sen a great deal, illustrates my claims. The main good thing that food does for people is that it nourishes them. Typically, of course, people become nourished by nourishing or feeding themselves, by exercising the capability of nourishing themselves which ownership of food confers on them. But the fact that food gives a person the capability to nourish himself is not the same fact as (and is usually less important than) the fact that it enables him to be nourished. To say that food enables him to be nourished is to say that it makes it possible for him to be nourished. That he characteristically actualizes that possibility himself is a further (and usually less important) fact. When, moreover, we ask how well nourished a person is, we are not asking how well he has nourished himself, even though the answer to the two questions will usually be the same; and we are usually primarily interested in the answer to the first question.[20]

The difference between midfare and capability (properly so called) will perhaps become more evident if we reflect a little about small babies. Small babies do not sustain themselves through exercises of capability. But it is false that, in the case of babies, goods generate utility and nothing else worth mentioning. When food is assigned for the consumption of either a baby or an adult, each is enabled to be nourished. The fact

[20] In one place ("Goods and People," p. 510), Sen makes one of the distinctions on which I am insisting: "while goods and services are valuable, they are not valuable in themselves. Their value rests on what they can do for people, or rather, what people can do with these goods and services." But why does Sen here reject his first and, in my view, superior suggestion in favor of the second? Because, I suggest, of an interest in advocating freedom, which is a desideratum different from midfare: see subsection *d* below.

that only the adult is able to nourish himself does not mean that he alone gets midfare. The baby gets it too. Hence midfare, the product of goods which, in turn, generates utility, is not coextensive with capability, and "capability" is therefore a bad name for midfare.

If food does not make my case strongly enough, since babies do suck and chew, think instead of clothes. No collaboration on the baby's part is needed when its parent confers the midfare of warmth and protection on it by dressing it. Or consider the midfare supplied by the nutriment in a hospital drip, to baby and adult alike, or, for that matter, by the rays of the sun. There is no relevant exercise of capability by benefited agents in these instances, but there is an important benefit to be described in nonwelfarist—midfare—terms. Hence the concept of capability is insufficiently general to capture one of the things that Sen wants to identify.

There are two powerful motivations for pointing to something other than either goods or utility when concerning oneself with egalitarian policy, but the motivations point at different things. There is good reason to look at what a person *can* achieve, independently of his actual state; *and* there is good reason not to reduce the evaluation of that *actual* state either to an examination of his stock of resources or to an assessment of his utility level. But these are distinct points, and the language of capability felicitously covers the first one only.

The ambiguity I have tried to expose appears in a number of Sen's dictions, including the apparently harmless phrase "what people get out of goods."[21] On one reading of it, under which 'get out of' means (roughly) 'extract,' getting things out of goods represents an exercise of capability. But 'get out of' can also mean, more passively, 'receive from,' and it does not require capability to get things out of goods in that sense. Goods (and welfare) theorists ignore (some of) what people get out of goods in both senses of the phrase, but while only the first sense relates to capability, the second denotes something at least as important.

c. In Sen's discourse, to have a capability is to be capable of achieving a range of what he calls "functionings." But Sen characterizes functionings differently at different times, and thereby adds further imprecision to the presentation of his view.

Sometimes, in keeping with the ordinary meaning of 'functioning,' and in line with Sen's original gloss on 'capability' as "being able to *do* certain basic things,"[22] a functioning is by definition an activity, something that a person does.[23] The questions "Can they read and write? Can

[21] See text to n. 6 above.

[22] "Equality of What?" p. 218 (italics added).

[23] "'Functionings' are what the person succeeds in *doing* with the commodities . . . at his or her command" (*Commodities and Capabilities*, p. 10).

they take part in the life of the community?"[24] inquire into people's functionings in this familiar sense of the term. But at other times, functionings are not by definition activities but all (desirable) states of persons, and "being well nourished," "being free from malaria," and "being free from avoidable morbidity"[25] are consequently entered as examples of functionings, although, not being activities, they are not functionings in the ordinary sense of the term. (Even though "I am free from malaria now" can be part of the answer to the question "How are you doing?" in its colloquial use.)

When Sen writes that "Functionings are . . . personal features; they tell us what a person is doing,"[26] he places his incompatible broad and narrow definitions of 'functioning' on either side of the semicolon. For not all personal features, and not all of the personal features that Sen wishes to encompass, are things that a person is doing. Unlike reading and writing, being free from malaria is not something that one does. Elsewhere, a broader definition of 'functionings' is offered, under which "they tell us what the person is doing or achieving,"[27] and it is true that being free from malaria is something that one *may* achieve. But it is surely of supreme (midfare) importance even when one cannot be credited with achieving it.

Sen himself notes that being free from malaria may be entirely due to "anti-epidemic public policy."[28] What he fails to note is the consequent impropriety of regarding it, in that instance, as something the person achieves, as the exercise of a capability of any kind. Yet Sen would surely not want to exclude heteronomously obtained freedom from malaria from the balance sheet of how a person "is doing." *And that proves that he has a concern to promote forms of midfare which does not derive from his concern to promote the claims of capability as such.* Indeed, one may go further: the lacks in people's lives which Sen is *most* concerned to draw to our attention are midfare lacks which are not lacks in capability proper, and the alleviation of which need not always proceed through an enhancement of the sufferer's capability. He is concerned with people who are "ill-fed, undernourished, unsheltered and ill,"[29] who lack "basic clothing, ability to be housed and sheltered, etc."[30] Being able to be housed is

[24] "The Living Standard," p. 84.

[25] Ibid., and see "Well-Being, Agency and Freedom," p. 197. These examples fall under the characterization of functionings as "activities . . . or states of existence or being" (ibid.). (In one place, Sen describes "being well nourished" not as a functioning but as a capability, but that is probably a slip: see *The Standard of Living*, p. 18.)

[26] "Rights and Capabilities," p. 317.

[27] "The Living Standard," p. 84.

[28] *Commodities and Capabilities*, p. 16.

[29] Ibid., p. 21

[30] Ibid., p. 73.

not the same thing as being able to house oneself. Entitlements to goods make desirable states possible for people. They generally realize these possibilities themselves, by exercising a capability to do so. But, with respect to the lacks which most exercise Sen, it is the possibilities that matter, and the corresponding capabilities matter only derivatively.

At one point[31] Sen extols the importance of "a person's ability to function without nutritional deficiency" and of "the capability of avoiding nutritional deficiency." Such functionings and avoidings are genuine activities,[32] but the generative desideratum here is not activity but simply lack of nutritional deficiency, the fundamental desirability of which is lost in these athletic phrasings. It is not hitting the nail on the head to say that food is desirable because it enables a person to avoid nutritional deficiency, as though performing that activity is the (one) important thing here. Decent living space, to change the example, is a primary good which helps to maintain a person in good health, and it often does that when it would be false to say that it helps him to maintain himself in good health. Whether he is doing that is an exquisitely subtle question, a negative answer to which is consistent with decent living space delivering its hygienic boon. More generally, the "kind of life I am living" cannot be identified with what I am "succeeding in 'doing' or 'being',"[33] unless we put scare-quotes around "succeeding" as well. There are many benefits I get which I do not literally succeed in getting.

It is true that the better nourished I am, the larger is the number of valuable activities of which I shall be capable. But that capability, the important capability which food confers, is a *result* of eating it. It is not the Sen capability associated with food, which is a capability to *use* food to achieve various "functionings": being nourished, conducting a ceremonial, entertaining friends.[34] One cannot infer from the central place in life—and midfare—of action and capacity that capability spreads across

[31] I am embarrassed to say that I have lost my record of where these phrases occur. [They occur in "The Living Standard," p. 85.—Ed.]

[32] The *ability* to function without nutritional deficiency is trickier. I have that ability if and only if there is something I am able to do and I lack nutritional deficiency. But, in general, the characterization of the result as an ability is owing to the first clause in that statement of necessary and sufficient conditions, rather than to my nutritional good order.

[33] *Commodities and Capabilities*, p. 28. Cf. ibid., p. 51, where "well-being" is described as depending on "the particular achievements of the person—the kind of 'being' he or she succeeds in having." This is entirely implausible when 'achievements' and 'succeeds' are taken literally, and (see subsection *d* below) Sen has a reason to want their literal meanings to resonate.

[34] At one point Sen writes that "the essence of the capabilities approach is to see commodity *consumption* as no more than a means to generating capabilities" ("Goods and People," p. 522 [italics added]), but that is either an aberration or an unsignaled change of doctrine. For elsewhere commodity *entitlement* generates capability, which is the power to use or consume the commodity in a variety of ways, each of which uses is a functioning. In

the entire space of midfare. And, as we have seen, not everything which merits attention under the broad midfare construal of Sen's contention is an activity or achievement.

We may conclude that, while Sen's focus on what goods do for people apart from the mental reaction they induce is original and illuminating, it is unnecessarily narrowed when the object of the focus is described in functioning/capability language. Comprehending as it does everything which "goods do for people,"[35] midfare cannot be identified either with capability or with what Sen calls "functioning," nor can it be factored into the two without a confusing stretching of the meanings of words.

d. Why did Sen use the language of capability and functioning to express claims which that language fits quite imperfectly? Because, I hypothesize, he had something in addition to midfare in mind, to wit, freedom, and he wrongly thought that attending to a person's midfare—to what he gets from goods apart from the utility upshot of getting it—is attending to how much freedom he has in the world. Both the misrepresentation of all desirable states as a result of the exercise of capability and the tendency to represent all desirable states as activities reflect an interest in freedom distinct from, but not clearly distinguished by Sen from, the move from both utility and goods to midfare.

There is a case for installing the notion of freedom within egalitarian discourse, but that is a different exercise from vindicating the claims of midfare as such. There are *two* powerful motivations for pointing to something other than either goods or utility in a comprehensive characterization of well-being, but the motivations justify two distinguishable deviations from each of those metrics: possession of goods and enjoyment or utility are not the only actual states that matter, and—here is the freedom motivation—it is not only actual states, but the range of states the agent can attain, that matter.

According to Sen, "the category of capabilities is the natural candidate for reflecting the idea of freedom to do,"[36] since "capability to function reflects what a person *can* do."[37] Hence "the concept of capabilities is a 'freedom' type notion,"[38] and the functioning vectors accessible to a person determine her "*well-being freedom*."[39] All that may be true of capability (more or less) strictly so called, but it is not true of 'capability'

---

the different conceptualization just quoted, capability is a consequence of what elsewhere is called a "functioning."

[35] See the catalog characterization of midfare at pp. 48–49 above.

[36] "Rights and Capabilities," p. 316. Cf. "Economics and the Family," p. 376.

[37] "Rights and Capabilities," p. 317.

[38] *Commodities and Capabilities*, p. 14.

[39] "Well-Being, Agency and Freedom," p. 201.

where the term is used to denote the entire midfare dimension between goods and utility. Sen intends capability to have an athletic character. He associates it with the Marxist idea of a person fulfilling his potential through activity, which is to be contrasted with the idea of a person finding his *summum bonum* in passive consumption.[40] But, in Sen's wider construal of it, as midfare, capability covers too much to provide "the perspective of 'freedom' in the positive sense."[41]

The ambiguity between capability as a form of freedom and capability as midfare was not resolved in Sen's contribution to the July 1988 WIDER symposium ("Capability and Well-Being"), to which, with characteristic generosity, he has allowed me to refer. Instead, and as I shall explain, his ambiguous use of 'capability' was matched by an ambiguous use of 'freedom.'

At p. 5 of his 1988 typescript, Sen says that "capability reflects a person's freedom to choose between different ways of living." That formulation more or less identifies capability with freedom of choice (how much it does so depends on what 'reflects' means here: it might mean 'is'). In line with that characterization of capability is Sen's description of the rich faster, who "has the capability to be well nourished, but chooses not to [be]."[42]

Elsewhere, however, something very different from the freedom to choose whether or not to eat, namely, freedom *from* hunger, is denominated a "capability."[43] In fact, though, freedom from hunger is *being* well nourished. It is not the ability to choose which the rich faster has: it is what he chooses not to have. Freedom from hunger is a desirable absence or privation, the sort of freedom which even beings that are not agents can have. Healthy plants have freedom from greenfly, and sound houses are free from dry rot. (Note that a person might even be described, in a special context, as free from nourishment, for example, when he wants to fast, or by captors who want him to starve.)

Unlike the freedom to choose whether or not to eat, freedom from hunger is not constitutively freedom to *do* anything. Sen speaks of *exercising* such "capabilities" as freedom from hunger and freedom from malaria.[44] But they are not freedoms that are *exercised*. Sen's application of the term 'capability' *both* to the freedom to *avoid* morbidity[45]

[40] For relevant citations of Marx, see "Development: Which Way Now?" p. 497; "Goods and People," p. 512; *The Standard of Living*, p. 37.

[41] "Economics and the Family," p. 376. The sentence continues: "who can *do* what, rather than who has what bundle of *commodities*, or who gets how much *utility*." My point is the simple one that what people can do with their commodities is not identical with what their commodities (can) do for them.

[42] "Capability and Well-Being," p. 38.

[43] Ibid., p. 41.

[44] Ibid.

[45] Ibid., p. 6.

and to freedom *from* morbidity[46] shows that, in the attempt to bring the very different issues with which he is concerned under the single rubric of "capability," he is led to make equivocal use of the term 'freedom.'[47]

When Sen introduced capability equality in "Equality of What?" he was modest about its claims. It was "a partial guide to the part of moral goodness that is associated with the idea of equality."[48] Five years later, his claim for the new perspective was much stronger. For, in the Dewey Lectures, Sen said that "the *primary* feature of well-being can be seen in terms of how a person can 'function,' taking that term in a very broad sense," and that "the accounting of functioning vectors" provides "a more plausible view of well-being" than competing conceptions do.[49] Elsewhere, we are advised that, in assessing "well-being and advantage," we should focus "on the capability to function, i.e. what a person can *do* or *be*." His utility is only *evidence* of a person's advantage in that central sense,[50] and the goods at his disposal (here called his "opulence") are only *causes* of that advantage.[51] The position of midfare between primary goods and utility, thus construed, is given as a reason for treating it as the central dimension of value.

These are strong claims, but they are easier to accept in that functionings are now explicitly described as "doings *and* beings" so that both "activities" and "states of existence or being" come under the "functioning" rubric.[52] What I cannot accept is the associated athleticism, which comes when Sen adds that "the central feature of well-being is the ability to achieve valuable functionings."[53] That overestimates the place of freedom and activity in well-being. As Sen writes elsewhere, "freedom is

[46] Ibid., p. 41.

[47] There is further evidence of the persisting ambiguity at pp. 17–19 of "Capability and Well-Being." At pp. 17–18, and in line with the definition of capability on p. 5, a capability set is characterized by the "various alternative combinations of beings and doings any one (combination) of which the person can *choose*" (italics added). But at pp. 18–19, it is allowed, in seeming contradiction of that characterization, that the realized combination in a capability set may or may not be chosen. What is "achieved" might not be "achieved on the basis of choice" (p. 19).

[48] "Equality of What?" p. 220.

[49] "Well-Being, Agency and Freedom," p. 197 (italics added), p. 221. See further ibid., p. 195, where there is an implied identification of "having 'well-being'" with functionings. Cf. *Commodities and Capabilities*, pp. 25, 51; *The Standard of Living*, p. 16.

[50] And often it is rather unreliable evidence, since people tend to adjust to adverse conditions: see pp. 46–47 above.

[51] *Commodities and Capabilities*, preface. Cf. ibid., p. 52. (Strictly, opulence is a magnitude which *supervenes* on command of goods: see ibid., p. 58.)

[52] "Well-Being, Agency and Freedom," p. 197 (italics added).

[53] Ibid., p. 200.

concerned with what one *can* do" and "with what one can *do*":[54] midfare fails, on both counts, as a representation of freedom.

e. I said earlier that there are two powerful motivations for pointing to something other than either goods or utility when concerning oneself with egalitarian policy: there are other actual states that count, and it is not only actual states that count. In the last section I have shown how confusion of those two points is visible in the attempt to express both in the language of freedom, which is appropriate to the second point only.

Under one exegetically plausible disambiguation of Sen's formulations, they recommend equality of capability to achieve functionings, where 'capability' carries something like its ordinary sense (and is therefore not confused with midfare), and where 'functionings' denote all desirable states, and not desirable activities only. So disambiguated, Sen's theory displays two departures from equality of welfare: there is a change of modality, in that capability or opportunity, rather than final achievement, is key; and there is an enrichment of the conception of what opportunities are *for*—not welfare alone, but more broadly conceived good states of the person. In this reconstruction, the error of forcing the concept of capability to denote both the element of opportunity and the move to a broader conception of advantage is eliminated.

When Sen first invoked capability, it was in the context of a proposal that we attend to "*basic* capability equality."[55] The relevant capability was of a fundamental sort, capability whose absence disables the person from satisfying his basic needs. Such need satisfaction is, while clearly related to the achievement of welfare, also irreducible to the latter: one may need something for which one has no desire and one may desire something which does not constitute a need. At the basic level, we can, with some confidence, rank capabilities in importance without paying attention to people's tastes. But, as Sen points out, capability rankings are more moot once we pass beyond the basic desiderata of a normal human life:

> when there is diversity of taste, it becomes harder to surmise about capability by simply observing achievement. For extreme poverty this problem is less serious. Valuing better nourishment, less illness and long life tend to be fairly universal, and also largely consistent with each other despite being distinct objectives. But in other cases of greater relevance to the richer countries—the informational problems with the capability approach can be quite serious.[56]

[54] "Rights and Capabilities," p. 318.
[55] That was the title of section 4 of "Equality of What?"
[56] "The Living Standard," p. 87.

For capabilities which go beyond need satisfaction, it is hard to see how rankings are possible without recourse to utility valuations of the relevant states. In a critical comment on Sen, Richard Arneson tries to exploit the dependence on preference of the value of "higher" capabilities:

> I doubt that the full set of my functioning capabilities [matters] for the assessment of my position. Whether or not my capabilities include the capability to trek to the South Pole, eat a meal at the most expensive restaurant in Omsk . . . matters not one bit to me, because I neither have nor have the slightest reason to anticipate I ever will have any desire to do any of these and myriad other things.[57]

Arneson infers that, insofar as the capability approach claims our attention, it is only as a different way of presenting the idea of equality of opportunity for welfare. But that conclusion is hasty. For one might hold that objective (nonwelfare) assessment of capability is possible at the basic level, even though, beyond that level, we evaluate capability according to the range of desires which it enables a person to satisfy. The capability which matters as such (that is, independently of its welfare consequences) is capability definitive of a normal human existence, capability whose absence spells nonsatisfaction of need. This answer to Arneson is anticipated by Sen:

> The index of capabilities can be sensitive to the strength of desires without converting everything into the metric of desires. The welfarist picture drops out everything other than desires. A non-welfarist over-all index of capabilities may not drop out desires and may well be sensitive to the strength of desires *without ignoring* other influences on the indexing.[58]

And, one might add, the sensitivity of the capability index to desire is inversely related to the degree of "basicness" of the region of capability space under exploration.

Still, if capability in its higher reaches waits on utility for its significance, it is in its more basic reaches that it makes its distinctive normative contribution, as Sen acknowledges: "The issue of capabilities—specifically 'material' capabilities—is particularly important in judging the

[57] "Equality and Equal Opportunity for Welfare," p. 93.

[58] "Rights and Capabilities," p. 319. Not only does Sen allow strength of desire to condition capability evaluation, but, somewhat curiously, he is also disposed to classify happiness itself as a functioning. "Being happy" is described as a "major functioning" at p. 13 of "Well-Being and Agency" (unpublished, 1987) and as a "momentous" one at p. 200 of "Well-Being, Agency and Freedom." See also "Goods and People," p. 512; *The Standard of Living*, pp. 8, 11, 14. See, too, *Commodities and Capabilities* (pp. 15, 52) for more tentative statements of happiness's credentials as a functioning.

standard of living of people in poor countries—it is also important in dealing with poverty in rich countries."[59] And even if utility and opulence offer more general, nondependent (on other metrics) assessments of people's conditions, because of not being restricted to the basic, the notion of basic capability equality may provide an apter reading of the egalitarian impulse than they do. The problem of characterizing well-being in general is not the same as the problem of the priorities of egalitarian justice, and basic midfare, if not basic capability as such, rather than goods bundles or utility quanta, surely is the first priority of justice.

f. In the last sentence of subsection *e*, I reintroduced the equivocation between capability and midfare. Here I shall explain why I did so, and why, more particularly, capability as such is not, in my view, the right thing for an egalitarian to focus on.

I have elsewhere proposed that the right thing to equalize is what I called "access to advantage."[60] In that proposal, 'advantage' is, like Sen's "functioning" in its wider construal, a heterogeneous collection of desirable states of the person reducible neither to his resources bundle nor to his welfare level. And, while 'access' includes what the term normally covers, I extend its meaning under a proviso that anything which a person actually has counts as something to which he has access, no matter how he came to have it, and, hence, even if his coming to have it involved no exploitation of access in the ordinary sense (nor, therefore, any exercise of capability). If, for example, one enjoys freedom from malaria because others have destroyed the malaria-causing insects, then, in my special sense, such freedom from malaria is something to which one has access. That special construal of access is motivated by the thought that egalitarians have to consider states of a person which he neither brought about nor ever was in a position to bring about, states which fall within category (3) of midfare, as it was subclassified above (desirable states caused directly, without any exercise of capability by the beneficiary). Under the disambiguation of Sen's position articulated in subsection *e* above, such states go unconsidered in the egalitarian reckoning (though Sen himself is, of course, supremely concerned about them).

Under equality of access to advantage, the normative accent is not on capability as such, but on a person not lacking an urgent desideratum through no fault of his own: capability to achieve the desideratum is a sufficient but not a necessary condition of not suffering such a lack. My own proposal strikes me as better attuned than capability equality to the

[59] "The Living Standard," p. 85.

[60] See "On the Currency," pp. 920–21 [pp. 18–19 of Chapter 1 of this volume—Ed.].

true shape of the egalitarian concern with such things as health, nourishment, and housing.

Equality of access to advantage is motivated by the idea that differential advantage is unjust save where it reflects differences in genuine choice (or, more or less, capability) on the part of relevant agents, but it is not genuine choice as such (or capability) which the view proposes to equalize. The idea motivating equality of access to advantage does not even imply that there actually is such a thing as genuine choice. Instead, it implies that if there is no such thing—because, for example, "hard determinism" is true—then all differential advantage is unjust. The fact that my view tolerates the possibility that genuine choice is a chimera makes salient its difference from Sen's. In my view, Sen has exaggerated the indispensability of the idea of freedom in the correct articulation of the egalitarian norm. No serious inequality obtains when everyone has everything she needs, even if she did not have to lift a finger to get it. Such a condition may be woeful in other ways, but it is not criticizable at the bar of egalitarian justice.[61]

[61] For their excellent criticism of a previous draft of the material in this article, I thank Richard Arneson, John Baker, Gerald Barnes, Will Kymlicka, David Lloyd-Thomas, John McMurtry, Thomas Scanlon, Amartya Sen, and Philippe Van Parijs.

AFTERWORD TO CHAPTERS ONE AND TWO

1. INTELLECTUAL ETHICS DEMAND a degree of follow-through on things that one has written: one should respond to criticism and, where necessary, amend one's position. But satisfying that demand can mean diminishing returns in illumination per unit of effort, and trade-off judgments sometimes have to be made.

In the case of the currency of equality problematic, I have decided against extensive revision, partly because of diminishing returns, but also because I am at present defeated by some of the knotty issues that Chapter 1 in particular raises. I do not know how to untie the knots without devoting all of my exiguous research time to the task, and I also do not know that I would succeed in untying them even if I did go full throttle. This Afterword records a limited rethink, on three issues: the heterogeneity of advantage; compensation for expensive tastes; and equality versus priority for the least well off.

2. Powerful examples establish the claim of resources against a pure equality of welfare metric, but equally powerful examples of welfare deficiency make a pure resources metric look Procrustean. My "solution" was to honor both resources and welfare, and perhaps other things too, in an open-ended conception of equality of access to advantage. The heterogeneity of that metric protects it against (some) counterexamples, but no method of aggregation of the different types of advantage was suggested, or may readily be envisaged, and the very heterogeneity that makes counterexamples absorbable also made me (see pp. 18–19 of Chapter 1), and still makes me, wonder whether what I offered is any kind of *theory*, as opposed to a repository of considerations with which an acceptable theory must come to terms.

Even so, I still think it impossible for an egalitarian distributor to ignore either resources or welfare. Consider the matter as it confronts some of those who distribute in practice, within egalitarianly minded British local housing authorities. For various good reasons there is an element of first-come-first-served in the distribution of public housing to British

Editor's note: This is an unpublished Afterword to the papers that have been reprinted as the first two chapters of this volume. Cohen wrote this Afterword in the early nineties when he had plans, which he later withdrew, to reprint these papers as chapters 11 and 12 of *Self-Ownership, Freedom, and Equality*.

residents who are badly housed. But other considerations also enter the reckoning, and they are instructively various.

Recall Amartya Sen's good argument (see pp. 46–47 of Chapter 2) against using subjectively conceived welfare (that is, in its usual interpretation, utility) as the metric for distribution: that courageous people who rise above resource adversity to a condition of comparative equanimity should not pay a resource penalty for their virtue. Sen was right to insist that materially deprived citizens have a claim to egalitarian compensation, whatever their level of utility may be. But within the set of those who have that claim, scarcity (natural and/or socially imposed) enforces priorities, and then the antiwelfarist stance looks less appropriate. In particular, and as the following examples attest, unmodified rejection of disutility as a ground for compensation has dubious implications for housing distribution.

Two families are in substandard accommodation, and both are in precisely the same housing need, by every objective criterion. But the Happy family's members are serene while the Sad family's are in great distress. Do you not agree that, if other things are equal, then an egalitarian social worker should put the Sad family higher up the waiting list? Suppose, alternatively, that the Sad family's existing accommodation, though distinctly substandard, is *better* than the Happy family's. Do you not, nevertheless, also agree that, within limits, the Sad family should be given some priority, that the worse accommodated Happy family sometimes could not reasonably reject the social worker's explanation that the Sads should enjoy preferment, because of how miserable they are? All this, as I said, within limits: the Happy folk might be justly outraged if they were asked to wait a further ten years in consequence of their robustness. But as long as it is reasonable to ask them to wait (say) a further six months, then the point is made that both resources *and* welfare should govern egalitarian housing policy.[1]

Now what is the lesson of such examples for correct general principles? It remains puzzling that a metric should include both resources, out of which people generate welfare, and welfare itself. Perhaps the right course is to develop a metric with complex lexicalities: in the housing example, we look at the resource position first (how bad is a person's current accommodation?), then her welfare matters, but only if it is below a certain level, yet how much it matters depends how bad other people's resource position is, and so on.

If a lexical solution is correct, then the question "Equality of what?," which set this inquiry rolling, might be regarded as misleading, even if

[1] Mark Philp has suggested to me that deference to the Sads may be mercy, not justice. Maybe the council is asking the Happies to be *merciful*.

not as, strictly speaking, misplaced. For a set of lexically ordered desiderata constitutes no *amount* of some single thing that people should be equal in (cf. pp. 18–19 of Chapter 1). If the right view is lexically structured, then "Equality of what?" misleads to the extent that it suggests that the egalitarian *distribuendum* must be a homogeneous quantity.

Some think that the puzzlingly heterogeneous answer which suggests itself when one asks, "Equality of what?," reflects excessive generality in the question. In particular, they think that the question is underdetermined because it specifies neither who (or what) the *distributor* is nor which *goods* are to be distributed. But attention to these dimensions of distribution will not extinguish the heterogeneous solution which seems natural in the housing cases offered above.

Consider, first, the issue of the distributor. Thomas Scanlon distinguishes five kinds of distributor for whom a question of equality might arise and for whom different answers to that question might be appropriate.[2] But the distributor in my inquiry is unitary. It is the state, or, as in the housing illustration, a public authority created by it.

Consider, now, the issue of variety of goods. That variety is pivotal in the approach to distribution defended in Michael Walzer's *Spheres of Justice*, which advances three general claims. First, that there are no universally valid principles of social justice: valid principles vary from society to society. Second, that the variation obtains because social justice is satisfied when the practices of a society conform to the principles expressed or implicit in the society's cultural self-understandings. That pair of relativist theses I reject. But the third claim, fused with the first two in Walzer's presentation, is more persuasive: that there are different spheres of justice, different sorts of goods (e.g., status, welfare, occupation) to be distributed, and that, in general, trade-offs across spheres are impermissible. If the poor are unjustly underresourced, injustice is not reduced but compounded if, by way of an attempt at compensation, the voting rights of the rich are reduced.

One may, then, believe in spheres in a non-Walzerian way: non-Walzerian, because one rejects the relativism in the first two claims that I distinguished. Justice can come in spheres, but justice within a sphere need not be essentially determined by how the particular society understands what goes on in that sphere. But, even when we grant Walzer's third claim, heterogeneity in defensible egalitarian distribution is not explained away. For the council house distribution example remains intact. It is of one good (housing) in one society, distributed by one agency. Distinctions between goods (and between distributors) are respected, but heterogeneity survives.

[2] [Cohen is probably referring to Scanlon's "Value, Desire, and the Quality of Life."—Ed.]

My most outrageous application of a heterogeneous metric was to Ronald Dworkin's Jude (see Section 4*d* of Chapter 1), who has "cheap expensive" tastes. Jude's trip to Spain should, I said, be subsidized, in the face of equality of (opportunity for) welfare (for he thereby gets more welfare [opportunity] than others have), but my recommendation about Jude also contradicts equality of resources, since, even when thus subsidized, Jude ends up with fewer resources than the norm. This would-be vindication of heterogeneity has been subjected to a strong challenge by Eric Rakowski.

Before I address Rakowski, let me note that treatment structurally like that which I proposed for Jude would not seem bizarre in the case of the Happy family. Suppose that the Happies voluntarily cultivate a taste for pets which means that they need more space than they otherwise would have done to achieve the level of welfare that exceeds what the Sads get with even more space than that. The Happies' demand for that intermediate quantity of space does not seem unreasonable, yet it also does not seem unreasonable to ask them (together with their pets) to continue to tolerate less space than what the Sads get. A pet-loving Happy family is in relevantly the same position as Jude.

Rakowski's example[3] is intended to parallel the Jude case and discredit the lesson I drew from it. A population divides, evenly, into blind and sighted people. Equality of opportunity for welfare obtains if and only if resources are divided, in a ratio of seven to three, in favor of the blind moiety. But the sighted develop a taste for bull fighting,[4] which means that resources must now be redivided, in a ratio of 5.1 to 4.9, to maintain the sighted people's welfare level.[5] As a result, the welfare of the blind people goes down.

So, too, of course, does that of other people in the original Jude example, and of the Sad family in the pets version of the council housing example. Now, the intuitive response to the council house example supports my recommendation regarding cheap expensive tastes, the intuitive response to Rakowski's example[6] goes against it, and the intuitive response to the original Jude example is, perhaps, moot. What gives Rakowski's example its apparent power?

[3] See his *Equal Justice*, p 55.

[4] Of, as it happens, a particularly ghastly kind: Rakowski diminishes the intellectual force of his example by emphasizing the gruesomeness of the taste that the sighted choose to develop, since, to the extent that the example depends on it, (some of) its sting can be drawn by treating the taste it features as offensive, in the sense of Section 3 of Chapter 1 of this volume.

[5] Nothing I said *requires* that it be maintained without loss, but let that pass.

[6] Even if we ignore the awfulness of the sighted people's acquired taste: see n. 4 above.

The answer, I suggest, is our belief that blindness is a massive welfare reducer. This means that the opportunity for welfare of the blind people cannot be very great, and that that of the sighted people at stage one of the example is also very small (since all start with equal opportunity for welfare). Accordingly, I have two ways of handling the example. One is to say that voluntarily acquired cheap expensive tastes should indeed be deferred to, but only after a threshold value of equal opportunity for welfare has been passed: an application of the lexical treatment of these matters suggested at pp. 62–63 above. That solution presupposes that there is normal scarcity in the society in question and/or that the illfare of the blind could never be overcome by lavishing resources on them. If, however, that presupposition is false, if there is money to hand to make blindness much less welfare-diminishing than we suppose it must be, then Rakowski's example begins to look more like the Jude one, and the intuitive response to it becomes more moot.

I provisionally reaffirm what I said about Jude, which I have not, indeed, shown to be true, but which is not exploded by Rakowski's ingenious example.

3. John Rawls responds as follows to the Arneson/Cohen position on expensive tastes:

> . . . that we can take responsibility for our ends is part of what free citizens may expect of one another. Taking responsibility for our tastes and preferences, *whether or not they have arisen from our actual choices*, is a special case of that responsibility. As citizens with realized moral powers, this is something we must learn to deal with. This still allows us to view as a special problem preferences and tastes that are incapacitating and render someone unable to cooperate normally in society. The situation is then a medical or psychiatric one and to be treated accordingly.[7]

This passage advances matters in one respect. For it is now clear that the relevant responsibility does not require past or present exercise of choice: as I noted (see n. 12 in Chapter 1), Rawls has been ambiguous on that count.

Now, the reflections in the passage are framed by a special "political" conception of personhood that has acquired increasing salience in Rawls's writings. We are dealing with "what free citizens may expect of one another" and not, perhaps, with what people as such, viewed

[7] *Political Liberalism*, p. 185 (my emphases), citing Daniels, "Equality of What," pp. 288–92.

outside the "political" optic, may reasonably expect. If those expectations coincide,[8] then the political conception of personhood plays no differentiating role in the passage. But if there is a discrepancy between the two expectations, then the fiction of responsibility (for that is what, I believe, it would then be) is not, I think, a good basis on which to discuss the demands of justice. This brusque dismissal of Rawls's political turn will alienate some readers, and I cannot go into the large methodological question at issue here. But I do not think the following pages rely overmuch on a rejection of the political conception of justice.

Rawls says that whether or not they reflect choice, and whether or not they are expensive, tastes raise no case for assistance unless they are debilitating, and then the appropriate assistance is not compensation but therapy, or cure. (Cure is not compensation since, among other things, the victim of the taste would not be allowed to take the money allocated for his cure and spend it on a holiday. And the point of cure is not to restore equality of [opportunity for] welfare.)

Now, when I used the standard Arrow example of the expensive taste for plovers' eggs, I did not think of it as *debilitating* (as opposed to more or less impoverishing, if satisfied). Indeed I said little about debilitating tastes as such, about which some remarks are now in order.

Tastes can debilitate (a) when and because they are satisfied, (b) when and because they are not satisfied, or (c) whether or not they are satisfied (i.e., just because one has them). Rawls does not say which alternative(s) he has in mind. But he cannot mean (b), since quite ordinary tastes (for example, for food) debilitate when they are not satisfied.[9] Accordingly Rawls must mean tastes which debilitate even if (and whether or not especially if) they are regularly satisfied, such as a taste for heroin.

Now that changes the subject from expensive tastes as such, and it is curious that, in a footnote to the text quoted at the outset of this section, Rawls continues to use the plovers' eggs illustration. For that is not a taste that debilitates even if it is satisfied, but at most only when it is not. And it would seem absurd to propose cure (that is, reschooling the sybarite out of such tastes, e.g., by behavior therapy) if, as is likely, that would cost much more than the plovers' eggs. If, on the other hand, reschooling would indeed be cheaper, then, so I said (see p. 18 of Chapter 1), not compensation but such reschooling should be offered to involuntary sybarites. So the Rawlsian approach to them turns out to be either ill-

[8] I think Rawls might agree that they coincide. In a footnote to the quoted text, he says that "it is a normal part of being human" (and not of being a citizen as such) "to cope with the preferences our upbringing leaves us with" (*Political Liberalism*, p. 185, n. 15).

[9] That debilitation, which can take the form of an obsessional craving, is not identical with debilitation because of lack of satisfaction of the *need* for food.

considered or already covered by the doctrine to which Rawls is here responding.

I said "*involuntary* sybarites," because, unlike Rawls in the passage under discussion, I countenance public solicitude toward the Arrow man only if his expensive taste is unchosen. Judging by the exhibited passage, Rawls is uninterested in that aspect of the matter. But his considered view might more closely follow Daniels's, when the latter writes that "*unchosen* preferences that make us worse off than others do not (generally) arouse egalitarian concerns unless they can be assimilated to the cases of psychological disabilities, that is, to a departure from normal functioning."[10]

Daniels later refines what he means by 'unchosen':

> I think Cohen misses the mark. It is not actual choice that matters, but the underlying capacity for forming and revising one's ends that is at issue. If we have independent reasons to believe that a preference, whether chosen or not, whether identified with or not, cannot be eliminated and is handicapping because of a broader, underlying handicapping condition, then we have reasons to make certain resources available as compensation. It is not the unchosen taste, or the fact that the taste is unchosen, that gives rise to the claim on us. Rather, it is the underlying mental or emotional disability, and the taste, chosen or not, is but a symptom.[11]

But Daniels's contrast between capacity for (surely something like) choice and actual choice is out of place here. For I never said that *actual* choice is required to defeat compensation for expensive tastes, but only that the agent could have chosen not to develop, or could choose to school himself out of, the taste (see p. 18 of Chapter 1), which is to say that he has a certain capacity: accordingly, Daniels's reference to capacity, as such, establishes no difference between us. What does is Daniels's insistence that the relevant (in)capacity be general.

But the insistence on a general incapacity seems to me both unmotivated and arbitrary. Unmotivated, because the Arrow person's craving might anyway be too *local* to implicate a general incapacity for self-direction which might be addressed therapeutically. And arbitrary,

[10] Daniels, "Equality of What," p. 288, emphasis added. Daniels does not say what qualification "(generally)" is meant to signify. If a qualification is intended, it could be consequential. But "(generally)" may be redundant, just a misleading forecast of the subsequent "unless."

[11] Ibid., p. 290. (To be consistent with what he says elsewhere, Daniels must mean allocating resources for cure when he speaks in this passage of making resources available as compensation.)

because why should a general incapacity justify assistance (be it compensation or cure—that is a separate matter) while a particular one (say, to shake off a nagging obsession) justifies none at all?

Speaking more generally, we do in practice make a sharp cut between self-possessed and other people, but it is an artificial one imposed by informational and other practical demands. In truth, there is, in principle, continuous variation here, across people with respect to how much control they have, and within people with respect to how self-governing they are, with respect to different tastes. And it seems to me to be a methodological mistake to mirror the demands of practice at the level of fundamental justifying theory. The theoretical problems are best approached with a set of continua in mind, and without putting a premium on the identification of absolute distinctions such as that between those who can and those who cannot control, or be held responsible for, their tastes and preferences.

Two more points. First, I note that the question I raised (see Section 3 of Chapter 1) about the *consistency* between Rawls's doctrine of responsibility for ends and his doctrine of nonresponsibility for (lack of) effort is addressed neither by Daniels nor by Rawls. I thought it mysterious that the "foresight and self-discipline" credited to citizens with respect to their preferences was not also credited to them with respect to their productive efforts—which would undermine a key premise in Rawls's egalitarianism. Does the absolute standard of undebilitated normality (whatever it is) apply only to man as consumer and not also, and, as before, damagingly, to man as producer? If "taking responsibility for our tastes and preferences . . . is a special case of" the "responsibility for our ends" which "free citizens may expect of one another,"[12] why is taking responsibility for the amount of productive effort that we find worthwhile not another such "special case"?

Finally, I respond to Daniels's insistence that the liberal principle that people be allowed to pursue their own conceptions of the good extends to raising "our children as we see fit."[13] This, he says, can have the consequence that opportunity for welfare (or advantage) is disequalized. But there is no way of avoiding that consequence, without invasive and illiberal interference in family life.

Well, to begin with, there is scope for intelligent compensation even in this apparently unpromising instance. Some kids develop tastes that are relatively cheap to satisfy: reading books, playing ball, walking in the country. Others, from less favorable backgrounds, need more expensive

[12] *Political Liberalism*, p. 185: see the fuller quotation at p. 65 above.
[13] Ibid., p. 291.

stimulation for enjoyment. Instead of letting them fend for themselves, decent public authorities fund recreation centers that the first sort will use less.[14]

That said, the more significant point is that it is unclear that Daniels has here provided even the beginning of an objection to equality of access to advantage, considered in the mode in which I advanced it, as a weak *equalisandum* proposal (see Section 2 of Chapter 1). It is a nice question whether the interest in pursuing our own conception of the good as manifested in autonomous child-rearing raises an *egalitarian* objection to equality of access to advantage. If it does not, then it is beside the polemical point.[15]

4. Derek Parfit's Lindley Lecture, and the larger body of (as yet mostly unpublished) work to which it belongs, represent a great breakthrough in political philosophy, comparable to the provision for the first time of a map of territory hitherto traveled only with the help of the sun, the stars, and primitive sextants.[16] Had I possessed Parfit's map before I wrote the present pair of chapters, many of their formulations would have been differently cast. Not all of the needed rectification will be supplied here. But I shall situate my own central claim in relation to the master distinction of Parfit's new work.

My central claim is that the right equality is equality of access to advantage. Put negatively, it is that the inequality that egalitarians seek to eliminate is of disadvantage that is due to brute luck. Parfit's master distinction is between equality and priority to the worst off. He documents profound equivocation between those desiderata (be they teleological aims or deontic norms)[17] across recent egalitarian writing, not excluding that of Rawls.

My central claim is cast in terms of equality as such, rather than in terms of priority to the worst off. Parfit's doubts about the independent value or authority of equality as such consequently apply to my central

[14] I live opposite one in London, so I know what I'm talking about. I tolerate the loud band on Thursday evenings because I believe in equality of access to advantage. If, however, they began to play *every* evening . . .

[15] For further effective response to Daniels, see Arneson, "Property Rights in Persons," pp. 219–22.

[16] [See Parfit, *Equality or Priority?* This Afterword was written after Parfit had delivered this lecture in 1991 but prior to its publication as a pamphlet in 1995. Cohen's remarks are informed by a longer and still unpublished manuscript by Parfit on the Priority View. I have slightly amended Cohen's text to make reference to the published version of the Lindley Lecture where appropriate and to eliminate his references to specific pages or paragraphs in Parfit's longer unpublished manuscript.—Ed.]

[17] The subdistinction expressed in that contrast has no bearing on present concerns.

claim. Now, I do not want to address those doubts here, and thereby adopt a position on the equality versus priority issue. I want merely to show that the pivotal notion in my proposal, involuntary disadvantage, can serve to state a prioritarian position. But, as indicated, I shall not assess the relative merits of the two positions we shall consequently have before us.

The principal point is that the concept of involuntary disadvantage, which served in Chapter 1 to define an *equalisandum*, can also be used to define a *minimandum* (something to be minimized), and thereby to yield a prioritarian view.

Egalitarians think inequality intrinsically bad or wrong, and prioritarians do not. But prioritarians are nevertheless exercised by actually existing inequality, because an inequality poses the issue of whether those at the tail end of it, the worst off, could be made better off by redistributing some of what the better off have.

Now, different kinds of inequality, or, what comes to the same thing, absences of different kinds of equality, exercise different prioritarians. And my prioritarian is exercised by lack of equal access to advantage, where access to advantage is equal if[18] all inequalities of advantage are due to fault or choice on the part of the relevant agents.

Prioritarians believe that an inequality raises a case to answer, that case being that someone is, apparently, worse off than anyone needs to be, and could be made better off through a redistribution. And my prioritarian thinks that there are two ways of rejecting that case. One is to say that, if the suggested redistribution were attempted, no one would be made better off. And the other is to say that the redistribution would be unfair because it would mean that the better off are paying for the worse off's choices or faults.

That, so I submit, is a coherent prioritarian position in which, as with any such position, there is something to be minimized, here not illfare or other deprivation as such but the amount of involuntary disadvantage from which a person suffers. Accordingly I reject Parfit's conclusion that "if our aim is to eliminate involuntary disadvantage, we must mean comparative disadvantage, and our aim must be equality."[19]

[18] Not "and only if," because of a complication that does not seem worth pursuing in detail here. The complication is that my prioritarian theorist questions *equality* of advantage that reflects relevantly differential responsibility. And sometimes, moreover, he will redistribute from the relatively disadvantaged to the relatively advantaged. But the minimand, involuntary disadvantage, remains the same throughout.

[19] Editor's note: Here Cohen is quoting from an unpublished manuscript. (See n. 15 above.) The published version of Parfit's Lindley Lecture does not contain this passage. Rather, Parfit writes the following on p. 27 of *Equality or Priority?*:

But disadvantage is not, as I intend it, a comparative matter,[20] in the strict sense in which Parfit uses that notion when articulating the Priority View, for which comparativity is strictly irrelevant.[21] Accordingly, it is not true that a concern with involuntary disadvantage mandates an egalitarian as opposed to a prioritarian view. Within a concern to eliminate involuntary disadvantage, a prioritarian view endorses minimization of the amount of involuntary disadvantage suffered by those who have most involuntary disadvantage.

Here is a model of the involuntary disadvantage version of the Priority View. Imagine that life is a series of episodes in each of which you prosper or fail and in each case what happens is either down to you or beyond your control. Each person undergoes the same number of such episodes, and prospering and failing are of the same value regardless of the person and regardless of the episode. For such a world, the view I have tried to articulate says: make the largest number of uncompensated *net* involuntary failures in any one life[22] as small as possible (where the number of net involuntary failures is reached by subtracting the number of involuntary successes from the number of involuntary failures). The coherence of that recipe satisfies me that Parfit's conclusion (see p. 70 above) is a mistake. (Of course, life is not such a series of episodes, and there are in real life awesome problems of measurement that the episodes-fantasy spirits away, that being its purpose. But I do not see why a prioritarian statement of the access view becomes impossible, as opposed to complicated, when those problems are allowed back in.)

. . . Cohen suggests that 'the right reading of egalitarianism' is that 'its purpose is to eliminate involuntary disadvantage'. He means by this comparative disadvantage: being worse off than others. That is an essentially relational idea. Only equality could eliminate such disadvantage. Cohen's view could not be re-expressed in the language of priority.

[20] See n. 18 of Chapter 1 of this volume.

[21] See his *Equality or Priority?*, pp. 22–23, where he writes that on the Priority View:

> benefits to the worse off matter more. . . . On this view, if I am worse off than you, benefits to me are more important. Is this *because* I am worse off than you? In one sense, yes. But this has nothing to do with my relation to you.
>
> It may help to use this analogy. People at higher altitudes find it harder to breathe. Is this because they are higher up than other people? In one sense, yes. But they would find it just as hard to breathe even if there were no other people who were lower down. In the same way, on the Priority View, benefits to the worse off matter more, but this is only because these people are at a lower *absolute* level. It is irrelevant that these people are worse off *than others*. Benefits to them would matter just as much even if there *were* no others who were better off.

[22] Assume here, for simplicity, that all lives are of the same duration.

Parfit says in his Lindley Lecture that a concern to eliminate inequalities due to brute luck sits ill with the Priority View, since the latter is not concerned with distributive patterns.[23] But while the Priority View finds distributive patterns of no *intrinsic* interest, it is certainly concerned with them in identifying who has the greater claim to support and how that claim should be satisfied, and the concept of luck is, in the access to advantage proposal, required to answer those questions.

[23] [See the passage from *Equality or Priority?* quoted in n. 18 above.—Ed.]

Chapter Three

SEN ON CAPABILITY, FREEDOM, AND CONTROL

In the present appreciation, I first describe the leading idea—'capability'—which Amartya Sen has brought to this field of discourse. I then take up the connection or lack of it between freedom and control.

1. Capability

What Sen calls "capability" is determined by the different forms of life that are possible for a person: a person's capability is a disjunction of the combinations available to her of what Sen calls "functionings," which are states of activity and/or being. These functionings vary, Sen says, "from most elementary ones, such as being well-nourished, avoiding escapable morbidity and premature mortality, etc., to quite complex and sophisticated achievements, such as having self-respect, being able to take part in the life of the community, and so on."[1]

Sen's very identification of the capability dimension of assessment was impressive, in the light of its previous complete neglect. Capability lies, causally, between income or primary goods or resources on the one hand and utility or welfare on the other. Focus on capability means emphasizing not goods as such, but what they enable a person to do, and it also means disemphasizing the (often vagariously induced) utility associated with his doing it. The trouble with a metric of goods or resources or income is that the point of goods (and so forth) is to generate possibilities of choice for the individual: much better, then, Sen argued, to look not at their generators but at those possibilities themselves, which do not vary uniformly with what generates them, because of variations in people's

Reprinted in part from "Amartya Sen's Unequal World," *New Left Review*, No. 203, January–February 1994, pp. 117–29. By kind permission of *New Left Review*.

Editor's note: This chapter is an abridged and retitled version of a review essay of Amartya Sen's *Inequality Reexamined*. All page references in this chapter are to *Inequality Reexamined* unless otherwise indicated.

[1] *Inequality Reexamined*, p. 5. It is indicative of Sen's primary focus on poverty that the list of "functionings" given here to illustrate that concept in general is virtually identical with the list used elsewhere (p. 110) to characterize poverty as such.

physical (climatic, topographical, etc.) and social circumstances, and in their biological constitutions. And the trouble with a metric of utility is that it is blind to the fact that people adjust their expectations downwardly when in poverty and upwardly when in wealth. This and other subjective vagaries mean that utility is not the right quantity to focus on: it is unfair to a poor person to resource him less because he has developed modest tastes and therefore needs less wherewithal to achieve a given level of welfare. What matters centrally is the causal intermediary, the effect of goods that causes utility: functioning, and capability, as such.[2]

A person's functionings matter because they *are* his life, considered apart from the utility he gets out of it. And capability matters at least instrumentally, since functionings matter, and adequate functioning can obtain only if it lies within a person's capability set. But capability also matters in three other ways. Freedom to choose is good in itself, apart from the goods it provides access to; freedom to choose with adequate functioning within the scope of that choice is a person's right; and capability also contributes *directly* to well-being, because a person's life is "richer" when the "opportunity of reflective choice" appears within it: capability is good not only, then, as a space of choice, but also because free choosing, a process that requires such a space, is itself good (pp. 40–42, 51–52).

Capability is a form of freedom, the freedom, specifically, to choose a set of functionings. When the value of that freedom is measured in terms of the forms of well-being those sets of functionings constitute, then what Sen calls a person's "well-being freedom" is displayed. But well-being freedom is not freedom as such. It must be distinguished from "agency freedom," which is a person's freedom to achieve whatever goals she has, including goals other than her own well-being. It diminishes a person's agency freedom that she cannot pursue a cause to which she is committed, but the restriction need not commensurately detract from her well-being freedom.

[2] There are two powerful motivations for pointing to something other than either goods or utility when concerning oneself with egalitarian policy, but the motivations point at different things. There is good reason to look at what a person *can* achieve, independently of his actual state; *and* there is good reason not to reduce the evaluation of that *actual* state either to an examination of his stock of resources or to an assessment of his utility level. These are distinct points, and they have often been conflated in Sen's presentation. (As I complained in "Equality of What?" [Chapter 2 of this volume—Ed.]. I shall not here resume the criticism pursued in that article of this and other minor dislocations in the conceptual scaffolding that Sen has erected, or respond to Sen's treatment of it in his "Capability and Well-Being" in *The Quality of Life*, or pass judgment on the extent to which the criticism applies to formulations offered in the book under review.)

2. Freedom without Control?

I turn to my selected subtheme: the relationship between freedom and control. Sen claims[3] that there is a significant form of personal freedom enjoyment of which does not involve (as freedom usually does, and is generally thought always to do) exercise of *control* over what happens by the relevant free agent. A supposed case in point is the freedom enjoyed by someone who lives in an environment without malaria. Sen does not mean, by that freedom, the freedom to do things that can be done only when malaria is absent, for, in that *consequent* freedom control is manifestly present.[4] He means the (supposed) freedom that a person enjoys just *in* that her environment has no malaria in it. This, Sen argues, is indeed a part of the person's freedom, even though she does not (and cannot) control whether there will be malaria in her environment. Sen used to call this (supposed) freedom, where control is missing, the freedom of *power*. Critics protested that the situation of a person benefiting from a salubrious environment no more manifests her power than it does her control. Sen now accedes to this criticism, drops the word 'power,' and calls his theme "effective freedom."

Sen has here, once again, identified an undoubtedly important and neglected phenomenon, but it is not freedom without control. In this section, I show that Sen's argument for the existence of such a freedom is unsuccessful, and I then indicate what I think is the true shape of the important phenomenon that he has discerned.

The failure of Sen's argument becomes apparent when we ask *why* a person benefiting from an environment rid of malaria qualifies in that respect as free. Sen vacillates between two different answers to that question, corresponding to two conditions, one strong and one weak, each of which he takes to be sufficient for "effective freedom." The strong condition indeed identifies a form of freedom, but one in which, contrary to what Sen requires, control is present, however (literally) remote. The weaker condition indeed involves no control, but also, *pari passu*, no freedom. Through failing to distinguish the two conditions Sen produces his fallacious result, that freedom can obtain without control over what happens.

[3] As he did in earlier essays: see, in particular, "Liberty as Control," section 5.

[4] See *Inequality Reexamined*, p. 67, n. 17, where Sen acknowledges that "freedoms that *result from not having malaria* [are] not in dispute" between him and actual and potential critics. The question is not whether you are freer in the absence of malaria (because you are free to do things you could otherwise not do), but whether its absence is itself part of your freedom. Unless this distinction is grasped, the criticism of Sen in this section will not be understood.

The stronger condition conjoins two elements, corresponding to the two phrases italicized by Sen in his statement of it: "As long as the levers of control are systematically exercised in line with what *I would choose* and *for that exact reason*, my 'effective freedom' is uncompromised, though my 'freedom as control' may be limited or absent" (pp. 64–65). In illustration of this point, Sen instances the relationship between me and a proofreader of my book, who corrects the text as he does because he knows I would want it to be corrected that way.[5]

Now it is true, in this example, that "the levers of control" are not "*directly* operated" by me (p. 64), but the fact that Sen emphasizes "directly" betrays that they are indirectly operated by me, which means that I do control what happens. I can be *free* without exercising the *levers* of control precisely because I can *control* without exercising the levers of control. (When I tell my obedient chauffeur where and how to drive I do not exercise the levers which control the car[6] but I nevertheless control what it does.) Satisfaction of the strong condition indeed yields freedom, but not freedom without control.

But Sen often uses a weaker condition for "effective freedom" or (supposed) freedom without control, which is yielded by preserving the first italicized element but deleting the second one in his statement of the strong condition which I gave two paragraphs ago. The weaker condition is that whoever controls what happens does what I would choose to do if I were in control, no matter for what reason, and, in particular, whether or not he "*knows* what my instructions *would have been if sought*" (p. 64). So, for example, it may conform to my will that my environment has been rid of malaria, even though I did not, and could not have, made it so, and even though those who did make it so were relevantly unmindful of my wishes in the matter. I believe that this phenomenon, in which things conform to my will although I do not myself exert it, is of great conceptual interest, but that it is not freedom.

An indication, apart from his actual formulations and examples, that Sen also uses the stated weaker condition for freedom without control is that, as I reported, he accepted the criticism that freedom without control could not be said to qualify as power. For satisfaction of the first condition, as illustrated in the proofreader case, does entail power: I do not let the proofreader operate unless I am satisfied that he will act as I want him to. (If the proofreader is imposed on me willy-nilly,[7] then at most the

[5] It is not entirely clear that Sen means us to take the proofreader example in this fashion, but it must be so construed for the phrase "*for that exact reason*" to have application.

[6] As opposed to the levers which control the chauffeur: my commands might be said to be such levers.

[7] It is unclear—see n. 5 above—whether or not Sen would regard that as a relevant variant of his proofreader example.

weaker condition holds, and freedom of choice disappears.) Another indication that Sen sometimes employs the weaker condition is his description of the relevant form of (supposed) freedom as "outcome-based" (p. 135). For the second element in the stronger condition for "effective freedom" ("*for that exact reason*") is a matter of process, not outcome.

Consider the malaria clearance case, in which the controlling agent is the state, or some state body. If the policy of malaria elimination is adopted democratically, then people, together, control what happens to them, and therefore exercise freedom and, for good measure, power; but Sen's claim, that there exists freedom without control, remains unillustrated. If, on the other hand, the malaria clearance is achieved by an undemocratic (but, at least in this respect, benign) administration, or, as Sen at one point suggests (p. 65), by an international agency under distant direction, then there is neither control nor freedom on the part of the benefiting people, but it remains true that what eventuates conforms to what they would choose, and is *pro tanto* commendable. Sen says that what he calls "effective freedom" is important because, in a modern complex society, there is much that we can secure not individually but only collectively.[8] As the contrast between democratic and other malaria clearance shows, that is not a reason for concluding that there exists freedom without control.

We have to do, in sum, with two phenomena, one more general than the other, and only the more specific one involves freedom. The specific one, in which things go as I will *because* it is my will, even though my hands are off the levers of control, is politically important but philosophically not very interesting. The more general phenomenon, in which things go in accordance with my will, but truly without my control, is very interesting conceptually, but not rightly called "freedom." I agree with Sen that the fact that a central aspect of a person's situation may conform to his will other than because he himself arranges or sustains that conformity opens a "momentous perspective" (p. 69). First, a bit more on why the perspective is not one of freedom. Then, an attempt to say why the perspective is nevertheless momentous.

Contrary to what Sen says, when a person gets an unchosen thing that she would have chosen, no "ability" on her part "to choose to live as [she] desires" is thereby indicated (p. 67). 'Ability' is here infelicitous in just the way that its cognate 'power' was: abilities, like powers, are things that are exercised, and there is, *ex hypothesi*, no relevant exercise of anything in this example, and nothing that proves the presence of an unexercised ability either. It is also false, in the pertinent sense,[9] that "if

[8] *Inequality Reexamined*, p. 65, and see "Liberty as Control," pp. 216, 218.

[9] The qualification is necessary because of the distinction made in n. 4 above.

people do desire a life without hunger or malaria, the elimination of these maladies through public policy does enhance their 'liberty to choose to live as they desire'."[10] "Ability to choose" and "liberty to choose" obtain only when it is possible to choose, and much of the interest of the phenomenon misdescribed in these dictions is that the agent has no choice in the matter (for example, of whether or not there is malaria in his environment). Especially when applying the weaker condition, Sen emphasizes absence of control, while insisting on liberty to choose, but liberty to choose entails control over what happens.

So, while I agree with Sen that the issue of whether people have what they would choose "is a momentous perspective," I do not think that when they have what they would choose they are *pro tanto* free. To see the true significance of the phenomenon to which Sen draws our attention, let us begin by distinguishing between a person's good and a person's will. Following a traffic accident, my Christian Scientist friend lies unconscious on the road. I must decide between taking him home, as I know he would wish me to, and taking him to hospital, as I think would do him more good. I do what conforms to his will if and only if I take him home. A person's will is how he would make things go if he could, whether or not he is in a position to make them go that way, whether or not it would be good for him if they go that way, and whatever interest or lack of it he has in his own good.[11]

Suppose, in the example above, that, because I respect my friend's will, I take him home. Then his fate conforms, thanks to me, to his will, but his will does not "systematically" (Sen's word)[12] determine his fate. For it was pure chance that it was I who came along, rather than, for example, a thief, or a differently minded friend who might have put the man's welfare first, or not known about his will.

Now, standardly,[13] when freedom is exercised, the agent exercising it aims to make the world (in the relevant respect) conform to his will. But what Sen correctly notes, and rightly emphasizes, is that the world may conform to a person's will other than as a result of his control (or, as we can therefore safely add, of his exercise of a freedom). This is shown by the Christian Scientist case, and, indeed, by a case in which, unlike what holds in that one, the world conforms to my will not only not as a result

[10] *Inequality Reexamined*, p. 67, quoting Berlin, *Four Essays on Liberty*, p. 179.

[11] The Christian Scientist's will does aim at his own (eternal) good, but we could imagine a different example, in which the accident victim would wish to be elsewhere than the hospital for self-sacrificing reasons.

[12] See the quotation from pp. 64–65 at p. 76 above.

[13] There are exceptions which have no bearing here: when (perhaps because I am acting under duress) I hope to fail, or when I am picking indifferently between possibilities and I do not care which one is realized.

of my exercise of a freedom but not at all because my will has the character it does: when a public authority, perhaps acting for my good, but not out of respect for my will, delivers things that I would choose to get if I had a choice in the matter.

The real substance of Sen's innovative focus, then, is that the standard aim of exercises of freedom is achievable not only through exercises of it but also by other means: a friend does what he knows is your will because it is your will, a benign (or otherwise) agency does what happens to be your will. In these cases, the standard effect of a successful exercise of freedom, conformity of the world to the will, occurs without any such exercise. But although the standard effect of a successful exercise of freedom, world/will conformity, is thereby wrought, it is not therefore right to call the person whose will is satisfied free, or to say that he has freedom without control. The Christian Scientist is not more free in being at home than he would be if he were in hospital, though his will is better satisfied. Freedom, the "ability to get what we value and want" (p. 64), obtains only when it is the agent who secures the conformity of the world to its will.

My will is how I would make things go if I could do so. If they go that way without my intervention, then, except in special cases, I will unambivalently welcome that. (Special cases are ones in which it matters to me that I be the person who secures what I will: I want it to be me, not someone else, who nurses my spouse back to health.) And the malaria case is not a relevantly special one: I shall not feel that I have missed an opportunity to eliminate noxious mosquitoes if the government does it for me (or even if it does it not strictly *for me*). There are two values associated with successful exercises of freedom. One is that the world conforms to my will and the other is that it is I who achieve that result. Sometimes the second value does not matter much, and the malaria example is a case in point.

There is a political reason why Sen insists on the phrasings that I have stigmatized as inappropriate. "Freedom," he says, "is one of the most powerful social ideas" (p. 69), and he is therefore concerned (so I hazard) to prevent ideological enemies of state intervention from obscuring the fact that freedom is among the benefits that such intervention can bring. Extreme right-wing ideologues regard all state intervention as diminishing freedom (even if some of them concede that intervention might be justified on other grounds). Against that, I agree with Sen that freedom is *pro tanto* enhanced when the state functions as an instrument of the democratic will. But what should be said to a less extreme ideologue, who might grant that point, but who finds no freedom in a malaria clearance which is not democratically instituted? Not what Sen would say to her, that she is blind to the fact that there is freedom here too. Rather this: that all or most of what would make this situation valuable if it did represent an exercise of freedom is present here. The ideologue is blind, specifically, to that. She so makes a fetish of freedom that she fails to notice that a large part of its value can be present when freedom itself does not obtain.[14]

[14] I am also unpersuaded by Sen's attempt to vindicate the phrase 'freedom from malaria' as fitting "into a broad general concept of freedom" (p. 68), and not just signifying absence of something undesired, like a cupboard that is free of dirt, but I shall not pursue that issue here. See my "Equality of What?" [pp. 55–56 of Chapter 2 of this volume—Ed.].

Chapter Four

EXPENSIVE TASTE RIDES AGAIN

Swiss researchers say an eating disorder associated with right anterior brain lesions can turn people with average food preferences into passionate culinary aficionados. "Gourmand syndrome" seems to affect a small percentage of patients with focal lesions involving cortical areas, basal ganglia, or limbic structures. Patients have persistent cravings for fine foods, explain researchers Marianne Regard (University Hospital, Zurich) and Theodor Landis (Hôpital Cantonal Universitaire de Genève, Geneva).

723 patients with known or suspected single cerebral lesions were studied by Regard and Landis. 36 had gourmand syndrome; of these, 34 had a lesion in the right anterior region. The study was initiated after the authors noted altered eating behaviour in two patients with right hemisphere haemorrhagic lesions. The first patient was a political journalist described as an average eater. During hospitalisation, his diary was filled with references to food and dining. After discharge, he gave up his old job and became a successful fine-dining columnist. The second patient was an athletic businessman who "preferred a tennis match to a fine dinner". While in hospital, he fantasised about dining in a certain well-known restaurant, which he proceeded to do the day after discharge.

—Marilynn Larkin, "Eating Passion Unleashed by Brain Lesions," p. 1607

The present paper is a reply to "Equality and Capability,"[1] in which Ronald Dworkin responded to some of the criticisms of his work that I made in "On the Currency of Egalitarian Justice."[2]

The first two sections of the paper are clarificatory. Section 1 distinguishes two broad criticisms of equality of welfare that Dworkin has developed, one surrounding the indeterminacy of the concept of welfare and one surrounding the problem of expensive taste. I express sympathy with

"Expensive Taste Rides Again." In Justine Burley, ed. *Dworkin and His Critics*. Oxford: Blackwell, 2004. By permission of Wiley-Blackwell.

[1] Which is chapter 7 of Dworkin's *Sovereign Virtue*. All pure page references in the present chapter are either to that book or to my "On the Currency": see the next footnote.

[2] Unless otherwise stated, all citations of my work in the present chapter are to that article. All such citations begin with the number '9,' and are therefore unconfusable with

the first criticism, and I argue that the second one must be assessed in abstraction from the first. Section 2 explains what the phrase 'expensive taste' means within the present debate. It is vital that it does not mean, here, what it ordinarily means. Confusion of its ordinary meaning with the meaning that it bears here produces a false understanding of the point of disagreement between Dworkin and me about expensive taste.

Section 3 states the view of expensive taste that I defended in "On the Currency," but it also articulates a significant revision of that view, one that makes my present position in one respect more distant from Dworkin's than it was in 1989. Section 4 discusses brute taste, that is, taste that is not guided by judgment. I claim that Dworkin has now abandoned his 1981 refusal to compensate for expensive brute taste, albeit without acknowledging that he has done so.

Section 5 refutes the principal argument that Dworkin deploys against compensation for expensive judgmental taste. That argument rejects the claim that uncompensated (and relevantly involuntary) expensive taste represents an injustice, on the ground that the stated claim requires people to conceive themselves as alienated from their own personalities. I show that no such bizarre self-conception follows from the mooted claim. Section 6 scouts some further arguments that Dworkin brings against compensation for expensive taste.

Section 7 refutes Dworkin's charge that equality of opportunity for welfare offers a "buzzes and ticks" picture of human well-being, according to which people have reason to care about two things only: pleasurable experiences, no matter what occasions them; and satisfying their desires, no matter what the objects of those desires happen to be.

Section 8 explains why the dispute about expensive taste matters: it bears deeply on the justice of the market process. The section also explores the consequences that equality of opportunity for welfare has for state action. Section 9 shows, against Dworkin's claims to the contrary, that neither my view—which is not equality of opportunity for welfare—nor equality of opportunity for welfare proper, collapses into equality of welfare.

Section 10 offers a fragment of a taxonomy that distinguishes contrasting degrees of control that people display over the acquisition and the persistence of their tastes. The taxonomy bears against one premise in Dworkin's argument that equality of opportunity for welfare collapses into equality of welfare. Section 11 reviews, and rejects, various arguments, only one of which is Dworkin's, for not compensating for expensive tastes.

---

citations of *Sovereign Virtue*. ["On the Currency" has been reprinted as Chapter 1 of this volume. Page references to that chapter are provided in square brackets throughout this chapter.—Ed.]

A Coda comments briefly on wider aspects of the "Equality of what?" question[3] and the Appendix reconstructs, and refutes, a variant of the "alienation" argument against compensation for expensive taste whose substance is due to Matthew Clayton and Andrew Williams.

Before I proceed to business, I wish to point out that, although Dworkin treats me, for (legitimate) convenience, as a proponent of equality of opportunity for welfare, I *rejected* equality of opportunity for welfare in "On the Currency." I affirmed not equality of opportunity for welfare, but equality of access to advantage,[4] under an understanding of "advantage" in which welfare, in various of its forms, is only a proper part of it. Welfare is, in my view, no more than a part of advantage because, as Dworkin has taught us, egalitarians are moved to eliminate disadvantages that are not reducible to welfare deficits. But I also think, against Dworkin, that welfare is a part of advantage because egalitarians are (equally legitimately) moved to compensate for the very fact that some people's welfare is lower than that of others. But the indicated simplifying treatment of my position by Dworkin will not matter in the present paper except in Section 10 below, and even there it won't matter very much. For the most part, I am happy, and it is also convenient for *me*, to accept, heuristically, the role of champion of equality of opportunity for welfare, for the restricted purpose of confronting the argument that is central to Dworkin's polemic against me, and which is addressed in Section 5.

A word about what will be meant by the sentence-form '*x* represents an injustice' here. It will not mean '*x* represents an injustice that ought to be rectified by the state.' (No one should in any case think that that's what '*x* represents an injustice' *ordinarily* means: the words 'that ought to be rectified by the state' surely *add* meaning to the phrase that they expand). It will mean, more elementarily, that the world is less than fully just by virtue of the presence of *x* in it. So, to be as clear as possible, if, in the sequel, I say such things as "compensation is required by egalitarian justice," I mean: for there to be egalitarian distributive justice, there must be compensation; and not: there must (unconditionally) be compensation, because of the (unoverridable and always implementable) requirements of egalitarian distributive justice.

1. Dworkin's "Equality of Welfare"[5] criticizes equality of welfare as a reading of the form of equality that is demanded by equal concern, but it

[3] Or, as I sometimes think it should be designated, "The 'Equality of what!?!' question."

[4] There is a fleeting acknowledgment of that distinction by Dworkin at p. 289: he did not dwell on it because he rightly judged that it is substantially irrelevant to our principal disagreement and also because, as he has argued forcefully (but not to me convincingly) in a private communication, it is, in his view, an unsustainable distinction.

[5] Originally published 1981 and reproduced as chapter 1 of *Sovereign Virtue*.

does so on at least two quite distinct grounds. The first ground of objection to equality of welfare can be called "the indeterminacy objection." It says that any tendency to embrace equality of welfare depends on lack of clarity with respect to what *kind* of welfare *equality* of welfare is to be understood as an equality *of*: whenever we try to specify the *kind* of welfare that people are to be equal in, we soon find ourselves formulating a plainly unacceptable view. So, for example, degree of what Dworkin calls *overall success* may appear attractive as the relevant reading of welfare, but not when we consider the case of people whose judgments of what constitutes overall success are either extravagant or extraordinarily modest. That case inclines us to favor the alternative reading of welfare that Dworkin calls *relative success*, but relative success loses its shine when we realize that people may achieve a high degree of relative success simply because they set their sights low. Summing up the lesson of this first line of criticism, Dworkin says that ". . . welfare has gained whatever appeal it has precisely by remaining abstract and therefore ambiguous: the ideal loses its appeal whenever a particular conception of welfare is specified, which presumably explains why those who defend it rarely attempt any such specification" (p. 285).[6]

Dworkin's second and entirely distinct ground of objection to equality of welfare is that it mandates provision for expensive tastes: the objection is that it is unfair to impose the cost of satisfying a given person's expensive taste on other people.

In "On the Currency" I criticized the expensive taste objection to equality of welfare, but I said little about the indeterminacy objection, beyond crediting Dworkin with a "masterful exposé of ambiguities in the concept of welfare" (p. 921, n. 24 [p. 18, n. 24]). So let me say, as I should have said in "Currency," that, in my view, the indeterminacy objection is extremely powerful. But, however strong or weak the indeterminacy objection to equality of welfare may be, the point I am here concerned to make is that the expensive taste objection requires assessment in its own properly separate terms. To test that objection against cases, we need to fix what we mean by 'welfare,' in a given case, which is not to say that we must mean one thing only by it, across all cases. We can discuss expensive *preference*, or expensive *rational* preference, or expensive *enjoyable mental state*, or expensive *subset* of goods that appear on a correct "objective list" of what is worthwhile in life. Whether or not, as Dworkin rather improbably suggests, the *whole* appeal of the welfare metric depends on its indeterminacy,[7] I believe that people find

[6] One good consequence of the publication in 1981 of "Equality of Welfare" is that a lot of hard work has since been devoted to such specification.

[7] I believe that anything that can plausibly be considered welfare (enjoyment, preference satisfaction, the objective value of a life, and maybe etcetera) is something that egalitarians

the expensive taste objection more powerful when particular examples of expensive taste are underspecified with respect to what 'welfare' is to mean in the description of the example. When we fix what welfare is, in a given example, we clarify and thereby strengthen the case for affirming that there can be injustice when and because people's resource bundles do not compensate for the fact that (a certain form of) welfare that is cheap for some is expensive for others.

2. To say that someone has expensive tastes, in the present meaning of the phrase, which is its meaning in Dworkin's article "Equality of Welfare," is to say that that person "need[s] more income" than others do "simply to achieve the same level of [some form of] welfare as those with less expensive tastes" (p. 48), be that form of welfare satisfaction of preference, or self-development, or good experience, or whatever other form of welfare is brought into view. But the ordinary understanding of the expression 'expensive taste' does not match the technical Dworkin-meaning that I just stated, and, to the extent that resonances from the ordinary meaning of the phrase continue to occupy the mind, the issue of whether uncompensated expensive taste represents an injustice risks being clouded.

Ordinarily, when we say that people have expensive tastes, we have in mind the lifestyle that they *actually* live, one characterized by fine-textile clothes, caviar, posh furniture, and so on. But their *actual* pattern of consumption may show not that their tastes are expensive in the *required* sense, but just that their bank balance is large. Nor is expensive taste in the required sense necessarily exhibited by someone who is not *willing* to *settle* for a lesser satisfaction, for example, for hamburger, instead of steak. For that is a matter not of the structure of such people's taste or preference as such, but, precisely, of their will. It is a matter of the *policy* that they adopt when seeking to satisfy their tastes.

A person's tastes are expensive in the required sense if and only if, as I have explained, they are such that it costs more to provide that person than to provide others with given levels of satisfaction or fulfillment. People who insist on expensive cigars and fine wines are not *eo ipso* possessed of expensive tastes, in the required sense. For they may thereby be insisting on a higher level of fulfillment than the norm. In the present acceptation, people have expensive tastes if, for example, ordinary cigars and cheap wine which give pleasure to most people leave them cold,

have reason to care about, and that that also helps to explain the illusion that equality of (some undifferentiated) welfare supplies the right metric of equality. (The pluralism of equality of access to advantage embraces all the welfares that there are, and also nonwelfare advantages. For more on that pluralism, see the final paragraph of the Coda.)

and they can get something like that pleasure (and, *ex hypothesi*, *not* a greater one) only with Havana cigars and Margaux.[8] People's expensive tastes, here, are a matter neither of their behavior nor of their will but of their constitution. They are a matter of what they are satisfied *by*, not of what they are satisfied *with*. (It does not prejudice the integrity of that distinction that it is often difficult to discern which limb of it applies, nor even that there may be cases with respect to which there is no "fact of the matter" to discern.)

An expensive taste, then, is a dispositional characteristic: not a disposition to action, like the disposition to choose steak rather than hamburger, but, to stay with that example, the disposition to get from steak only what others get from something as cheap as hamburger. Expensive tastes, in the specified sense, militate against, because they reduce the opportunity for, a fulfilling life. For any given income you are worse off in terms of satisfaction or fulfillment if you have expensive tastes.

So: do not picture people who consume steak and thereby get premium-level satisfaction and nevertheless present its cost as an injustice. People like that, who whine that their tastes are expensive in the ordinary sense of the phrase, give expensive taste in the appropriately technical sense a bad name that it doesn't deserve. Instead, picture people who consume hamburger but fail to get ordinary satisfaction from it and who present the high price they have to pay for the steak that would bring them up to mere par as an injustice.

Now, someone who loves cheap wine may hate ordinary cigars, and someone who is satisfied by ordinary cigars may need Margaux for ordinary-level wine pleasure. More generally, each person's satisfaction function will likely be an amalgam of cheap and expensive tastes, and few may have expensive tastes in an aggregate sense, when one considers the vast variety of commodities that are available to people. That fact is relevant to practical politics. It is certainly a reason for not worrying too much, in many practical contexts,[9] about compensating people for expensive tastes, particularly in the light of the invasiveness of the procedures that would sometimes have to be set in train to discover how cheap or expensive (in the *required* sense) a given person's tastes are. But the self-same fact is irrelevant to the philosophical question, which is

[8] I infer that Margaux is an unordinary wine because it is the one that David Niven ordinarily drank: see his various memoirs.

[9] But not all. Under Dworkin's characterization of expensive taste (see the first paragraph of this section) a person who is burdened with an expensive taste needs more resources to reach the same level of welfare as another. But people may be afflicted by expensive taste not because given commodities provide them with smaller *increments* of welfare but because they are generally miserable. A wide menu of commodities is unlikely to extinguish their welfare deficit.

whether or not, *ceteris paribus*, an expensive taste warrants compensation. Dworkin rejects compensation for expensive taste as a matter of *principle*, not on the grounds that a principle which might dictate their compensation is never *in fact* satisfied (because everyone can find *some* reasonably priced things that satisfy them as much as other people are satisfied by things that they find unsatisfying). I criticize Dworkin's principled position. Expensive tastes may be peripheral to the *practice* of justice, but the concept of expensive taste nevertheless raises questions at the heart of the *theory* of justice.

3. Dworkin believes that expensive tastes do not warrant compensation, from an egalitarian point of view. Against that, I said the following (p. 923 [p. 21], and cf. p. 920 [p. 18]):

> I distinguish among expensive tastes according to whether or not their bearer can reasonably be held responsible for them. There are those which he could not have helped forming and/or could not now unform, and then there are those for which, by contrast, he can be held responsible, because he could have forestalled them and/or because he could now unlearn them.

I now want to improve that statement, in two respects. I want to improve the *formulation* of its first sentence, but I also want to enter a *substantial* correction to the second sentence, one that also affects how the first sentence is to be understood.

The improvement as to formulation expands the first sentence by deleting "them" and adding "the fact that her tastes are expensive." It is, as I made abundantly clear elsewhere in "Currency,"[10] precisely *that* fact for which the question of responsibility is crucial.

Secondly, and more substantively, the statement needs improvement because it confuses a *general* criterion for deciding whether people should pay for their expensive tastes, which is described in the (now amended) first sentence of the statement, with a more *specific* criterion, described in its second sentence, and one that I now think is appropriate only to a subset of expensive tastes.

Let me explain. While the first sentence applies, so I think, to *all* expensive tastes, the second, which specifies the first *entirely* in terms of choice and will, is appropriate, I belatedly see, only in the case of tastes

[10] "A typical unrich bearer of an expensive musical taste would regard it as a piece of bad luck *not that he has the taste itself but that it happens to be expensive* (I emphasize those words because, simple as the distinction they formulate may be, it is one that undermines a lot of Dworkin's rhetoric about expensive tastes). . . . He can take responsibility for the taste, for his personality being that way, while reasonably denying responsibility for needing a lot of resources to satisfy it" (p. 927 [p. 25]).

that do not embody judgments of valuation, and which I shall call *brute* tastes, such as my own liking for Diet Coke, which embodies no particular *approval* of it. With respect to tastes that *are* informed by valuational judgment,[11] we can still ask whether their bearers could have avoided developing them or could be asked to rid themselves of them, and the answers will be variously relevant, but I no longer think that the mere fact that people chose to develop and/or could now school themselves out of an expensive judgmental taste means that they should pick up the tab for it, and that is *precisely* because they *did* and *do* identify with it, and therefore cannot *reasonably* be expected to have not developed it or to rid themselves of it.[12] So what Dworkin gives as a reason for *withholding* compensation—the subjects' approving identification with their expensive taste—is something that I regard as a reason for offering it, since, where identification *is* present, it is, standardly,[13] the agents' very bad luck that a preference with which they strongly identify happens to be expensive, and to expect them to forgo or to restrict satisfaction of that preference (because it is expensive) is, therefore, to ask them to accept an alienation from what is deep in them.[14] Accordingly, the significant revision of my view of expensive taste that I offer here renders my position more different from Dworkin's than it was in 1989.

Let me, then, set forth the flagship statement in its revised form:

> I distinguish among expensive tastes according to whether or not their bearers can reasonably be held responsible for the fact that their tastes are expensive. There are those that they could not have helped forming and/or could not now unform without violating their own judgment, and then there are those for whose cost, by contrast, they can be held responsible, because they could have forestalled their development, and/or because they could now quite readily unlearn them, without violating their own judgment.

[11] I take the distinction between the two types of taste (but not the word "brute," in this use of it) from Dworkin: see, e.g., pp. 290–91, and for more extended discussion, where they are called "volitional" and "critical" tastes, see pp. 216ff., 242ff.

[12] I am here influenced by Price's penetrating criticism of my "On the Currency" in section III of his "Egalitarian Justice, Luck, and the Costs of Chosen Ends." As Price points out, it might have been just someone's "bad luck that those preferences that he believed he ought to cultivate turned out to be [and might have happened to be from the start—G. A. Cohen] expensive preferences" (p. 272): thereby "the successful pursuit of the projects he finds important (and, so, *chose* to pursue), unlike the successful pursuit of the chosen projects of others, is frustrated by factors completely beyond his control" (p. 271).

[13] That is, barring the special case where people *welcome* the fact that their taste is expensive—see pp. 937–38 [pp. 35–36].

[14] For a particularly compelling illustration of this point, see the quotation from Justine Burley at the end of this paper.

The result, I acknowledge, is hardly a determinate theory, as opposed to a sketch for constructing one, but, incomplete as it is, the statement will do for present purposes.

4. I return to expensive *judgmental* taste in Section 5. But first I want to say something about brute taste, the taste that does not track a judgment of the value of its object.

In his 1981 articles Dworkin set himself against compensation for *all* tastes, whether brute or judgmental, other than those pathological ones which qualify as such because their bearer would prefer not to have them.[15] "Equality of resources," he said, "offers no . . . reason for correcting for the contingencies that determine how expensive or frustrating someone's preferences turn out to be" (p. 69). And that went for such brute expensive tastes as (suppose in a given case it is a brute one) a desire for plovers' eggs belonging to someone cursed with a propensity to find chickens' eggs disgusting. The only qualification on this rigor was signaled by this footnote: "See, however, the discussion of handicaps below, which recognizes that certain kinds of preferences, which people wish they did not have, may call for compensation as handicaps" (p. 478, n. 4). The footnote implies that compensation is in order *only* when people disidentify with (that is, wish they did not have) their own tastes.

Now people who find chickens' eggs disgusting may not regret having that reaction *as such*: they might even approve of it. If they wish that they did not have it, that is probably because the alternative to which the reaction drives them, namely, plovers' eggs, are so expensive. But that hardly qualifies their desire for plovers' eggs as a *craving*, either in the ordinary sense of that word or as Dworkin intended his use of it. And if regretting the special expense that one of my tastes imposes on me *did* make that taste a craving, then virtually *all* expensive tastes would attract compensation[16] under this widened understanding of Dworkin's compensate-for-cravings proviso.

To motivate my counterview, which is that *all* appropriately involuntary brute expensive tastes warrant compensation, suppose that there are only two edible things on Dworkin's island,[17] eggs and fish. Eggs are abundant, but fish are scarce. Consequently, fish are expensive and eggs are very cheap. Most people love eggs, but Harry hates them. Most people mostly eat eggs, reserving fish for special occasions, and they consequently have plenty of clamshells left to pay for other things, such as shelter, clothing,

[15] Dworkin calls such tastes "cravings": see pp. 81–83, and my response at pp. 925–27 [pp. 23–25].

[16] The exceptional case was mentioned in n. 13 above.

[17] The island, and the auction that occurs on it, are described at pp. 65ff.

recreation, and so forth. Unlike them, Harry has a tough choice, which is between regularly eating fish and therefore having little of anything else, and eating lots of eggs, at the cost of gagging when he nourishes himself. We may suppose that it is because of how his taste buds work that he gags, although we could equally well suppose that he gags because eggs remind him of his mother, whom he (perhaps rightly) could not bear. What we rule out is that he gags because he judges eggs to be an inferior sort of food: he has nothing against eating eggs, except that they make him gag. Although the example is stylized and peculiar, it stands here for the unpeculiar phenomenon of different people (through no fault, or merit, of their own) finding the same consumables differentially satisfying, and therefore being differentially placed with respect to what they can get out of life with a given income. And, in my view, that phenomenon explodes the pretension of Dworkin's auction to being an engine of distributive justice. It shows that equality of resources should give way to equality of opportunity for welfare, because identical quantities of resources are capable of satisfying people to different degrees, since people are made differently, both naturally and socially, not only (a fact to which Dworkin is sensitive) in their capacities to produce, but also (the fact to which he is insensitive) in their capacities to obtain fulfillment.

Relative to his 1981 auction treatment of taste, chapter 7 of *Sovereign Virtue* represents a remarkable and consequential U-turn. For, although he does not acknowledge this, Dworkin has *in effect* given up completely on brute taste, and now defends noncompensation for judgmental taste only. Under a regime of compensation for brute expensive tastes, people impose the costs of servicing their tastes on other people in just the way they were not supposed to do (except in the case of cravings). Yet what Dworkin says in *Sovereign Virtue* (2000, p. 288) about the person who finds his tap water repugnantly sour is entirely generalizable:

> Suppose someone cannot stand the taste of ordinary water from the tap—it tastes unbearably sour to him—and he therefore chooses to buy more expensive bottled water. It is true that he has a choice whether or not to do that. But he did not choose to have the property—a special sensory reaction—that made the choice not to do so distasteful. That physiological condition is his bad luck, and he should therefore be compensated for his misfortune: he should be given extra resource [*sic*] so that he will not be worse off buying bottled water than others are who make do with tap water.

But there is no relevant difference between finding tap water sour and finding (hens') eggs disgusting. And if, as Dworkin says, "[t]he unfortunate man whose tap water tastes sour would prefer not to have that disability: his condition is a handicap, and equality of resources would regard it as such . . . " (p. 291), then that can *only* be because bottled water is expensive, so that what he regrets is that he has an expensive taste, and it is to precisely *that* object of regret that equality (here misnamed: "of resources") is responding. If the water drinker is handicapped, then so is Harry the egg hater. But then—this is why I called Dworkin's U-turn consequential—Dworkin's market treatment of goods that supply brute satisfaction falls to the (in my view morally superior) principle: to each according to what they need for their satisfaction. In the huge domain of brute taste, market prices cease to embody justice. The scope of Dworkin's auction shrivels.

Note that one may identify with a preference (by which I here mean, roughly, be glad that one has it), disidentify with it (by which I here mean, roughly, wish that one did not have it), or possess neither attitude. In Dworkin (1981) you pay for your preference *unless you disidentify with it*, in which case it qualifies as a handicapping craving. But in Dworkin (2000) you pay for your preference *if you identify with it*, and not if you neither identify nor disidentify with it, this last being the condition of typical haters of tap water and hens' eggs.[18] And, as I said, that greatly reduces the writ of the market.

Let me now deal with another of Dworkin's responses to a "Currency" discussion of a case of brute taste. I argued (pp. 918ff. [pp. 16ff.]) that Dworkin could not countenance compensation for nondisabling pain, for pain, that is, that does not prevent people from pursuing their plans, since such pain constitutes no resource deficit. Dworkin responds (p. 297) that

> everyone would agree that a decent life, whatever its other features, is one that is free from serious and enduring physical or mental pain or discomfort, and having a physical or mental infirmity or condition that makes pain or depression or discomfort inescapable without expensive medicine or clothing is therefore an evident and straightforward handicap.

And he draws this lesson: "If the community gives someone money for medicine to relieve pain, it does so not in order to make his welfare or well-being equal to anyone else's, but because his physical constitution handicaps his ability to lead the life he wishes to lead" (p. 491, n. 11).

In my view, the quoted formulations run together two contrasts that must be kept apart for the sake of a proper assessment of the impact of what is here said on the matter in dispute. There is the contrast between, on the one hand, making a person's "welfare or well-being *equal* to anyone else's," with the emphasis on *equal*, and, on the other hand, ensuring that a person achieve a decent level of life, *however* that level is to be

[18] That is, once we set aside as *ultra vires* their wish not to have the tastes they do *because* they are expensive: see the third paragraph of the present section.

measured. That contrast is not material to the present dispute. The contrast that bears here is, rather, between aiming at remedying a deficiency in welfare, and aiming at remedying a deficiency in something else.[19] And on this, the only relevant count, what Dworkin says is ineffective. You do not turn a welfare consideration into a resource consideration by appealing to the fact that the source of the illfare in question is a person's physical constitution. What is claimed to be compensation for resource deficit is *not* compensation for welfare deficit in another guise when resources are valued independently of their bearer's particular wishes, which is how the market values them. But we get the stated mere guise when "resources" of physical constitution are treated as handicapping a person's "ability to lead the life he wishes to lead," and *that* means, *ex hypothesi*, in the relevant context, nothing more than that he wishes to lead a life without the deleterious welfare effects of that constitution. If I say that people should be compensated for desiring fine foods, and Dworkin responds that they should be compensated for the constitution that makes them want them,[20] then he disagrees with me in appearance only. Nor is it any kind of reply to my objection that people would *insure* against serious pain (p. 297): a deficit doesn't count as a resource deficit just because people would insure against it.[21]

For the rest of this paper I ignore the large concession documented here and I treat chapter 7 of *Sovereign Virtue* as a full defense of Dworkin's original view. For he continues to criticize my position as though he has not made the stated concession, and I have said what I wanted to say about that concession here.

5. Let us now focus on expensive judgmental taste, with respect to which Dworkin undoubtedly stands his ground. He continues to hold that costly judgmental preferences warrant no subsidy when they constitute, as they

[19] In Susan Hurley's terms, we are here disputing the *currency* of distribution, not its *pattern*. See her *Justice, Luck, and Knowledge*, chapter 6. Examples of the former are resources, welfare, capabilities, and so on. Examples of the latter are equality, "sufficiency," and maximin. (It might be thought curious that Dworkin, who is not a sufficientarian, but a relational egalitarian, should here introduce an element of sufficiency into his view, but that, as I said, is not the matter in issue between us.)

[20] For example, for the state of their cerebral cortices, rather than for "gourmand syndrome" as such: see the epigraph to this chapter.

[21] Bernard Williams suggested to me (personal communication, December 4, 2002) that the relevant difference between handicaps (ordinarily so called) and satisfaction-reducing expensive tastes might be "between giving up or not getting something nice as opposed to having to put up with or being subjected to something nasty." I think that there is a lot of plausibility in that, but it is not a thought that a *relational* egalitarian like Dworkin can exploit in the present polemic, since equalizing, as opposed to providing some sort of sufficiency, or a decent level of life, is indifferent to any distinction that may obtain between the less pleasant and the more nasty.

normally do, preferences with which the agent identifies, preferences, that is, which the agent would not wish to lack. Dworkin thinks, in my view falsely, that it is of the nature of preferences that they do not relevantly reflect choice,[22] so he does not think that compensation for expensive preferences is out of order *because* they have a *chosen* character. It is, rather, because to demand compensation for an expensive judgmental preference is to treat it as a burden or a disability, and therefore to repudiate it, which is not something that a person whose preference is informed by a judgment which endorses the value of its object can in general coherently do. To my urging that expensive preference may be relevantly unchosen bad luck, Dworkin replies that although it is indeed unchosen, the agents cannot regard it as a piece of bad luck for which they should be compensated, on pain of incoherently repudiating their own personality, on pain of confessing to a most bizarre alienation from themselves.

But this move is entirely unpersuasive, since the relevant bad luck does not lie in the mere *having* of the preference. As I tried to make clear in "On the Currency" (see again n. 10 [of this Chapter—Ed.]), the person regards the relevant taste as bad luck *only* in the light of its price. And people can certainly without any self-misrepresentation or incoherence ask for compensation for (what might be, in every relevant sense) the *circumstance* that their taste is expensive. Whether or not it is weird to regret one's preference for reading certain kinds of books (that *happen* to be expensive),[23] there is nothing weird or self-alienating in regretting precisely this: that the kinds one wants to read are expensive. Accordingly, so many of us think, libraries should not charge people more who borrow more expensive books, since people cannot reasonably be held responsible for the property of the object of their book preference that it is expensive. Perhaps the stated antimarket policy, which does compensate for expensive taste, is mistaken, but it is no argument against it that the library readers must represent themselves as dissociated from their own taste if they support such a policy. That is no argument against the antimarket policy, for the simple reason that no such dissociation is in fact displayed.

The bulk of Dworkin's reply to me, and the whole of his extended allegory of "buzzes and ticks,"[24] misrepresents me as supposing that the person with an expensive taste that raises a case for compensation regrets having the taste, rather than merely that it is expensive.

Toward the end of his reply to me, Dworkin does bring that critical distinction to the fore, when he reports what he importantly misdescribes as a "new argument" (p. 298) that I put against equality of resources:

[22] See p. 289. I take up this disagreement in Section 11.

[23] I use parentheses to mark off a feature of the books that plays no role in the preference for them under specification here.

[24] For more on which, see Section 7.

> Cohen's final objection to equality of resources . . . says that *even* if people cannot sensibly claim that they have suffered bad luck in *having* the tastes and ambitions that they do, they can certainly claim that they have suffered bad luck when, in virtue of other people's competing tastes and ambitions, what they want is expensive. (p. 297, emphases added)

But Dworkin's "even if" is out of place, for I never say that people might be thought to suffer bad luck *just* in having the tastes that are in fact expensive. The regret I had in mind was wholly and solely that their tastes are *expensive*: perhaps I was not always explicit about that because I so took it for granted that price is the proper object of their regret. I did not say, and would never say, for example, that it is the *very fact* that he likes photography which is a burden to Paul (pp. 926–27 [pp. 24–25]). The locus of his burden is the entirely different fact that photography is an *expensive* hobby. Accordingly, what Dworkin calls my "final objection" is not, as he represents it, a *distinct* objection. It is my central objection to Dworkin's unwillingness to compensate for expensive tastes: that they may be tastes that we cannot reasonably expect their bearer to shed and that plunge them in what is straightforwardly the *circumstance* that satisfying their tastes is expensive, and regret about this circumstance is transparently coherent.

Consider this passage:

> It would strike us as bizarre for someone to say that he should be pitied, or compensated by his fellow citizens, because he had the bad luck to have decided that he should help his friends in need, or that Mozart is more intriguing than hip-hop, or that a life well lived includes foreign travel. (p. 290)

It might indeed be absurd for Mozart-lovers to regard their love for Mozart as *itself* bad luck. But there is nothing absurd, there is no dissociation from their own personality, when they expresses regret that Mozart CDs are more expensive than Madonna CDs. What the Mozart-lovers or the opera-lovers (p. 292) regret is not that their whole personality affirms their love of Mozart or of opera, but that what their whole personality (*legitimately*) affirms is expensive. Nor need anyone regret "loyalty to his friends" (p. 291), as such. What they may regret is that the friends have moved to Scotland, so that the exercise of loyalty to them costs so much more in time and money than it would if they were still in London: if they think some rail travel should be subsidized for this sort of reason, it remains false that they are repudiating, or affecting to repudiate, their own convictions, any more than bereaved air travelers repudiate their desire to show solidarity with their loved ones when they request and accept the low ticket price that some airlines charge for last-minute bookings to attend funerals.

Although "complex tastes are" indeed "interwoven with judgments of endorsement and approval" (p. 291), it simply doesn't follow that those judgments are prejudiced or denied by a request for, or an offer of, subsidy for the cost of satisfying complex tastes. A taste for reading art books rather than dime novels is, as tastes go, pretty complex, but one might think, with no trace of self-alienation, that one should not pay extra because it costs more for the library to stock art books than it does for it to stock dime novels. The art book lover *is* unfairly handicapped if libraries charge readers according to the market cost of what they read, and that is one good reason[25] why libraries, in the real world, subsidize tastes for expensive books by charging a uniform entrance fee, be it zero or some positive amount. It is precisely because lovers of art books quite reasonably *do* identify with their expensive book preference, it is because they cannot reasonably be expected to divest themselves of it, that the relevant readers have a case for support, regardless of whether they could have avoided or could now divest themselves of that preference.[26]

So it is no reason to deny support that the claimants in question identify with their preferences. But I do not say the polar opposite of what Dworkin does: I do not say that wherever there is an expensive identification, there is a case for support. And, as I have already acknowledged, I was certainly wrong, in "Currency," to distinguish the cases merely according to presence and absence of will, although I think they do count. It may, for example, also be important in our response to art book lovers, that their preference runs to books that merely *happen* to be expensive, that they do not, be it noted, prefer them for Louis-like snobbish reasons[27] that justify less sympathy.

I would add that the unsubsidized art book lovers might or might not prefer, all things (including prices) considered, to have other preferences over books: that will depend on many things, including the size of their bank balance and how they *now* rate being relatively poor but reading what they *now* like to read against the comforts of a less literate solvency.[28] (There is an intensity of dissatisfaction that Socrates might suffer that might well make him, or, at any rate me, prefer to be a satisfied pig.)

[25] There are no doubt other reasons for the policy: perhaps we charge no or low fees to everyone for the perfectionist reason that we approve of education; or we charge the same fee to all for the sake of administrative simplicity; or low fees have a public good justification (because educated people are a boon to others); and so on. But what requires focus here is what we should think of a library which resolved to charge according to the book's cost: would we not regard that as, *inter* whatever *alia*, *unfair?*

[26] I here apply the revision in my view that I described in Section 3.

[27] See Section 6.

[28] Dworkin himself points out (p. 30) that people might prefer pursuing preferences for what they judge to be inferior things that they are likely to fulfill to pursuing preferences whose objects they regard as superior.

But in either case, that is, whatever their preferences across their preferences may be, it is no reason for charging them more that they must misrepresent themselves as alienated from their preference if they ask to pay less, since no such misrepresentation is required.

Suppose that the members of a minority group appeal to the local municipality for funds to sustain a recreation center, be it because they are very poor or because they happen to believe that such things should be paid for by the state: the motive and justifiability, all things considered, of their request are not in point here. Dworkin must say, what is preposterous, that they thereby distance themselves from their own culture and/or that they show a preference for lacking that culture, all things considered. And things stand no differently, as far as alienation is concerned, with respect to less cultural expensive preference, whether or not justice calls for compensation in *either* instance.

I must point out that when I say that compensation for expensive taste is warranted, I do not mean that the state should establish a comprehensive program to provide it, since epistemic and practical obstacles rule that out: see, further, Section 9 below. I mean, instead, that, absent compensation, an injustice obtains,[29] one, however, that, so I have just implied, it may be unwise in many cases to seek to eradicate, because it may be hard to identify, and hard and/or invasive to treat. So I am not saying that people's trips to their friends, or their practice of helping others, or their love of Mozart, *should* be subsidized. For all that I have argued here, there might be (as I am sure there are) excellent reasons for not doing so. But Dworkin's alienation reason is not one of them.

6. I must now reply to Dworkin's objections to what he misnames my "new argument" (p. 298). But, before I reply to them, let me say that it is noteworthy, it is, indeed, of the first importance, that those objections abandon the "alienation" motif that frames Dworkin's earlier discussion in chapter 7 of *Sovereign Virtue*. And that confirms, what I have already urged, the utter irrelevance of the alienation motif for our dispute. If Dworkin had thought it relevant against what he describes as (merely) my "final objection," but what is, in fact, simply my objection, he would have continued to press the alienation motif. But he did not continue to press it. So it isn't relevant to what is called my "final objection." So it isn't relevant at all, since what Dworkin calls my "final objection" *is* my objection.

In response to my objection, Dworkin (p. 298) invokes an analogy with politics:

[29] See the final paragraph of the introductory section above.

> The mix of personal ambitions, attitudes, and preferences that I find in my community, or the overall state of the world's resources, is not in itself either fair or unfair to me; on the contrary, that mix is among the facts that fix what it is fair or unfair for me to do or to have. This is plain in politics: it would be absurd for me to claim unfairness or injustice in the fact that so few others share my tastes in civic architecture or my views on foreign policy that I am on the losing side of every vote on these matters.

I cannot disagree with Dworkin's insistence that what it is fair for me to have depends on the condition both of other people and of the world: what follows "on the contrary" is undeniable, and the dispute concerns not its truth but the right way to respect that truth, be it equality of resources, equality of welfare, or something else. But an unadjusted market that reflects the relevant "mix" may nevertheless be unfair to me, even if the mix *itself* isn't. (If one added people's *talents* to the "mix," then Dworkin would readily agree with that.) So "on the contrary" in the first sentence of the exhibited paragraph proposes a false contrast.

Dworkin's substantive point is carried by his second sentence, which presents the analogy with voting, an analogy that may not be fully appropriate, but which I accept for the sake of argument. Let me then point out that, if Dworkin were right in what he says here about voting, then there would be no problem of the permanent minority in politics, and no need to write constitutions that constrain the ambit of majority decision. Note, further, that in a polity that displays a rift in architectural taste, a Palladian majority that cares about justice might defer to a Gothic-loving minority and allow some civic architecture to be Gothic,[30] and it might also, in the same spirit, legislate subsidies on books which only a minority desire and whose market price is therefore inordinately high. *Even if* a majority could *legitimately* deny a minority its recreation center, or the books it likes, there would still be a case for saying that it was thereby acting oppressively. The majority would then not be paying the social cost of its choice, which, on any sensible conception of social cost, must include the deprivation visited on members of the minority.[31] And there is indeed no relevant difference, here, between being at the short end of the electoral process and being at the

[30] A punctiliously fair-minded Palladian majority might make half the architecture Gothic, so that all see what they like half the time.

[31] Dworkin represents the auction, and the market more generally, as inducing the result that what I pay for the elements in my bundle represents the costs to others of my choices. And so it may do, in *money* (or clamshell) terms. But the intuitive force of the idea arguably depends on an interpretation of cost in *welfare* terms. If so, Dworkin is not entitled to draw on that intuitive force.

short end of the market process. Dworkin's analogy with politics therefore suggests the opposite of what he wants it to suggest. The injustices visited on minorities by an oppressively majoritarian *state* are matched by the different sorts of constraint that *market* processes impose on people's opportunities to secure what they value, of which I shall say more in Section 8 below.

Will Kymlicka points out that "the viability of [some minority] societal cultures may be undermined by economic and political decisions made by the majority. They could be outbid or outvoted on resources and policies that are crucial to the survival of their societal cultures."[32]

And that is also true of those who have a minority taste in non- (or less) cultural (in the relevantly ethnic sense) aspects of life, such as for old-fashioned local shopping, or countrysides with hedges, or vegan food, and so on. The survival of *their* preferred ways may also be subject to threat from majority preference, whether that threat expresses itself politically or more anonymously, through the market.

Dworkin also claims (p. 298) that my "final objection" undermines any prospect I may cherish of distinguishing between tastes for which compensation is in order and tastes for which compensation is not in order:

> This argument, if successful, would certainly undermine my claim that expensive tastes should not entitle anyone to extra resource. But it would also, on its own, sweep away Cohen's own distinction between equality of opportunity for welfare and plain equality of welfare. Even if we accepted his claim that some people, like Louis, have chosen their own champagne tastes, we would also have to concede that such people have not chosen that these tastes be expensive: They can sensibly complain that it is their bad luck that, in virtue of the scarcity of soil of the right kind and orientation, champagne is more expensive than beer. Indeed everyone, no matter how cheap his tastes and ambitions are to satisfy, can complain that it is his bad luck that other people's tastes, or the fortunes of supply and demand, are not such that his own tastes would be cheaper still.

Louis *may* not have chosen *that* his tastes be expensive: whether that is so depends on details in the structure of his snobbery that are not disclosed to us in "Equality of Welfare." But he is said by Dworkin to have chosen to develop tastes that he knew would be expensive,[33] his reason for having done so being something at least closely related to their expense. And

[32] *Multicultural Citizenship*, p. 109.

[33] It is not I but Dworkin who says that Louis "sets out deliberately to cultivate" champagne tastes (p. 49: the point receives special emphasis on p. 50). Accordingly, "even if we accepted," in the third sentence of the text quoted above, is out of order: "*deliberately* cultivated expensive taste" denotes no invention of mine.

that is a perfectly natural reason for hesitating to compensate him. It is *not* mere bad luck that *his* tastes are expensive, since it is true *ex hypothesi* that he could have avoided expensive tastes, and it is significant that his reason for developing them relates to their expensiveness.

Let me also respond to the final sentence of the quoted paragraph above. It is irrelevant whether or not it constitutes bad luck that my tastes, though cheap, are more expensive than they would be if supply of and/or demand for their objects were different. What matters here is bad luck that raises an issue of justice, and identifying *such* luck requires a comparison with the luck that *other* people have, which goes unrepresented in Dworkin's parting sentence. What matters is whether I have the bad luck to be saddled with tastes that are *more* expensive to satisfy than, on the whole, other people's tastes are.

Before we proceed further, let me sum up the polemical position. Dworkin's central argument[34] runs as follows.

(1) Harry genuinely prefers expensive *A* to cheap *B*.
∴ (2) He cannot honestly repudiate that preference.

But

(3) To ask for help in satisfying a preference is to regard it as a handicap, and, therefore, to distance oneself from it in a fashion that implies repudiation.
∴ (4) Harry cannot coherently ask for such help.
∴ (5) We should not supply such help.[35]

My main objection to this argument is that, whatever may be said about the inference from (1) to (2), premise (3) is false, for reasons that were laid out in Section 5. At one point (see the exposition of "strategy 2" on p. 937 [p. 35]) I *conjectured* that one might wish to challenge the inference from (4) to (5), as a means of handling a peculiar sort of preference, one, that is, whose high cost is *welcomed* by its bearer. But I expressly favored a different solution[36] to that problematic preference from the one that denies the inference from (4) to (5). At p. 295 Dworkin misdescribes the unaffirmed conjecture as something that I affirm. But even if I had affirmed it, and was not merely raising it as one of three alternative

[34] He also has some subsidiary arguments, to which I have just replied, against my *real* (and misnamed "new") argument, to wit, the analogy with majority voting, the "self-undermining" claim, and a particular spin on "luck."

[35] See the Appendix for a variant understanding of Dworkin's argument which merits independent consideration.

[36] Namely, "strategy 3":

This final strategy is to revise the view I have defended, as follows. Instead of saying, "compensate for disadvantages which are not traceable to the subject's choice," say,

treatments of a peculiar sort of example, each of which struck me as deserving of consideration, the thought in question would be independent of our main disagreement, which concerns expensive preferences whose expensiveness their bearer indeed regrets.

7. I turn to what Dworkin calls "buzzes" and "ticks," buzzes being episodes of experiential enjoyment *as such* and ticks being satisfactions of preference *as such*, that is, considered independently of, respectively, the source of the enjoyment and the object of the preference. Dworkin thinks that I am committed to believing that buzzes and/or ticks are what people do or should care about, to the extent that I think that egalitarians should be concerned about each of experiential enjoyment and preference satisfaction, as such.

Dworkin is right that it is an insane metaphysic of the person that gives buzzes and ticks the stated centrality. But I am not committed to that metaphysic, and it is interesting that, in "Equality of Welfare," Dworkin did not accuse believers in the eponymous ideal of trafficking in that metaphysic. (The passage quoted in n. 40 shows that he could not, in all consistency, have made that accusation.)

The reason why egalitarians whose metric is or includes welfare are committed to no such metaphysic is that welfare, *even* buzz-and-tick defined, might be a good metric of just equality even if it isn't the right metric by which to run one's life. Thomas Scanlon points out that other people can aim at my well-being *as such* in a way that I do not myself aim at it: I aim at its constituents, and normally, moreover, not *as* (prospective) constituents of my well-being, but as what they specifically are, as such (this particular career, that holiday, this chocolate bar, etc.).[37] And the egalitarian distributor can, like Scanlon's other people, aim at ensuring equality within a dimension which is not the dimension in which people's primary[38] aims are located.

The buzz/ticks parody of my view has whatever properly intellectual force it does through being a representation of some such argument as the following:

"compensate for disadvantages which are not traceable to the subject's choice *and* which the subject would choose not to suffer from." The revisionary element is the second clause. In the revised view, choice appears at two levels, actual and counterfactual. (p. 937 [p. 35])

[37] See his *What We Owe to Each Other*, chapter 3, section 4.

[38] The qualification "primary" is necessary because it is reasonable to suppose that people commonly (thus I do, even if Socrates didn't: see p. 95 above) *also* have some second-order concern as to whether or not their preferences *whatever they may be* are satisfied. You don't have to believe any ridiculous buzz/tick metaphysic to appreciate that measured truth.

(1) Sensible human beings don't care exclusively or even centrally about buzzes and ticks as such.
(2) The egalitarian distributor must distribute according to what sensible people care about, as such.
∴ (3) The egalitarian distributor should not have regard to buzzes and ticks as such.

The first premise of that argument, one with which I agree, is beautifully set out by Dworkin. But the second premise, which is also required, isn't mentioned in "Equality and Capability," and Scanlon's point shows that it is a false premise. It is, moreover, a premise that Dworkin himself must reject, since his egalitarian distributor distributes according to a metric of resources, and, as Dworkin well realizes, balanced people do not care about *resources* as such.[39] During Oxford seminars in the late 1980s Amartya Sen used to object to equality of resources on the ground that resources are not what people care about. Dworkin used to respond (e.g., on June 1, 1987) by rightly denying premise (2) above.[40]

A final point, on buzzes, ticks, and judgment. Some utilitarians, and many economists, underestimate the role of judgment in desire: they are deserving butts of Dworkin's "buzz/tick" parody. Dworkin rightly emphasizes the role of judgment in desire, but he also undoubtedly overestimates it. The idea that the thrill that one gets from jazz is "predicated on [the] judgment . . . that good jazz is wonderful" (p. 293) is bizarre. I get a kick from certain works of rock and roll that I consider to be pretty worthless. Endorsement of the objects of desire doesn't run so far across the map as Dworkin appears to believe.

Where judgment endorses a desire, a regret about the cost of one's desire doesn't undermine that judgment, because the regret attaches to *that* cost. And where, as in my rock and roll case, there is no endorsement by judgment, where a pure "buzz" is indeed in question, the idea that asking for it to be subsidized involves some sort of unrealistic "dissociation from personality" (p. 290) is a manifest nonstarter.

8. For all that I have said, it may seem peculiar that a person, that is, me, whom most people would account more radically egalitarian than Dworkin is, should be tender, where Dworkin is tough, toward those who have expensive tastes. And, independently of which *side* I am on in

[39] See the contemptuous reference to preoccupation with "bank account wealth" at p. 107.

[40] Cf. pp. 19–20: "We may believe that genuine equality requires that people be made equal in their success (or enjoyment) without believing that essential well-being, properly understood, is just a matter of success (or enjoyment)."

this dispute, it might also seem odd that I should have spent so much time and energy on what might seem to be such an unimportant issue.

The answer to the first puzzlement follows from the clarification given in Section 2 above of what an expensive taste, *here*, is: expensive tastes, in the unordinary meaning of the phrase that operates here, militate against the quality of a person's life. Typically, if not always, they generate an involuntary welfare deficit, and it is not peculiar that a radical egalitarian should be exercised by involuntary welfare deficits.

But why—I turn here to the second puzzlement—should I concern myself with what might nevertheless seem to be so tiny an issue? The answer is that it is not a tiny issue at all: the correct assessment of the justice of the market is at stake here. Dworkin regards market process as integral to the specification of what distributive justice is:[41] it is his endorsement of the market that enforces his rejection of the claims of expensive taste.[42] Egalitarians like me, by contrast, see the market as at best a mere brute luck machine, and are correspondingly obliged to highlight the misfortune of those who are saddled with expensive tastes.

To see why I disagree with Dworkin about the justice of the market, consider, once again, a library which subsidizes some at the (money) expense of others by charging the same rate per borrowed book regardless of which book, be it cheap or expensive, a member borrows. There are, as I have acknowledged (see n. 25), reasons for a uniform entry price that are not telling here, such as an aversion to the pettiness, and costs, of setting individual rates for books and keeping detailed accounts. But I think that a distinct good reason is that which books people find fulfilling is not a matter of people's choices, but of their culturally and socially developed constitutions. It is, of course, a matter of choice, if anything is, that some members borrow expensive art books when they could have borrowed inexpensive novels. But it would not normally reflect relevant exercises of their will that novels fail to engage their powers in the way that art books do. When, as is usual, libraries charge the same price to all comers, few regard those who choose expensive books as taking unfair advantage of the subsidy on them. Egalitarians believe that there is a fairness case for one price, and more generally, for nonmarket pricing of *many* activities that people pursue, the ground for a uniform and therefore redistributive price being relevantly unchosen or otherwise defensible variations in the cost of satisfying people's tastes and fulfilling their aspirations. The distributive norm that I favor takes part of its inspiration from the socialist slogan, "To each according to their needs—according, that is, to what

[41] "[T]he idea of an economic market, as a device for setting prices for a vast variety of goods and services, must be at the center of any attractive theoretical development of equality of resources" (p. 66).

[42] I ignore, once again, Dworkin's (effective) volte-face on brute tastes: see Section 4.

they need for fulfillment in life," which is an antimarket slogan. Need satisfaction, thus capaciously understood, is a major element within what I have called "advantage."

When there are charges for use according to cost, then some are unfairly penalized for expensive tastes that they could not, and cannot, help having, or, more generally,[43] that they cannot reasonably be expected not to pursue: that is the case against market allocation here. Because of the vagaries and variations of preference, markets do not deliver justice, but that is not to say that there exists a practicable alternative that does so. To see that, let us distinguish between general and special subsidies: *general* subsidies reduce the cost of a given good to *all* comers, and therefore not only to those whose taste for that good is in the relevant way expensive; *special* subsidies are to those particular consumers of a given good whose taste for it is expensive. Now, special subsidies are in most cases multiply impractical. For one thing, it would almost certainly be impossible for the state to determine which tastes reflect disqualifying choice and which do not. For another, it could not easily determine whether a person, as he is now constituted, *needs* more resources than others do, for comparable effect or, on the contrary, simply *demands* more satisfaction than they do from life.[44] If, moreover, the state could indeed determine such things, it could do so only through a monstrous invasion of privacy that would not be justified, in my view, by the contemplated particular gain in egalitarian justice. What our tastes, *as individuals*, are, and how we got them, should, therefore, largely not be the state's business. (Note that library subsidies target groups, not individuals as such.)

But while individual subsidies are not on, general subsidies are, like the market, insensitive to individual variations in levels of fulfillment. So we produce some injustice whether we leave the market alone or interfere with it in a generally subsidizing way. If we wish to serve justice as well as we reasonably can, then we have to try to guess when taste differences make general subsidy *more* just than market upshots, and in some cases, such as that of libraries, my guess is that justice is indeed better served by our actual practice of subsidy: it is less insensitive to individual need than the market is. If we fix in our minds the form of welfare that we are supposing the library delivers, be it reading enjoyment, or preference fulfillment, or self-development, then the case for a general subsidy seems to me to be overwhelming. We must not be misled, inappropriately, by vagueness about what 'welfare' might mean here: we must not let the expensive taste objection to equality of welfare ride piggyback on the indeterminacy objection (see Section 1 above). (The library example is importantly different from a case where someone needs expensive cigars

[43] See Section 3.

[44] I invoke here the will/constitution distinction that I made at pp. 85–86 above.

to get what others get from cheap ones, for we may suppose that everyone prefers expensive to cheap cigars, whereas people differ not only in the degrees of satisfaction—or whatever—that they get from different books but also in their preference orderings over them. Partly for that reason, the library case is the appropriate model for how to treat different, and differentially expensive, cultural needs.[45])

Dworkin does not himself believe in pure *laissez-faire*, since he thinks that, so far as possible, people should be compensated for handicaps and for poor earning capacity before they enter the market. But he thinks that the market produces justice insofar as its prices reflect the play of people's tastes and ambitions. So he claims[46] that his auction produces stainless justice, when people differ only in their (comprehensively unrepudiated) tastes, but not in their capacities, whereas I believe that, for example, it is unjust if I have to pay more for figs than you do for apples simply because few people like figs and many like apples—always assuming that you get from apples more or less what I get from figs. In my view, markets can "produce" justice only in the Pickwickian sense that they do so when in some unattainable possible world they are so comprehensively rigged that they induce a distribution which qualifies as just for reasons which have nothing to do with how market prices form.

In sum: Dworkin believes that the market constitutes its results as just when pretrading assets are suitably equalized, where that equalization is blind to differences of taste, but I believe that, while market results may be more or less just, the market plays no part in the *constitution* of justice, precisely because it is blind to how well it satisfies different tastes and aspirations.

Some will balk at the idea that what is claimed to be a demand of justice is not something that the state, or, indeed, any other agent, is in a position to deliver. I cannot here defend the methodology that allows such a result. But it merits comment that Dworkin could not (and, so I believe, would not) object to my position on any such methodological basis. For he himself believes that egalitarian justice justifies compensation for expensive tastes whose bearer is disposed to repudiate them, and he can no more infer, in all due realism, that the state should comprehensively see to such compensation than I can realistically propose that it compensate with precision for unrepudiated expensive taste whose cost their bearer cannot reasonably be asked to shoulder.

Although I agree with Dworkin that the state cannot put particular individuals' tastes on its agenda, our reasons for that common stance could not be more different. For it is false, on my view, that people's

[45] Which is a topic that I explore in "Expensive Tastes and Multiculturalism."

[46] Or claimed: see the discussion in Section 4.

(unrepudiated) tastes are not the state's business *because* it is reasonable to expect them to take responsibility for those tastes, no matter how they came to have them, and no matter what they can do about them now. Instead, they must perforce pick up the tab for them because they cannot reasonably be the state's business.

9. Dworkin writes (p. 286):

> One group of critics—I shall use G. A. Cohen's version as representative—proposes that citizens should be equal, not in the welfare they achieve, but in the opportunity that each has to achieve welfare. As we shall see, that supposedly different ideal turns out to be equality of welfare under another name.

What we come to see, according to Dworkin, is that no one really *chooses* her tastes or preferences, and, so his argument continues, since equality of opportunity for welfare differs from equality of welfare only because the former refuses to compensate for certain tastes (chosen ones) that the latter compensates, it follows that there turns out to be no difference between the two positions.

There are two objections (*i* and *ii* below) to the claim that equality of opportunity for welfare collapses into equality of welfare for the stated reason. They are also objections to the claim that *my* view (equal access to advantage) collapses into that. And there is a third reason (*iii* below) for objecting to the claim that my view in particular collapses into equality of welfare.

i. *P* does not become *q* "under another name" because *r* is true and the conjunction of *p* and *r* implies *q* (the relevant values of those variables here are, respectively, *there should be equality of opportunity for welfare* [*p*], *there should be equality of welfare* [*q*], and *people never really choose their tastes* [*r*]). It is a matter of principle for equality of opportunity for welfare that tastes are compensated for only if and when and because they are (to put it crudely) not chosen, however often (including never) they are *in fact* chosen, and equality of welfare denies that principle. That deep difference of principle would survive even if it should turn out that all tastes are unchosen: we would still be faced with "a distinct political ideal" (p. 289), or, at any rate, a distinct conception of justice.

ii. We *can*, as I shall show in Section 10, distinguish relevantly different *degrees* of care and choice in preference formation. To be sure, we never quite simply *choose* a preference or a taste, in the way that we choose actions: preferences, unlike actions, and like all the things that aren't actions, are not immediately subject to the will. But there remain more nuanced things to be said about preference and the will.

iii. I am not, in any case, a proponent of equality of opportunity for welfare, but, rather, of equality of access to advantage, according to which there should be equality of opportunity not for welfare alone but for a vector which includes that, *and* resources, *and* need satisfaction, and, perhaps, other advantages. And that makes my own view proof against the mooted collapse. *Even if* no tastes were affected by the will, even if *ii* above were false, my view would remain trebly removed from equality of welfare: first, for the reason given in *i* above; second, because I do not think welfare is the only element that belongs in an egalitarian metric; and finally because there would *still* be scope for distribution-affecting choice, on my view (as, of course, on Dworkin's, but not according to plain equality of welfare), with respect to things *other* than preferences.

10. I now take up the task laid down two paragraphs back, that of showing that some preferences reflect more will than others do, in a way that bears on justice. But before I do so, I wish to reiterate and emphasize that any disagreement that Dworkin and I may have concerning the dynamics of preference formation is quite surplus to my disagreement with him about whether preferences that fall outside the governance of the will should be compensated. Even if we agreed that preferences never do in a relevant way reflect will, our root *normative* disagreement would persist.

I say that some preferences reflect will *more* than others do: I do not say that any preferences are (just like that) *chosen*. That would contradict the nature of preference. It is conceptually excluded that we should (just) *choose* our preferences (as opposed to the objects that they prompt us to pursue). But we can devote more or less control to the development of our preferences, and be differentially responsible for their cost as a result.

Consider, for example, Shirley, who relishes hamburger and steak in the same different degrees that the rest of us do. She knows that if she eats steak all the time it will lose its special zing and become no more satisfying than hamburger is. But for a while there will be extra pleasure, and Shirley's resources are ample enough for her to embark on the stated course: indeed, she has it in mind occasionally to buy super-duper steak once ordinary steak has come to taste, for her, the way hamburger does now. She is warned that the temporary gains she contemplates will be nullified if her income drops, and she is aware that there is some chance that it will.[47] But she embraces that risk, and, in the event, her income does happen to drop, so that she is landed with an expensive taste that is difficult for her to satisfy. Her predicament cannot plausibly be represented as a matter of mere bad luck, and we should be as reluctant to compensate her as we are to compensate losing gamblers who gambled with their eyes open.

Unlike Shirley, Dworkin's Louis (Bourbon) does not gamble on getting *more* welfare at the cost of developing an expensive taste. On the contrary: he "sets out deliberately to cultivate some taste or ambition he does not now have, but which will be expensive in the sense that once it has been cultivated he will not have as much welfare . . . as he had before unless he acquires more wealth" (p. 49). Louis originally, perhaps, hates caviar, but, being attracted to it because of its snob value, he trains himself to like it. That is an entirely coherent, even somewhat familiar, story, and, so it seems to me, justice should look less kindly on the proposition that he be sold caviar at a discount than on the proposition that Louisa, who came by the same taste inadvertently, should be given that discount.

It may, however, be unfair to characterize what Dworkin calls Louis's "taste for refined tastes" as a piece of snobbery. Perhaps he is moved by a certain more admirable ideal of consumption. If so, then my own disposition would be to treat him more indulgently (see Section 3 above).

So we may indeed distinguish between tastes for whose cost we hold people responsible because they could readily and reasonably have avoided developing them or could now be reasonably expected to develop cheaper ones (which means: learn to gain an ordinary degree of satisfaction from cheaper things), and tastes where responsibility is relevantly absent and/or where judgment is relevantly present and where compensation is therefore required by egalitarian justice. To be sure, you might find it unrealistic, and in any case likely to be special pleading, for people to say that they just *cannot* get from hamburger what others get from it (as opposed to that they are unwilling to *settle* for a lesser satisfaction). But the epistemic—and even conceptual problems[48]—that arise here do not affect the content of justice.

Sometimes no relevant choice obtained or obtains. If you were brought up on baseball, you did not deliberately develop a taste for it, and it may be impossible for you to come to enjoy cricket, irrespective of any

[47] Compare and contrast Richard Arneson's person who voluntarily cultivates "a preference for spending [her] leisure hours driving about in [her] car at a time when gas is cheap, when it is unforeseeable that the price of gas will later skyrocket." ("Liberalism, Distributive Subjectivism, and Equal Opportunity for Welfare," p. 186.)

[48] See the end of the third paragraph of Section 2.

judgments you may now make about the comparative value of those sports. But in other cases, nothing similar is true.

Suppose that I am hypnotized into an expensive taste, and, for good measure, into the endorsement of the value of its object that, so Dworkin thinks, puts it beyond the reach of legitimate compensation. It seems to me plain that it would offend against egalitarian justice to deny me the extra means that are required to satisfy it (although, *ex hypothesi*, it is not a Dworkin-compensable "obsession," or "craving":[49] an endorsing judgment obtains). But, importantly, that is merely an extreme case, at the far end of a continuum of absence and presence of will in taste formation, rather than something that in no way resembles ordinary processes of the genesis of preference and desire.

In responding to my claim, illustrated above, that preferences vary with respect to how much they represent will, Dworkin has not expressly addressed the motif of schooling oneself out of an expensive taste. But he has addressed the issue of responsibility for acquiring a taste in the first place. He has remarked that "people who deliberately cultivate tastes do so out of opinions they did not in the pertinent sense cultivate but had."[50] That remark is supposed to upset my insistence on the distinction, and its importance for justice, between tastes for which people can, and ones for which they cannot, be held responsible. But I do not think that Dworkin's remark, whatever truth may lie in it, does upset the required distinction.

It would do so only if it were generally true that responsibility for the consequences of a choice requires responsibility for the (always more or less constraining) situation in which it is made, and we normally suppose no such thing. Of course we do not choose out of the blue to develop our tastes, but it does not follow, and it is false, that we never have a significant choice with respect to whether or not we develop them. When any sort of choice of anything occurs, we normally modulate any resulting assignment of responsibility according to the character of the alternatives that the chooser had, and I believe that we can proceed in that fashion here. Louis chooses to develop a certain taste in the light of a "taste for refined tastes." That makes him a very special case, but set that aside. The feature to focus on here is that he indeed chooses a certain course of action, that of developing a certain taste, in the light of a (further) taste. Dworkin thinks that people choose *courses of action* in the light of their tastes, yet he also thinks that, despite *that* unchosen background to their choices, they may reasonably be held responsible for (some of) the consequences of those actions. I treat Louis's choosing to develop an expensive taste, in the light of a further taste, in precisely that fashion.

[49] See the beginning of Section 4.

[50] Text of Oxford seminar talk, January 24, 1994, and cf. p. 289.

You do not escape responsibility for the costs of your choice by virtue of the mere fact that you made that choice *against a choice-affecting background*. But *also*, the mere fact that you made a choice, and could have chosen otherwise (for example, not to buy that steak), no more shows that subsidy is out of order than does the *mere* fact that you could have chosen not to buy that wheelchair show that subsidy is out of order. In each case facts in the background to the choice, facts about degrees of control, and about the cost of alternatives, affect the proper allocation of responsibility for the consequences of the choice.

My strategy has been to propose a reckoning of presence and absence of responsibility for the costs of expensive taste that in material part imitates our quotidian treatment of responsibility in more familiar domains. It is false that the only relevant questions about choice and responsibility are whether or not something (an action, a preference) is, simply, *chosen* (that is, *tout court*), and that the only relevant upshot is whether the agent is responsible, *tout court*. Here, as elsewhere, we make judgments of *degree* of responsibility, and they are based on *graded* and *shaded* judgments about choice. It always bears on the matter of responsibility that a person chose a certain course, but it is also always pertinent how *genuine* that choice was (see p. 934 [p. 32]) *and* how constraining the circumstances were in which it was made. The genuineness of a choice is a function of the chooser's knowledge, self-possession, and so forth. And the point about constraining circumstances is illustrated by the case of the juvenile delinquent from a deprived background who undoubtedly chose to commit the crime, but our response to whom is conditioned by knowledge of what his alternatives were, and of how, for example, they differed from those of someone from the middle class, who had, as we say, many advantages. For a relevantly comparable contrast in the domain of expensive taste formation, consider the difference between someone who would have had to make a special effort to avoid developing a dependence on steak and someone whose taste for hamburger was ensured by the unavailability of steak.[51]

It is, of course, an extremely complex question what the shape of the function is which, in our ordinary thought, takes us from data about what lies inside and outside of a choice to an assignment of (some degree) of responsibility for its consequences: I cannot discuss that here (or anywhere else). But nothing says that we cannot operate that function

[51] It might be objected that I here support a reactionary view to the effect that people whose tastes are cheap, people who get satisfaction from modest things, should not be permitted, or, at any rate encouraged, to expand their horizons: the Etonian steak lover gets his steak because he needs it, but the street boy is condemned to eternal hamburger. My reply to the objection is that different dimensions of justice tell against one another here. It is indeed an injustice that *A*'s scope for development is worse than *B*'s, but it remains an independent injustice if *A* has the good fortune, lacking to *B*, of access to cheap contentment.

(which has more than two values) for the case of expensive choice and the taste that lies behind it. To be sure, it may be that it is only in unusual cases of taste formation that responsibility, on quotidian criteria, is in order. And it may also be true that the quotidian criteria which I have applied to the special case of taste and choice disintegrate, in the general case, under metaphysical interrogation. But I need not say that people *are*, in general, responsible for their expensive tastes. And if, indeed, we never are, whether because the metaphysics of the will says that we are responsible for nothing, or for more particular reasons, then, on my view they *always* constitute a complaint, from the point of view of distributive justice. The final *judgment* of justice depends on the facts of responsibility, but the ultimate *principle* of justice (compensate if and only if it is not reasonable to hold disadvantaged people responsible for their plight) is independent of those facts.[52]

11. I close with brief comments on several arguments to be found in the literature for regarding expensive tastes as outside the scope of compensatory justice.

> Argument (1): Since people choose which tastes to pursue, they have the opportunity to pursue others, and there is therefore no call to subsidize their expensive tastes.[53]

Argument (1) confuses the truth that you decide what tastes to pursue (that is, what objects of taste to acquire) with the falsehood (in the general case) that you decide what tastes to have. Different lifestyles are (within situational constraints) indeed chosen, but the preferences guiding those choices are not usually commensurately subject to the agent's control, and this has implications for justice.

Argument (1) is attributed to Dworkin by Kymlicka, among others, and with some textual basis: Dworkin offers noncongruent formulations on this matter, some of which more than suggest argument (1). (See pp. 927–31 [pp. 25–29] for substantiation of that noncongruency claim.) But argument (1) is not Dworkin's considered position, which is that tastes

[52] See, further, my "Facts and Principles." If, as I think he does, Dworkin means, by 'determinism,' 'hard determinism,' then I agree with him that "we all reject determinism, all the time," but I do not think that our affirmation or rejection of hard determinism has any bearing at the deepest level of *normative* philosophy. (The quotation from Dworkin appears at p. 107 of his "Sovereign Virtue Revisited"), and see ibid., pp. 118–19, for evidence that he means 'hard determinism' in particular (whether or not he thinks that soft determinism is coherent). For my own rejection of hard determinism, see p. 76, n. 14 of my "Why Not Socialism?"

[53] I discern argument (1) at p. 369 of Rawls's "Social Unity and Primary Goods" [page reference to version reprinted in Rawls's *Collected Papers*—Ed.]. See my p. 913 [p. 10] *et circa*, for discussion of the Rawls text.

are substantially unchosen—their bearer has little discretion with respect to their development—but that, for argument (4)-type reasons (the fact, barring special cases, that they are not repudiated), they should not be subsidized.

> Argument (2): To subsidize some tastes, and, therefore, tax others, would be to violate that neutrality across conceptions of the good which it is the duty of liberal states to maintain.

Richard Arneson has shown that argument (2) misapplies the concept of neutrality.[54] The policy of equality of opportunity for welfare is thoroughly neutral, even though it allows subsidy to those whose welfare costs more because of the structure of their tastes.

> Argument (3): Whether or not you choose your tastes, it is part of your proper responsibility as an adult to cope with them. They are a private, not a public matter.

Argument (3) is suggested by this passage in Rawls's *Political Liberalism*:

> . . . that we can take responsibility for our ends is part of what free citizens may expect of one another. Taking responsibility for our tastes and preferences, whether or not they have arisen from our actual choices, is a special case of that responsibility. As citizens with realized moral powers, this is something we must learn to deal with. . . . We don't say that because the preferences arose from upbringing and not from choice that [*sic*] society owes us compensation. Rather, it is a normal part of being human to cope with the preferences our upbringing leaves us with.[55]

But to the extent that this contention differs from argument (1), it is nothing but an appeal to popular opinion. People no doubt do think about the matter as Rawls says they do, but no justification of that familiar way of thinking is provided here. Why is the misfortune of expensive taste an essentially private matter when the misfortune of expensive mobility is not?

In my view, the Rawls passage gets things backward. The right argument says: it is extremely difficult and/or unacceptably intrusive to determine whether a person's tastes are expensive *and* how much they are responsible for them; therefore the state cannot and/or should not seek to make determinations of that sort; therefore people must (on the whole) take responsibility for the costs of their tastes. But Rawls propounds the opposite argument which says that *because* it is right to hold people re-

[54] See his "Liberalism, Distributive Subjectivism, and Equal Opportunity for Welfare."
[55] *Political Liberalism*, p. 185.

sponsible for their tastes, the state should not intervene here. (Compare the last paragraph of Section 8 above.)

> Argument (4): It is incoherent for people with (at any rate judgmental) expensive tastes to represent them as handicaps or disadvantages that warrant subsidy. They would thereby be repudiating as a burden what they *ex hypothesi* affirm as a desideratum.

Argument (4), which is put by Dworkin, depends, I have argued, on failure to make pertinent distinctions. Those who need expensive things for satisfaction would not, indeed, normally regard their very desire for them as a handicap. What handicaps them is that they are expensive. And no repudiation of their desire for them, or dissociation from their own personality, attaches to their representation of that as a handicapping circumstance.

Coda

I have not in this essay argued positively for the view that I set out in "On the Currency," nor indeed, except in small part, for the (somewhat sketchy) descendant view which replaces it and which is described in Section 3 above. What I have principally done is to refute one argument against equality of (opportunity for) welfare, namely, the expensive taste argument, and *pari passu*, to support one argument against equality of resources: that it is unfair to people who cannot reasonably be expected to pay the cost of satisfying their own expensive tastes.

I close with some remarks about the architectonic of Dworkin's magisterial 1981 diptych. It is of great importance to the apparent success of his case that he examines equality of welfare *first*. It is undoubtedly comprehensively demolished, in any *single one* of its interpretations,[56] so that the way then appears clear to propose equality of resources as an alternative. But the latter is not argued for positively, and it is also not subjected to the same test by counterexample that equality of welfare faced. And if one urges against equality of resources that people who are equal in resources will frequently be unequal in welfare in ways that look unfair, then Dworkin rules the objection out on the ground that equality of welfare has *already* been refuted.

But if that latter move appears sound, then that is only because of the *order* in which the competing equalities were examined. If Dworkin

[56] Dworkin also rejects an "ecumenical" view under which egalitarianism has regard to *several* types of welfare (pp. 47–48). I do not find his reasons for rejecting it cogent, but saying why would take us too far afield.

had considered equality of resources *first*, it would have faced counter-examples that could not be dismissed simply because of their welfarist character. (Note that the force of a welfare-inspired objection to equality of resources does not depend on an affirmation of [unqualified] *equality* of [opportunity for] welfare.)

It is because welfare equality can lead to crazy resource results and resource equality can lead to crazy welfare results that I was moved to float a pluralistic answer to the "Equality of what?" question. That question may be misframed, because, for example, distributive justice comes in uncombinable "spheres."[57] But *if*, what I increasingly doubt, Sen[58] and Dworkin's question is sound, then I remain confident that a heterogeneous plurality is the answer.[59]

Appendix

In parallel efforts, Matthew Clayton and Andrew Williams have sought to refurbish the "endorsing judgment" objection to compensation for expensive taste.[60] Their argument, here reconstructed, stepwise, by me, can be stated with respect to the case of Paul and Fred (p. 923 [pp. 20–21]). Paul's unchosen recreational taste is for expensive photography, while Fred's is for inexpensive fishing. As I understand the Clayton/Williams argument, it has, when rendered fully explicit, four premises and a validly derived conclusion:

(1) Paul merits compensation only if he can ask Fred for compensation.

(2) Paul cannot ask Fred for compensation unless he thinks himself worse off than Fred.[61]

[57] Cf. Walzer, *Spheres of Justice*. Note that a belief that the goods that figure in distributive justice cannot be aggregated implies neither Walzer's particular differentiation of such goods nor his relativizing view that goods count as such in virtue of "social meanings."

[58] Sen, "Equality of What?"

[59] I expressed doubt at p. 921 [pp. 18–19] about my own answer to the question, because of its awkward pluralism. I remain uncertain as to whether that pluralism is sustainable, and, hence, whether the Sen/Dworkin question *is* sound. A tentative defense of the pluralism is available in a document called "Afterword to chapters XI and XII," which I can supply on request. [This is the "Afterword to Chapters 1 and 2" of this volume.—Ed.]

[60] Clayton, "The Resources of Liberal Equality"; Williams, "Equality for the Ambitious."

[61] Williams: "the basic idea underlying the continuity test is that a political community should regard certain conditions as disadvantaging some of its members only if those members' own views about what it is to live well also imply that those conditions disadvantage them" ("Equality for the Ambitious," p. 387). Cf. Clayton, "The Resources of Liberal Equality," p. 77.

(3) Paul cannot think himself worse off than Fred unless he would rather be in Fred's shoes.[62]
(4) But Paul would not rather be in Fred's shoes. He does not want to love fishing rather than photography.
∴ (5) Paul cannot ask Fred for compensation.

I shall not reject premise (1). I believe that it is false *at most* in the peculiar cases typified by Scanlon's suffering-welcoming worshipper,[63] and perhaps also in cases where a person's false beliefs prejudice his welfare but at the same time make it incoherent for him to request relief. But such are not the cases that induce the disagreement between Dworkin and me.

"Worse off" in premise (2) is underspecified. It is true only if we add, at the end: worse off in some justice-sensitive respect. But the argument requires that we add: worse off, all things considered, since that is how "worse off" in premise (3) must be read. But when (2) is read in the required fashion, equality of resources itself contradicts (2). Underresourced people need not think, when demanding the compensation that Dworkin licenses, that they are all things considered worse off than relevant others. They need be worse off only in resources terms.[64] And Dworkin has no monopoly on the idea that you can be worse off precisely in the justice-sensitive respect without thinking yourself worse off *tout court*. There is a certain sort of welfare in which Paul is deficient: he fulfills his leisure needs less well than Fred does,[65] but he need not think himself comprehensively worse off even if in other respects he is on a par with Fred. If Dworkin's continuity test indeed implies premise (2),[66] under the "all things considered" interpretations of (2) that the Clayton/Williams argument requires, then so much the worse for the continuity test.

The very "shoes" metaphor that is used to formulate premise (3) exposes the falsehood of that premise. I can think myself better off in my shoes than I would be in yours while nevertheless thinking myself worse off in mine than you are in yours: yours fit your feet better than mine do.

[62] Clayton: ". . . an individual can plausibly claim that she is less advantaged than another in virtue of having a physical impairment or taste only if she would prefer to have the other's physical resources or taste" ("The Resources of Liberal Equality," p. 75; cf. Williams, "Equality for the Ambitious," p. 379).

[63] See pp. 937–38 [pp. 35–36]. Williams focuses too much on this bizarre example: Paul/Fred is the significant case.

[64] Recall Dworkin's refutation of Sen's objection to equality of resources: see p. 101 above.

[65] *Even if*—what need not be true: see the comment below on premise (4)—he prefers having those needs and having them less well satisfied than having Fred's needs, better satisfied.

[66] See n. 61 above.

To speak without metaphor, (3) is relevantly false because I can think myself better off with my preferences ill-satisfied than I would be with your preferences well-satisfied. An important example of this structure of preference is provided by Justine Burley:

> . . . when it comes to reproductive capacities for example, the greater financial burdens imposed on women by virtue of their unique biological endowments probably will not be compensated on Dworkin's view. A woman's complaint is only deemed legitimate if there is penis envy, as it were. If she affirms her possession of female reproductive capacities, if, that is, she affirms the fact that she is a woman, we cannot say that there is any injustice along Dworkinian lines when *actually* there is. To demand that a woman *want to be a man* to support compensation is simply ridiculous.[67]

Finally, premise (4) is not always true. As I noted in Sections 5 and 7, Paul can care *both* about the source of his satisfaction (he prefers it to be photography rather than fishing) *and* about the extent of his satisfaction. They are both, plainly, desiderata, and he can trade them off against each other (without thereby showing himself to be a buzz or a tick addict). Differently put: there is value *both* in pursuing what is more valuable *and* in getting whatever it is one pursues—one might have to add: as long as it has *some* value; but that wouldn't affect my argument against (4). And Paul might be sufficiently exercised by that second value that he indeed prefers to be in Fred's shoes.[68]

[67] Justine Burley, private communication, May 1995.

[68] I am grateful to Daniel Attas, John Baker, Alex Callinicos, Miriam Cohen Christofidis, Michèle Cohen, Ronald Dworkin, Cécile Fabre, Kerah Gordon-Solmon, Will Kymlicka, Michael Otsuka, Derek Parfit, John Roemer, Hillel Steiner, Zofia Stemplowska, Peter Vallentyne, Andrew Williams, Bernard Williams, and Erik Wright for helpful discussion. Some of the text in Sections 2, 4, 8, and 9 of this chapter provide a modified version of pp. 83–88 of my "Expensive Tastes and Multiculturalism."

Chapter Five

LUCK AND EQUALITY

1. In Chapter 6 ("Why the Aim to Neutralize Luck Cannot Provide a Basis for Egalitarianism") of her *Justice, Luck, and Knowledge*, Susan Hurley defends two claims: that "the aim to neutralize luck [does not] contribute to identifying and specifying what egalitarianism is," and that it also provides no "independent non-question-begging reason or justification for egalitarianism" (p. 147).[1] In the present response, I reject the first of Hurley's claims, and I show that the second, while true, lacks polemical force.

I said, in "On the Currency of Egalitarian Justice" [reprinted as Chapter 1 of this volume—Ed.], that

> *a large part* of the fundamental egalitarian aim is to extinguish the effect of brute luck on distribution. Brute luck is an enemy of just equality, and, since effects of genuine choice contrast with brute luck, genuine choice excuses otherwise unacceptable inequalities. (p. 931 [p. 29 of Chapter 1—Ed.], emphases added, with post-Hurley hindsight)

I have learned from Hurley, but I nevertheless stand by the substance of that statement, on a reasonable understanding of what that substance is. I do not claim that I had the stated understanding clearly in mind when I wrote my 1989 paper. Hurley has helped me to identify what I should have had in mind when I wrote it.

Egalitarians, so I said in "Currency," object to all and only those inequalities that do not appropriately reflect choice. They object to inequalities that are caused by (brute) luck[2] not merely because they are inequalities (since they accept inequalities that reflect choice), nor *merely* because they are effects of luck (since they would accept some *equalities*—and,

"Luck and Equality: A Reply to Hurley." *Philosophy and Phenomenological Research* 72 (2006): 439–46. By permission of Wiley & Sons.

[1] [Unless otherwise indicated, all page references in this chapter are to Hurley's book.—Ed.]

[2] Throughout, I use 'luck' to mean 'brute luck,' the luck which, unlike that of a deliberate gamble, we cannot reasonably be expected to avoid or to escape. And, unless the context indicates otherwise, I always mean, by *X*'s good or bad luck, *X*'s luck as compared to that of other people.

as it were, all noninequalities[3]—that are caused by luck). So—it bears repeating—they object to the inequalities to which they object because they are inequalities caused by luck: that it is caused by luck specifies the inequality to which they object, and the aim to neutralize luck *does*, therefore, contribute to specifying their egalitarianism (whether or not it is a *justification* of egalitarianism that it extinguishes the effect of luck on distribution).

What have come to be known as "luck egalitarians" focus on the *difference* between people's advantages, and they count that difference just if and only if it accords with a certain pattern in the relevant people's choices. All innate and otherwise (in the broadest possible sense) inherited differences of advantage are, accordingly, unjust. And, among differences of advantage that are not inherited, we have two just cases: one in which the required accord obtains because choice fully explains the difference, and one in which (brute) luck, too, played a role, but, luckily enough, it was to nobody's advantage, compared to anybody else. So you could say that luck egalitarians count uninherited differences of advantage as just if and only if the differences are not at all due to luck.

Accordingly, I see no case for Hurley's contention (p. 147) that luck plays no role in the specification of the egalitarian aim. In a variant of that claim, Hurley says that "the aim to neutralize luck" *indeed* specifies the desired equality, but only "trivially" (p. 156). But every defining specification of anything is trivial in that innocuous sense: it is, for example, a trivial specification of reticulated giraffes that they are reticulated. And we lack here, what Hurley thinks we have, on this basis, a reason for saying that "the aim to neutralize interpersonal bad luck begs the question of justification" (p. 157), if only because, when specification is the enterprise, justification is not in question. Unlike an argument, a specification *can't* "beg the question" (ibid.), yet Hurley seems to mean the accusation of question-beggingness to apply not only against the argument claim but also against the specification claim. (I say "seems" because the relevant paragraph moves without noticeable segue from the specification issue to the argument issue, and I am caused to wonder whether, in writing it, Hurley maintained the—polemically crucial—separation between the two issues in her mind.)[4]

[3]Luck might cause one person to have more freckles than another: that is (in itself) neither an equality nor an inequality between them.

[4]I believe there are a number of other places where Hurley fudges the specification/argument distinction. Consider, for example, the first two sentences of the final paragraph of Hurley's chapter (p. 180). "[T]hat equality should be taken as a default position when people are not responsible for what they have" *does* straightforwardly specify an egalitarian position. To say that "considerations of responsibility and luck do not provide a basis

2. Now Hurley also claims—and with this claim I agree—that it is not an *argument* for egalitarianism that it extinguishes the effect of luck on distribution (where 'luck' contrasts with 'genuine choice'). I agree that that is not a good argument, but let us be clear *why* it is not a good argument.

Someone might say that it is not a good argument for this reason: if *equalizing* against the grain of luck extinguishes luck's effect on distribution, then so, too, does *any unequalizing* or *equality-indifferent* restructuring of what luck scatters about, such as, for example, the restructuring proposed by utilitarianism. It is, accordingly, no argument for egalitarianism (in particular) that it extinguishes the effect of luck. Any principle does that, merely by being effectively applied.

But that objection to the argument claim is invalid. To be sure, enforcing utilitarianism sweeps away the (initial) results of luck, but unlike luck egalitarianism, utilitarianism replaces those results with further, different luck. For luck, in the relevant sense, is benefit and burden in disaccord with choice, and utilitarianism does not eliminate the offending discord: when utilitarianism is enforced, it can be my good luck, compared to others, that my utility function makes me an apt recipient of lavish resources, from a utilitarian point of view: it may be my good luck that I am what has been called a "utility monster,"[5] which is to say that my utility function converts resources into utility with spectacular efficiency. To be sure, the utilitarian can say, about a happenstance distribution: "This came about by luck, not by application of the utilitarian principle." But being produced by "luck," as far as that sentence is concerned, contrasts with being produced by the application of whatever principle might be in question: here, the utilitarian one. It is not the luck of a relevant absence of choice, and it is *that* luck which the egalitarianism in contention here targets.

So I reject *that* objection, the objection based on the existence of competing luck-extinguishers, to the claim that it is an *argument* for egalitarianism that it extinguishes the effects of luck on distribution. I reject that objection because it equivocates on the word 'luck.' But I nevertheless agree with Hurley that luck extinction is no argument for egalitarianism, and I want to insist that I never claimed otherwise. I never said that it was an *argument* for egalitarianism that it extinguishes the effect of luck on distribution.[6] That it extinguishes the influence of luck is no

for" (p. 180; cf. "no luck-related *reason*" at the bottom of p. 156) that position is merely incoherent, when *specification* is in question.

(In the paragraph above I respond to the first horn of the dilemma that Hurley sets out at pp. 156–57. A response to the second horn of the luck neutralizer's dilemma had to be excluded for reasons of space.)

[5] See Nozick, *Anarchy, State, and Utopia*, p. 41.

[6] But that is not to say that I *deliberately* refrained from saying so: I simply had not thought about that question. This is but one respect in which Hurley's challenging work

more an argument for egalitarianism than that it promotes utility is an argument for utilitarianism, and in each case for the same reason, to wit, that the cited feature is too definitive of the position in question to *justify* the position in question. If we set aside exotic projects in ethics that would parallel Max Black's inductive justification of induction,[7] then it cannot be an *argument* for utilitarianism that its implementation maximizes happiness.[8] It is, nevertheless, a *specification* of utilitarianism that it does so. And it is, of course, precisely *because* utilitarianism directs happiness-maximization that its propensity to maximize happiness would not justify it: the goal is too *integral* to utilitarianism to be available as a justification of it.

In parallel fashion, luck extinction cannot be an argument for egalitarianism precisely because, *pace* Hurley, it does specify egalitarianism. The specification of this egalitarianism involves essential reference to luck, where 'luck' contrasts, constitutively, with the responsibility for outcomes that comes with genuine choice.[9] Since luck egalitarianism accounts it an unfairness when some are better off than others through no fault or choice of their own, the relevant contrast with 'luck' is 'choice,' complexly understood: other contrasts with luck, such as 'naturally determined,' are simply irrelevant. (In certain instances, luck contrasts with counterfactual choice: I leave that pregnant complication aside here: see "On the Currency," pp. 936–38 [pp. 34–36 of Chapter 1—Ed.].)

Whether genuine responsibility ever actually obtains is a matter on which luck egalitarians can be neutral,[10] but, if there is indeed no such thing as genuine responsibility, then the luck egalitarian proposes what the flat egalitarian—who believes that justice consists in unmodified equality—proposes. Hurley writes that "if responsibility is impossible, then everything must be a matter of luck and it is impossible to neutralize luck" (p. 175). And it is true that everything would then be a matter of luck in the sense that everything would be unchosen. But distributions could still be in accord or in disaccord with the principle that only differential responsibility can justify inequality. And that is

has, so I believe, improved my understanding of these matters, and forced me to try to be more clear about what I thought and think.

[7] See "Inductive Support of Inductive Rules," in his *Problems of Analysis*.

[8] It might nevertheless be an argument *against* it that its implementation *fails* to maximize happiness: see Parfit, *Reasons and Persons*, chapter 1.

[9] Various luck egalitarianisms can interpret the different dimensions of that view differently, through different answers to such questions as: what is genuine choice? what is a properly equal option set? For a brilliant treatment of the second question, see Vandenbroucke, "Responsibility: Rule-Currency."

[10] I am entirely unconvinced by Hurley's claim that "the aim to neutralize the effects of luck treats everything as a matter of luck" (p. 172).

the substantive normative point, whether or not genuine responsibility ever actually obtains.

3. Three related features distinguish the egalitarianism of Dworkin, Cohen, and the then[11] young Arneson, from other ones. First, their egalitarianism, so-called luck egalitarianism, recommends the equality it affirms, an equality of (differently interpreted) opportunity or access, *as such*: it does not recommend it merely in the light of claims about the *consequences* of adherence to the recommended egalitarian principle. Second, luck egalitarianism purports to identify what is distributively *just*, and, third, its prescriptions are inspired by certain intuitions about *fairness*.

Not every egalitarianism has the stated features. There is, for example, a form of egalitarianism that is based on fraternity[12] and that lacks all three. This fraternity-based egalitarianism depends on the claim that significant divergences in people's fortunes discourage community: the principle of equality is not, in the relevant sense, fundamental within that fraternity-based egalitarianism, an egalitarianism which is, moreover, not submitted as an answer to the question what distributive justice is, and one which is not inspired by intuitions about fairness.

Not being inspired by intuitions about fairness, fraternity-based egalitarianism *might* ignore the criticism that unmodified equality is unfair because it provides the same benefits for the idle grasshopper as it gives to the industrious ant.[13] Luck egalitarianism arises as a response to that criticism, from an initially cruder egalitarian standpoint. But, as Ronald Dworkin has argued, the shift to an egalitarianism that is sensitive to issues of responsibility is demanded by a proper understanding of the ideal of equality *itself*: it is not a development that represents a *compromise* with the ideal of equality.

We can, for expository purposes, present what might be called a *dialectical* story of how luck egalitarianism arises. The luck egalitarian begins by being revolted by what she considers to be the injustice of actual social inequality. It comes, she protests, from the sheer luck of inheritance and circumstance: it has nothing to do with people's choices. It seems to me

[11] That is, in 1989, when his "Equality and Equal Opportunity for Welfare" appeared in *Philosophical Studies*.

[12] Cf. Miller, *Principles of Social Justice*, chapter 11.

[13] The fraternity egalitarian may make various responses to the unfairness objection. She might say that she does not care about fairness, or that she thinks it's a confused concept. But she might also acknowledge the force of the objection, and propose a trade-off between fraternity and fairness. She might then allow responsibility-induced inequalities, within the limits of an imperfect but tolerably robust preservation of community: see my "Why Not Socialism?" pp. 63–66, where such a compromise is stated more (but not very) formally.

merely perverse to deny the intelligibility of outrage at the unfairness of mere luck causing a huge social inequality. We can argue about the correct further construal of the content of that outrage, but that its proper object is inequality caused by luck seems to me evident, and there is nothing defeatingly "trivial" (see Section 1 above) about saying so.

Possessed of the premise that luck has caused enormous unjust inequality, the traditional egalitarian proposes, rather rashly, and in the name of fairness: plain, ordinary equality. But now a responsibility objection is pressed against her: why should those, like the grasshopper and the ant, with exactly the same initial advantages, and who merely *chose* differently, be forced back to equality if an inequality ensues? Why should one person pay for another's truly optional choices? Since the question appeals to the very conception of fairness that inspired her initial protest against inequality, the egalitarian who rides under the banner of fairness cannot, as the fraternity egalitarian might, ignore the objection that the question formulates. So, in deference to fairness, the relevant egalitarian says that she's against inequalities in the absence of appropriately differential responsibility (just as, she now realizes, she is also against *e*qualities in the presence of appropriately differential responsibility). But that *is* to say that she's against inequalities if and only if they're a matter of luck. She is against luck *in the name of fairness*: if we add that explanation of the egalitarian hostility to luck, then Hurley's case against the *specification* claim is retired. Since we are against luck *in the name of fairness*, we have to rejig what luck produces in a specific way, by, that is, removing or counterbalancing the inequalities that are caused by luck in particular.

Since there is a symmetry in the luck egalitarian's attitude to plain, ordinary equality and plain, ordinary inequality—both are bad if and only if they are in disaccord with choice—it might seem that it is not luck but *equality* that plays no role in specifying luck egalitarianism. Why, indeed, is unjust inequality, rather than unjust equality, salient in statements of luck egalitarianism and in luck-egalitarian sentiment?

For several reasons. First, there is a historical reason: huge inequalities cried out for rectification at the bar of justice, given what was known about their origin. Nothing similar was true of any equalities. Second, there remains in contemporary society typically much more offensive inequality than offensive equality: there are reasons for objecting more strongly to the corporate welfare bum than to the able-bodied plain welfare bum who gets as much as the working stiff does. Luck egalitarians may, moreover, entertain a view of the maximum *amount* of inequality that choice could justify, and, whatever that view may be, inequalities above a certain size will constitute very *large* injustices, while equality itself might never constitute a *large* injustice: the injustice it causes could not be larger than the injustice at the border of the stated permissible extent of inequality. (So, for example, if the maximal permissible inequality is of measure ten, then the injustice of an unjust *e*quality could never exceed ten, whereas that ten norm would impose no limit on how unjust an *in*equality could be.)

4. The liaison between fairness-driven egalitarianism and hostility to luck enables a criticism of Hurley's employment of the distinction between *what* is to be distributed (that is, *which* goods are to be distributed: what she calls the *currency* of distribution)[14] and *how* it is to be distributed (that is, the desired *pattern* of the distribution, which might be equalizing, or maximinizing, or maximizing, etc.).

Hurley argues that even if the aspiration to extinguish the effect of luck controlled the currency of distribution, it would not follow that it determines its pattern. But *if* we are against luck *because* luck is unfair, then a bridge from currency to pattern comes into view. For consider. Suppose, as Hurley does, that we could divide goods up into those for which people are responsible and those for which they are not responsible. Then, says Hurley, we might use only the goods for which people are *not* responsible as the *currency* of justice, but *pattern* the distribution of those goods according to nonegalitarian norms. And what Hurley says is perfectly true, as a thesis in logic. But the conception of fairness that *drives* the stated initial choice of *currency* surely *also* recommends an egalitarian *pattern*. If it is *fair* for people to keep, before any redistribution is set in train, what and only what they are responsible for, *because* they are responsible for it, then the same conception of fairness *also* requires that the *rest* be distributed equally, because to distribute otherwise is to benefit people in disaccord with their exercises of responsibility. Since the fundamental distinction for an egalitarian is between choice and luck in the shaping of people's fates, the egalitarian deplores contrasts of advantage that do not result from choice, and it is the fundamental status for her of *that* distinction which explains why canceling luck plays both a currency and a patterning role in her thought. (And the patterning role is the more fundamental one. It is *because* we want a pattern of reward that accords with choice that we use luck as a filter when we answer Hurley's "currency" question.)

[14] Hurley (pp. 149–50) is mistaken that I used 'currency' to denote the goods that are to be distributed in "On the Currency." There 'currency' meant what Sen and Dworkin mean by 'metric,' where resources, utility, and capability constitute different metrics. Hurley means by 'currency' not the metric by which goods are to be distributed but the to-be-distributed objects themselves. Correspondingly, she misinterprets my *equalisandum* as those things that people are to have equal amounts of, as opposed to that respect in which people are to be rendered equal, which is what I meant by (the Anglicized Latin) '*equalisandum*.'

In this section, I use 'currency' in Hurley's sense.

The point just made illustrates the general truth that logical consistency does not entail consistency of rationale. Consider, in further illustration of this truth, what Hurley calls the *inequality-default* view, in which cancellation of luck determines the pattern but not the currency:

> This view . . . . takes an unequal distribution as the default position: aristocrats should have more than peasants, whether this is a matter of luck or not. Departures from this inequality, including equality, need to be justified by responsibility. (p. 154)

The stated view is undoubtedly logically consistent, but it faces a challenging question, to wit, why are *departures* from the initial inequality justified if and only if they reflect responsibility when that initial choice of default position flouts issues of responsibility? I do not say that nothing can be said in reply to that question. But I insist that plenty needs to be said, by contrast with what holds for a view that uses responsibility *both* to determine the currency *and* to specify the pattern. (Note that the semi-feudal view that Hurley states here almost certainly could not demand a responsibility-sensitive pattern in the name of *fairness*.)[15]

[15] I thank Nir Eyal, Keith Hyams, Michael Otsuka, and Peter Vallentyne for comments on an earlier draft.

Chapter Six

FAIRNESS AND LEGITIMACY IN JUSTICE, AND: DOES OPTION LUCK EVER PRESERVE JUSTICE?

"What's fair ain't necessarily right."
—*Toni Morrison, Beloved, p. 256*

FOR A LONG TIME I was preoccupied with the idea of self-ownership and, connectedly, with entitlement theories of justice. A major influence was, of course, Robert Nozick's *Anarchy, State, and Utopia*. But an earlier influence in the same direction began to exercise itself on me when I met Hillel Steiner in 1968. He was visiting my then London home with his then wife whom I had known since childhood: it was through her that we first came to know each other. Hillel described the germs of an arresting point of view that was later expressed in a series of articles. I was intrigued, impressed, and resistant.

The most significant articles, in my opinion, that emerged from the germination of those years were "The Natural Right to Equal Freedom," "The Natural Right to the Means of Production," and "The Structure of a Set of Compossible Rights." The last of those three merits special admiration. The majestic project of "Structure" was to derive a complete answer to the question, what is justice? on the basis of two premises: that people have equal fundamental rights, and that it is a condition of a coherent set of rights that all rights in the set can be exercised simultaneously, in whatever way the right-holders choose. "Structure" was the founding document, or manifesto, of what came to be known as "Left Libertarianism," a libertarianism that affirms self-ownership together with a radically egalitarian regime over worldly resources. And if "Structure" was Steiner's Manifesto, then *An Essay on Rights* was his *Capital*. (I do not say that the philosophical project of "Structure" was successful. I think it fails to prove what it sets out to prove, which is something that it has in common with Leibniz's *Monadology*, Kant's *Grundlegung*, Plato's *Republic*, and, indeed, Marx's *Capital*.)

"Fairness and Legitimacy in Justice, And: Does Option Luck Ever Preserve Justice?" In S. de Wijze, M. H. Kramer, and I. Carter, eds. *Hillel Steiner and the Anatomy of Justice*. New York: Routledge, 2009. By permission of Taylor & Francis.

The present paper is a set of variations on a theme to which I was introduced by Hillel.

• • •

It seems to me that four leading ideas that play a role in philosophical debate about just distribution are not always treated in proper distinction from one another, to the detriment of clarity in our thinking about justice. The four ideas are justice, unanimity, fairness, and what I shall call "legitimacy," which is the property that something has when, to put it roughly, no one has the right to complain about its character, or, perhaps a little less roughly, when no one has a just grievance against it.

Here is one likely locus of error. Fairness is frequently treated as necessary for justice, and unanimity is treated as sufficient for legitimacy, and therefore, in turn, for justice. But unless, what I shall deny, a distribution is legitimate only if it is fair, the stated relations among the four designated notions cannot obtain. Fairness might be necessary for one kind of justice, and legitimacy might be sufficient for another kind of justice, but one cannot say, on pain of equivocation, that fairness is necessary for justice and legitimacy is sufficient for it, since what's legitimate, to put the point with Morrisonian pungency, "ain't necessarily" fair.

In short, different kinds of justice get confused, and, so I shall argue, this may have a bearing on the question of whether option luck preserves justice.

1. New (I Think) Light on the Wilt Chamberlain Argument

In 1977 I published an article called "Robert Nozick and Wilt Chamberlain: How Patterns Preserve Liberty":[1] my subtitle was in intended contradiction of the title-message of Nozick's Wilt Chamberlain section, which is called "How Liberty Upsets Patterns."[2] But that intention, I avow below, was somewhat ill-considered.

I began the article with a quotation from the Russian Marxist George Plekhanov, because I was proud that a Marxist, a predecessor in the tradition from which I had come, had, as I then thought, so succinctly anticipated, and then replied to, a central strain in libertarian argument. I shall begin once again with the Plekhanov quote, but this time with more of it:

[1] Reprinted with revisions in Cohen, *Self-Ownership, Freedom, and Equality*. Page references in this chapter are to this revised version.

[2] *Anarchy, State, and Utopia*, pp. 160–64.

> . . . look at the conclusion to which the so-called *labour principle of property*, extolled by our Narodnik literature, leads. Only that belongs to me which has been created by my labour. Nothing can be more just than that. And it is no less just that I use the thing I have created at my own free discretion: I use it myself or I exchange it for something else, which for some reason I need more. It is equally just, then, that I make use of the thing I have secured by exchange—again at my free discretion—as I find pleasant, best and advantageous. Let us now suppose that I have sold the product of my own labour for money, and have used the money to hire a labourer, i.e., I have bought somebody else's labour-power. Having taken advantage of this labour-power of another, I turn out to be the owner of value which is considerably higher than the value I spent on its purchase. This, on the one hand, is very just, because it has already been recognized, after all, that I can use what I have secured by exchange as is best and most advantageous for myself: and, on the other hand, it is very unjust, because I am exploiting the labour of *another* and thereby negating the principle which lay at the foundation of my conception of justice. The property acquired by my personal labour bears me the property created by the labour of another. *Summum jus, summa injuria*. And such *injuria* springs up by the very nature of things in the economy of almost any well-to-do handicraftsman, almost every prosperous peasant.
>
> And so *every phenomenon, by the action of those same forces which condition its existence, sooner or later, but inevitably, is transformed into its own opposite*.[3]

I do not agree with the "dialectical" (Plekhanov's characterization of it, a little later) generalization with which the excerpt concludes, but in this paper I do say something similar about the particular example that Plekhanov uses in the excerpt to illustrate what he thinks is dialectic. I argue that there is a deep incoherence in the idea that "whatever arises from a just situation by just steps is itself just": I claim that its apparently axiomatic status depends upon an equivocation on 'just.' If we purge the equivocation, what we have left is an unconvincing dialectical (or not) would-be paradox.

• • •

"Whatever arises" says Robert Nozick, "from a just situation by just steps is itself just."[4] Hence, so he argues, if we assume that the initial

[3] Plekhanov, *The Development of the Monist View*, pp. 94–95, original emphases.
[4] *Anarchy, State, and Utopia*, p. 151.

distribution in his famous Wilt Chamberlain story is just, then, unless, implausibly, we find some injustice within or surrounding the fans' decisions to pay to watch Wilt play, we must deem the resulting distribution to be just.

Now one might think that the Wilt Chamberlain argument is intended as a paradox. For the initial distribution counts as just because it is, let us assume, egalitarian:[5] it is just under the principle that a distribution is just if and only if it is egalitarian. But the final distribution violates that very principle. In its paradox construal, the Chamberlain argument runs as follows:

(1) Whatever arises from a just situation by just steps is itself just.
(2) The initial situation in the Chamberlain example is just according to your favorite egalitarian principle.
(3) The payments that transform the initial situation into the final situation constitute just steps.
∴ (4) The final situation is just.

But

(5) The final situation contradicts your favorite egalitarian principle.
∴ (6) Your favorite egalitarian principle is self-contradictory (or something like that).

Yet Nozick does not conclude that the initial egalitarian principle has *no* force, that, in a certain manner, it refutes itself. He concludes, more modestly, that "it is not clear how those holding alternative conceptions of distributive justice can reject the entitlement theory of justice in holdings."[6] He does not present his argument as a paradox.

And, indeed, whether or not one is an egalitarian, one should not readily accept that egalitarianism is paradoxical, that, together with other, supposedly undeniable premises,[7] one can derive a rejection of egalitarianism from egalitarianism itself. So there is a reason for suspecting that the justice that putatively characterizes the result of the Chamberlain transaction is not the justice that characterizes the situation that obtains before the transaction unrolls. Such a difference between kinds of justice would eliminate the appearance of paradox, even though it would not show that the argument achieves nothing, nor, in particular, that egalitarians need not countenance entitlement at all.

[5] The assumption is merely for the sake of simplicity. The present observations are robust across all criteria for characterizing the initial distribution as just.

[6] *Anarchy, State, and Utopia*, p. 160.

[7] The putatively undeniable premises are (1) and (3) and (5). (2), being a postulate, is neither deniable nor undeniable.

Before I elaborate the "different kinds of justice" proposal, let me remark that the claim that even egalitarians must acknowledge an *element* of entitlement in their view of justice is bound to be true. For Robert van der Veen and Philippe Van Parijs have shown that, although Nozick calls his theory an "entitlement theory," and thereby means to contrast it with theories that aren't entitlement theories, the truth is that all theories of just distribution have an entitlement, or historical, component *and* a nonhistorical component: on *any* theory of justice, one cannot tell whether a distribution is just by examining its profile alone, with no information about how that profile came to be.[8]

Consider, then, the paradox-dissolving proposal that the justice of the initial situation is not the same kind of justice as the justice of the final situation. It seems to me easy to vindicate. For, to begin with, the word 'just' is clearly subject to different criteria when it is applied to initial distributions from the criteria that decide whether steps are just: whereas the initial distribution is judged just or otherwise by looking at who has what, steps are judged just or otherwise by looking at who has done what to, or with, whom. (To illustrate the difference of criteria, reflect that, to put the matter crudely, equality is completely different from voluntariness.) It follows, of course, that the final situation isn't judged just *simply* by looking at who has what. It is judged just by virtue of the just content of the initial distribution and the just character of the actions that transform the initial distribution into the final distribution.

But what sort of justice characterizes the final situation? Do we have a name for it? Not a short one, but the justice in question is the property that a situation has when no one has a right to complain against its character, when no one has a just grievance against it, and I shall call that property *legitimacy*, for short, here.[9] And it need not, in my view, be a contradiction (though, unlike me, some may think it is always false) to say: "This outcome is unjust, but nobody can complain about it." That

[8] See van der Veen and Van Parijs, "Entitlement Theories of Justice." They acknowledge, ibid., pp. 73–74, that the entitlement component in a theory may be "strong" or "weak," but that does not prejudice the significance for my purposes of the truth that they expose. It is not clear from Nozick's words (see the quotation two paragraphs back) whether he means to conclude something stronger than the van der Veen/Van Parijs conclusion: does he mean by his words that "those holding alternative conceptions" must (comprehensively) abandon those conceptions, or merely, as the Benelux (or Bene) authors state, that they must make some *room* for entitlement within their (thus revised) conceptions?

[9] Note that what I here call "legitimacy" is not legitimacy in the usual sense: 'legitimacy' is simply the most (though imperfectly) suitable single word I could think of to denote what I mean. Legitimacy is, standardly, the right to exercise political power, and that is not the same thing as a universal absence of the right to complain against its exercise, or, *a fortiori*, against anything else. (The fact that there is no single word that means 'universal absence of a right to complain' has, of course, no effect on anything argued here.)

need not be a contradiction because 'unjust' need not mean 'susceptible to legitimate complaint.'

Let me try to vindicate that noncontradiction claim. Suppose that a democracy enacts a (not too) unjust law. I thought it was unjust when I voted against it, but I think that the state may now rightly impose it. I have been given no reason to stop believing that the law is unjust, now it's been voted for, in the sense in which I previously believed it was unjust: that belief did not entail the further belief that a majority of my fellow citizens would recognize the injustice of the proposed law. So, if I now think the law is just, which is to say, justly imposed, and I'm clear-minded, then I don't think the law is just in the sense in which I initially thought—and still think—it unjust. It is just in the quite different sense that it is legitimate.

I said that what I call 'legitimacy' is the property that something has when no one has the right to complain about it. But that formulation needs further refinement. We may have a right to complain when a legitimate outcome is unfair or ugly or costly and so forth, but that does not mean that we then have a right to complain in the sense that I contemplate. Zosia Stemplowska[10] suggested that I should mean that we cannot complain if the outcome's reversal is not *enforced*. I mean that as a minimum, but more work is needed here.

Nozick asks, about people's shares: "what [were they] for except to do something with?"[11] Well, of course the shares were given to people for them to do something with, but it does not follow that they could not, unfortunately from the point of view of the principles of the original distributors, use their shares so as to produce a result that contradicts those principles.

But why would the distributors, supposing that they had the power to forbid that use, *let* the agents use their shares in that way? Almost certainly for reasons of freedom, not justice. Contrary to what some political philosophers like to think, freedom and justice *can* conflict, and you can hold an egalitarian view of justice while giving special priority to freedom as far as legitimacy is concerned. (Such an egalitarian might not *always* put freedom before justice, for she might sometimes put [other] justice before [that special justice that is] legitimacy.)

Consider doctors who were educated at state expense and who take their services abroad. We may deplore that, but, on grounds of freedom, we may be loath to restrict their ability to do so. And we may grant that freedom consistently with thinking that the doctors behave unfairly and unjustly when they do what we believe they should be granted the

[10] Private communication, December 2007.

[11] *Anarchy, State, and Utopia*, p. 161.

freedom to do. But we need not think that the doctors we educate should be free to go abroad because they have a *right* to go abroad. What we rather think is that they *should* have a right to go abroad *because* they should be free to go abroad. But the rights that they *should have* are, transparently, not rights that they (just) have, rights, that is, that are conferred by justice, rather than by (merely) the law.

Given what I permissibly meant by 'liberty' in the 1977 article, I was right that, in the words of its subtitle, "Patterns Preserve Liberty": pattern-upsetting market choice can reduce people's scope of (future) choice, and therefore, and in that sense, their liberty. But it does not follow that, given what *he* permissibly meant by 'liberty,' namely, the freedom to do as one wishes as long as one harms no one,[12] Nozick was wrong when he said that liberty upsets patterns. I did argue for that *further* claim (one not proven by the vindication of my subtitle) in a *different* way, on the basis of considerations that were quite independent of the thought expressed in my subtitle, in the 1977 article.[13] But I was wrong to think that my subtitle *itself* contradicted everything important that Nozick said.

The foregoing deconstruction of the claim that whatever arises from a just situation by just steps is itself just leaves intact a structurally similar claim. For consider. Fairness is sufficient for what I have called "legitimacy"[14] in an initial distribution, and, since the initial Chamberlain distribution is fair, it is indeed legitimate, and so are the steps that turn it into the final distribution, which is therefore *itself* legitimate, because *whatever arises from a legitimate distribution by legitimate steps is itself legitimate*. Unlike Nozick's slogan about justice, which it imitates, *that* slogan does not suffer from equivocation: the criterion of legitimacy is the same throughout.

Someone commented that the italicized substitute gives Nozick everything that he wants. But that isn't so. Nozick wants the Chamberlain example to show that egalitarianism violates all three of liberty, justice, and the Pareto Principle, even though he does not clearly distinguish those

[12] Except in certain specific ways, such as by outcompeting them and thereby driving them out of business, but that qualification is beside the point here.

[13] See *Self-Ownership, Freedom, and Equality*, pp. 28–31.

[14] Which here, recall, is the property something has when no one has a just complaint against it. (It might be objected that fairness in an initial distribution does not suffice for legitimacy. For suppose that an unequal distribution that is strongly [or even weakly] Pareto-superior to the given fair and equal one is feasible: those who fail to obtain what they would in that Pareto-superior distribution might be thought to have a just grievance against the given fair distribution. If you agree with that objection, you can read "fairness" in the sentence in the text, and in comparable occurrences in this piece, as: fairness that is not Pareto-inferior to some other feasible initial distribution.)

different purposes of his parable.[15] And the claim about legitimacy that I italicized in the last paragraph vindicates none of those three theses.

The van der Veen/Van Parijs insight that I reported above runs very deep. Perhaps one may put it this way. Consider distributions that are not actually willed by the relevant parties, including, therefore, those that *could* not be willed by the parties: such distributions count as "fair," in the broadest sense of the word, when they are appropriate to everything to which a distribution ought to be appropriate (given, as it is given here, that how the parties will is not in question). And the authors' point is that there always *is* both a necessarily unwilled initial distribution to consider, *and* rules that permit agents to transform it, by appropriate "steps," that is, by exercises and executions of will. And the criteria of fairness in initial distribution, whatever they are, can be comparatively independent of the criteria for evaluating the justice of steps, and the former are therefore not identical with the criteria that qualify the final distribution as just (that is, legitimate).

2. Dworkin on Option Luck

The foregoing reflections have implications for the question that forms the second part of my title.

According to Ronald Dworkin, justice requires some sort of initial equality of distribution, but certain inequalities are nevertheless just, some of them being those inequalities that result from option luck, or gambles, against a starting point of equality. *Option luck*, Dworkin believes, preserves justice, but *brute luck* overturns it. Dworkin distinguishes the two as follows: "Option luck is a matter of how deliberate and calculated gambles turn out—whether someone gains or loses through accepting an isolated risk he or she should have anticipated and might have declined. Brute luck [by contrast] is a matter of how risks fall out that are not in that sense deliberate gambles."[16]

Dworkin does not specify the "sense" in which brute luck does not count as the result of a deliberate gamble, and a large critical literature has been generated by that lacuna. It will suffice, here, to convey what brute luck is by paradigmatic illustration: brute luck is illustrated by the case of a brick that falls on your head in a not particularly dangerous place.

Now, strong arguments have been advanced for the claim that, contrary to what Dworkin says, option luck against a just background does

[15] See Cohen, *Rescuing Justice and Equality*, chapter 4, section 7.

[16] Dworkin, *Sovereign Virtue*, p. 73.

not *always* preserve justice, but does so *at most* under rather demanding conditions.[17] I shall not explore that claim here, for the question, does option luck *always* preserve justice?, is not my question. My question is: does option luck (even) *sometimes*, or, in other words, *ever*, preserve justice? Or, more precisely, does it ever do so other than by accident, because it *happens* to replicate the pre–option luck distribution? In such a case justice indeed continues to obtain, but not *because* the outcome is a result of option luck, not because option luck has in a strong sense *preserved* justice, but simply because it happens not to have destroyed it. I shall mean 'preserve' in its stronger sense throughout what follows.

In order to pursue my subtitle question, I focus on a paradigm case of putatively justice-preserving option luck. I believe that, if option luck does not preserve justice in the case upon which I shall focus, then it never does, and we can then safely return a negative answer to the question that appears in my title. To anticipate, and bearing in mind the argument of Section 1, I am inclined to the view that option luck does not preserve the justice that renders the pregambling situation just.

Imagine, then, two people, *A* and *B*, who are relevantly identical with respect to their assets, their circumstances, their tastes, and so forth: they are, that is, identical in every respect that bears on distributive justice, and the distribution of goods between them is perfectly equal and perfectly just. Let's say that each has $100,000. Now one taste that *A* and *B* share is for gambling. And each gambles half of his assets against half of the other's, on a 50-50 toss. Dworkin would claim that the resulting distribution is entirely just, because of its origin in option luck against a background of equality, and despite the fact that one of the people emerges with $150,000, which is three times the assets that the other one comes to have, and however dire the resulting state of that other person may be.

3. The Anti-Dworkin Argument

I shall shortly present an argument (the "anti-Dworkin" argument) against Dworkin's view.[18] But, before I come to the argument, we need some background. Suppose, as Dworkin does, that we regard a certain form of equality in distribution as just, *at least* provided that the people to whom the distribution applies do not will otherwise, that is, at least provided that they are either all in favor of equality or, at any rate, none

[17] See Lippert-Rasmussen, "Arneson on Equality of Opportunity for Welfare," especially pp. 482–87; Lippert-Rasmussen, "Egalitarianism, Option Luck, and Responsibility"; Otsuka, "Luck, Insurance, and Equality"; and Otsuka, "Equality, Ambition, and Insurance."

[18] Which was originally presented to me by Arnold Zuboff, but the elaborations of it here are, for better or worse, mine.

of them is against it, and (this is the intended force of "*at least*") whether or not equality would remain just *even* if their wills were opposed to equality. Now suppose that the holdings of a set of people are characterized by the relevant equality, but that they *do* will otherwise, and, in particular, they unanimously will that all the members of the group give half their assets to Sarah and Jane,[19] not because they think that is fair, but because Sarah and Jane are fair (in the other sense), and they like to bestow gifts on the fair.

Many would say, and I among them, that the upshot is unfair, and everyone must agree that it is not fair by the criteria that rendered the original distribution fair. Still, the result is legitimate, in the defined sense: no one has a right to complain about the outcome, since everyone voted for the transactions that brought the outcome about.

The result of the Sarah/Jane transfer will not be just by the criteria that endowed the unanimous choice in favor of Sarah and Jane with legitimating power, which was the justice of the initial situation. The initial just situation renders unanimity legitimating,[20] and the actual unanimity renders the outcome legitimate, but not by the criteria that made the initial situation just. Those steps indeed render the outcome in some sense(s) just, but do they render it just in any sense beyond the legitimacy sense? The legitimacy of the outcome has no tendency to remove its unfairness: instead, it ensures that nobody has the right to *complain* about that unfairness. So if unfairness (always, that is, even in *this* sort of case) implies injustice, then the upshot, though legitimate, is (in one way) unjust. And does unfairness not always imply *some* sort of injustice, even if not an injustice, all things considered?

Most would agree that, in the Sarah/Jane example, unanimity trumps *equality*, which is to say that it would be wrong for anyone (say, for example, an exogenous party) to force a return to equality from the unanimously endorsed (and therefore legitimate) unequal result. But there are two opposed understandings of what a unanimity that trumps *equality* does to *justice*. One might think either *i* or *ii*:

i. The unequal outcome is not entirely just (because it is unfair) but it is legitimate. With respect to legitimacy, unanimous will trumps the justice of fairness.

ii. The unequal outcome is both legitimate and entirely just. Unanimous will confers unqualified justice on an unequal outcome that would otherwise be an unjust outcome.

[19] Ironically or otherwise, the example is a modified version of Dworkin's famous Sarah example: see Dworkin, "Is There a Right to Pornography," pp. 202–5.

[20] Absent an initial just situation, unanimity might merely reflect unjustly differential bargaining power: the highwayman and I are unanimous that I will hand over the money.

Dworkin holds the *ii* view. Note that the *ii* view is, at least *prima facie*, consistent both with affirming and with denying that the outcome is unfair.

Other pertinent illustrations of equality-upsetting unanimity: I wholly voluntarily enslave myself to you or agree to work for you for a wage that would not be just in the absence of that agreement. This might be because I love you, and/or because I do not care about justice. Or I accede to what I know to be, *at least* if I were *not* to accede to it, an unjust arrangement, and I accede to it simply because I refuse to demean myself by insisting on my rights in the face of my ornery opposite number, you. (I was first in line, but I allowed you to go ahead, because you're such a kvetch.) As before, there are two contrasting things that we might think about what's happening in these cases. We might, once again, think (analogues of) either *i* or *ii* (the unanimity in these cases being the concordance in favor of my enslavement, or of your queue jumping, of the wills of, in those cases, a pair of people).

Now, the anti-Dworkin argument says that the gambling case belongs with the (other) unanimity cases. It says that, as regards justice, we should say the same about both, with respect to the choice between *i* and *ii*. It presents the gambling case as one in which a concordance of wills overturns what would otherwise be a just distribution. *And* the anti-Dworkin argument *also* says, in line with the view expounded in Section 1 above, that *i*, rather than *ii*, tells the truth about the unanimity cases. It follows that, if the losing gambler has no complaint, he has no complaint *not* because the outcome is just in the sense in which the initial situation was just, but because he, the loser, agreed to the procedure that produced the circumstance that has befallen him. Accordingly, option luck never preserves the justice that precedes its operation. For, as I suggested in the fifth paragraph of Section 2 above, if option luck doesn't preserve justice in the entirely symmetrical two-person gamble case, then it doesn't do so anywhere.

4. A Discriminating Response to the Anti-Dworkin Argument

Let us now consider a possible response to the anti-Dworkin argument. Dworkin thinks that the outcome is just both in the unanimity cases[21] and in the gambling case. The anti-Dworkin argument of Section 3 disagrees with him in both cases. But there are two logically possible, and

[21] Though not, perhaps, in the slavery example: being a liberal rather than a libertarian, Dworkin might seek to impugn that outcome.

more or less embraced (by somebody), *discriminating responses* to the anti-Dworkin argument that merit an airing. The first defends what Dworkin says about gambling while rejecting what he says about the effect of unanimity in general, and the second, contrariwise, rejects what he says about gambling while defending what he says about unanimity in general.

According to the first discriminating response, I indeed *legitimate* an injustice when I willingly enslave myself to you, and when I let you go in line ahead of me: to that extent, Dworkin is mistaken. But, the response continues, and by contrast, *i* is not the correct description of the gambling case: there is a relevant structural difference between the two types of case, whose consequence is that unanimity does *not* confer the *same* justice property on its outcome as is conferred on their outcomes by fair and voluntary gambles. I call this response "discriminating" because it rejects what Dworkin says about unanimity in order to protect, by way of a supposed contrast, what he says about gambling.

The assimilation made by the anti-Dworkin argument of Section 3 says that the claim that the result of option luck is just is simply a special case of the claim that anything that's consented to is just: the case for the justice of the relevant outcome, whatever the quality of that case may be, is the same in the two instances. But the discriminating response says that the voluntariness of a 50-50 gamble might be thought to make the gamble preserve justice in the initial sense even if that justice is not preserved by unanimous will in the (other) unanimity cases.

In the unanimity cases, everyone agrees to what would otherwise be unquestionably unjust. But what the gambler agrees to is a 50-50 chance, an equal chance, and that's certainly *not* unquestionably unjust. Crucially, for our purposes, the gambler is agreeing to a *gamble*, and, indeed, to what virtually anyone would call a *fair* gamble, and, therefore, a just procedure. The gambler is not agreeing directly, but only indirectly, to an outcome. So, this discriminating response concludes, unlike what holds in the unanimity cases, what the will directly endorses in the gambling case is *not* (at least otherwise) manifestly unjust: what the will endorses directly in the gambling case is, by contrast with the unanimity cases, something that is not otherwise unquestionably unjust, namely, a seemingly fair procedure, a procedure in which no one is at a disadvantage.

5. Two Objections to That First Discriminating Response

The first discriminating response to the anti-Dworkin argument can be construed as an argument with a premise and a conclusion, as follows:

(1) Unlike what holds for the unanimity cases, the gamblers do not will a result that is, considered independently of their willings, unfair.

∴ (2) Unlike what holds for the unanimity cases, the upshot of the gamble is not unfair.

The first objection questions the premise of that discriminating argument and the second questions the inference to its conclusion.

The first objection questions the supposed independent fairness of the 50-50 gamble procedure. The objector says: if, as you think, the fact that the 50-50 gamble *is* fair[22] because 50-50, then why is voluntariness needed to *make* the gamble fair? Why isn't an *imposed* 50-50 gamble[23] *also* fair?[24] And, she might say, in the same vein, since the *outcome* of this supposedly fair gamble is supposed to be just: if the fact that the gamble is 50-50 makes the outcome of the gamble just, why is *consent* to that gamble *also* needed to make its outcome just? Why is not the outcome of an *imposed* 50-50 gamble also just?

The second objection, which is to the inference of the discriminator's argument, will be stated in Section 7 below. Whereas I shall judge that the objection stated above does not succeed, the second objection strikes me as weighty. I nevertheless canvass the first objection, because it appears to me to raise some interesting issues.

6. Defending the First Discriminating Response against the First Objection

The first objection to the discriminating response misdescribes what the discriminator said about the 50-50 gamble, in her attempt to contrast it with the outcome that is directly willed in the unanimity cases. She did not say that a 50-50 gamble is just because fair, whether or not it is imposed. She said the weaker, yet still relevant, thing that the gamble is not, considered independently of whether it is willed, unquestionably unjust, by contrast with, for example, your occupying what should be my position in the queue.

[22] One might question whether it suffices for a gamble to be fair that it is 50-50. Perhaps a 60-40 gamble might be considered fair when the parties to it are appropriately differentially risk-averse. But I need no doctrine of what constitutes a fair gamble here. I need just the concept of a fair gamble, and, in the given circumstances, a 50-50 gamble qualifies as fair because *A* and *B* are fully similar.

[23] Or, if an "imposed gamble" is an oxymoron, an imposed 50-50 risk procedure.

[24] The outcome of an imposed 50-50 gamble is (arguably, but subject to what is said in n. 22 above) just (or as just as things can be) when the good is indivisible. But we may nevertheless regard that outcome as merely the best available second-best with regard to justice.

If that sounds mysterious, an example might help. Suppose that a pound of apples are, by any standard,[25] worth precisely a dollar. Despite their being worth that, I don't like apples, and it's therefore not OK for you to take my dollar by force and saddle me with a pound of apples. For such a use of force would override (my taste or preference and consequently, here) my will. It would also not be OK for you to impose the apples and take the dollar even *if* I *did* prefer the apples to a dollar (or, *a fortiori*, even if I were indifferent between them), because those moves might *also* contradict my will: it is not an axiom that one always wills what one prefers. What's true is that *if* I want to buy apples, then one dollar per pound is the fair price. Gambling, similarly, is a matter of one's taste about risk, and, therefore, a matter where my will counts. The true parallel is not between a voluntary 50-50 gamble and the unanimity cases. Instead, a voluntary 50-50 gamble is like a decision to purchase apples at a fair price, and it is a voluntarily *unfair* gamble that resembles the unanimity cases.

You may not agree that there is such a thing as *the* fair price of an apple. But I do not need to claim that much, for the purposes of vindicating the concept exercised in the foregoing paragraph. I need only say that (at least) certain prices for apples are, by contrast with other prices, not unquestionably unjust, considered independently of whether those terms are willed: and that seems to be obviously true. In any case, enough has been said to show that the first objection to the argument against the discriminating view that what's willed in the gamble is fair fails.

The general claim suggested by the apples case is that outcomes that are not judged unjust on will-independent grounds (like the outcome in the apple purchase example, and the outcome of my will, that is, the 50-50 chance itself, in the gambling case), may be judged unjust on will-dependent grounds. The gamble is just only if the parties' wills favor gambling. Two things are required here for justice: that the outcome of my will (a dollar for a pound of apples, a gamble of 50-50) is not *independently* unjust, *and* concordant wills.

To rehearse, briefly, what has been a somewhat sinuous exposition. The anti-Dworkin argument assimilates the gamble to the fairness-upsetting unanimity cases. The first discriminating response counters that what the wills endorse, directly, in the gambling case, is a fair gamble, a gamble that could not *itself* be called unjust, by contrast with what the wills endorse in the unanimity cases. The anti-Dworkinite replies that, in that case, the 50-50 chance should be just even if it is imposed. But the discriminator responds that this doesn't follow: some things are just only if the will endorses them, but they are then undoubtedly just. So the anti-Dworkinite fails to vindicate his original assimilation. So far, then,

[25] And therefore not merely by the standard of market happenstance.

the mooted proposal, to wit, that the voluntariness of a 50-50 gamble might be thought to make the gamble preserve justice even if justice is not preserved by voluntariness in the unanimity cases, remains on the table: it might be that some option luck preserves justice, even if unanimous willing of an unequal result doesn't do so.

7. A Second Objection to the First Discriminating Response

But there is a distinct objection to the discriminator's argument, which is that its inference is questionable.

True, and as the discriminating response insists, the willing gamblers, unlike the unanimous voters, don't directly will an unfairness, but why should it follow that the *upshot* of the gamble is not unfair? Why may one not say, within the assumption that fairness/unfairness is a matter of the profile of the distribution, that the gamblers' wills, if implemented, *ensure* an unfairness, one way or the other, and the difference between willing an unfairness and willing what ensures an unfairness isn't deep? In *each* case, it might be possible to say, for all that the discriminator has shown, that the result is legitimate but unfair, as the anti-Dworkinite claimed.

Michael Otsuka is a patron of the first discriminating position. He rejects the claim that unanimity preserves justice (in the sense of fairness): he accepts the force of such examples as the Sarah/Jane transfer. But Otsuka believes that, contrary to what was suggested in the paragraph above, the difference between directly willing an inequality and willing what (merely) ensures an inequality is indeed deep: he regards it as a key difference between the cases that, in the Sarah/Jane case, people vote for what all know will be a distribution that is unequal *in favor of known people*, namely, Sarah and Jane. In the gambling case, the relevantly analogous proposition is false: the gamblers do know that the gamble will produce an inequality, but neither knows who will benefit from that inequality. Contrast a gamble in which one party knows how the dice will fall. The result of that gamble is not, for Otsuka, fair, precisely because now, as in the Sarah/Jane case, the full profile of the inequality is foreknown.

I hover between accepting and rejecting Otsuka's distinction.

8. An Opposite Discriminating Response to the Anti-Dworkin Argument

Nozick and Dworkin believe that the outcome is just, without qualification, both in the unanimity cases and in the willing gambling case. The anti-Dworkinite believes that the outcome is not in every respect just in either the unanimity case or the gambling case. The first discriminating response holds that the outcome is not just in the unanimity case but is just in the gambling case. An anonymous[26] luck egalitarian who affirms the Temkin/Cohen formulation of luck egalitarianism, under which an outcome is just if it shows no inequality that is nobody's fault or choice,[27] has suggested the interesting fourth view, which is a second and opposite discriminating response to the anti-Dworkin argument, that the outcome is just in the unanimity case but not in the gambling case.[28]

Anonymous reasons as follows: In the unanimity case there's a good sense in which no one is worse off than anyone else through no fault of her own, since each voted for the inequality, and it would not have obtained without her vote. In the gamble, by contrast, the inequality isn't *itself* willed, and, for Anonymous, that makes a crucial difference: it means that, in a relevant sense, someone *is* worse off through no fault of her own, but, rather, because of the way that the dice fell, and that the result is therefore *not* just. So, according to Anonymous, far from unanimous choice being a paradigm of a legitimating justice-subverter to which option luck might be assimilated, option luck subverts justice whereas unanimous consent does not. And note that option luck subverts justice, for Anonymous, precisely because its outcome is not directly willed: she/he makes the *opposite* contrast to the one that the first discriminating response makes.

[26] I anonymize her/him because she/he withdrew from the claim when she/he had read a draft of this section.

[27] In his article "Inequality," Temkin wrote: "I believe egalitarians have the deep and (for them) compelling view that it is a bad thing—unjust and unfair—for some to be worse off than others through no fault of their own" (p. 101). In my "On the Currency," I broadened the idea, saying that inequalities are unjust when they reflect no fault or *choice* on the part of the relevant agents: "choice" is broader than fault, which is, roughly, at any rate in this context, faultful choosing. (See "On the Currency," p. 916 [p. 13 of Chapter 1 of this volume—Ed.], for a relevant case of choice that isn't a case of fault.) In his book *Inequality*, Temkin repeats the shorter "Inequality" formulation, but he adds a footnote in which he says that he shall mean, by "through no fault of their own," "through no fault or choice of their own" (*Inequality*, p. 13).

[28] A tabulation of the four logically possible views may be useful:

	Gambling Case outcome	Unanimity Case outcome
Nozick/Dworkin	Just	Just
Zuboff	Not Just	Not Just
Otsuka	Just	Not Just
Anonymous	Not Just	Just

In order to test the Anonymous view, let us move to a different example. Suppose that the initial distribution is equal, but we, all of us, have a choice whether or not to legislate in favor of permitting Pareto improvements, and it is foreknown what Pareto improvements there would be, and how people would differentially benefit from them. Then we might vote for permitting Pareto improvements wholeheartedly, or, on the other hand, we might regret that inequalities are to ensue, but nevertheless vote for permitting Pareto. But in the latter case, it is questionable *both* that we unanimously *will* the result (true, we unanimously *choose* it, but we do not *will* it, in the fullest possible sense) *and* that, even if we do, the result is just.

Now that may not be a lethal criticism, since Anonymous might enrich what she/he claims to be a sufficient condition of justice and thereby exclude the regret case. But one may nevertheless question the contrast between even an enriched version of the Anonymous claim about unanimity and the gambling case. Does it not challenge the Anonymous view that one may say to the unlucky gambler: you can't say it isn't your fault, since you willingly gambled? Something is surely my fault if my will was necessary and sufficient for it in the context (that, here, of others willing similarly) and I do so will.

And consider: if I agree to split the produce of a field 25:75 with a person who has put in equal farming time (and everything else is equal), then the share-out is just according to Anonymous, but if I agree to a 50:50 (or any other odds) gamble with him with the winner taking 75 percent of the produce, then the share-out is unjust. That claim of distinction between the cases is highly counterintuitive.

The underlying value, so Anonymous herself/himself says, is fairness, and I don't see why Anonymous's unanimous legislators cannot acknowledge that they are voting for an unfair result.

9. Does It Matter?

Someone might wonder whether the *(i)*/*(ii)* distinction, which was drawn near the beginning of Section 3 above, *matters*.[29] Suppose I say, in line with *(i)*, that the losing gambler suffers from an injustice, about which, however, he has no complaint. How, then, is what I say *interesting*, given that I shall treat both winning and losing gamblers exactly as I would if I thought that losing gamblers were *not* suffering from an injustice? We can say three things here, the objection continues: first, what we might

[29] Perhaps, indeed, the same someone who thinks that transforming Nozick's claims about justice into ones about legitimacy gives him everything that he wants.

call *fairness justice* requires, to put it simply, an equal distribution, so the outcome of the gamble is not just in the fairness sense; second, what we might call *legitimacy justice* endorses the outcome of the gamble, because a voluntary gamble, against a background of justice, is a fair procedure; and, third, the right thing to do is to respect the gamble's outcome. Is there a fourth question, as to whether the outcome is just, *tout court*? Once we've said the three things that were just distinguished, isn't the (*i*)/(*ii*) distinction a distinction without a difference?

Well, whether the gambler is suffering an injustice might be thought interesting for both theoretical and, *pace* what was said above, practical reasons.

First, the distinction might be interesting for the purely theoretical reason that it's interesting to know what justice is.

Second, and rather importantly, the distinction can ground an objection to capitalism that goes beyond the transparently true claim that capitalist inequality is extensively due to brute luck. One can add that much capitalist inequality shows injustice even when it is due to option luck: the additional objection could not be made if fairness and legitimacy had not been separated as *aspects* of justice. That second reason for saying that the (*i*)/(*ii*) distinction matters is at least theoretical, but also, in some contexts, practical.

Third, the (*i*)/(*ii*) distinction possesses a certain range of practical relevance. Maybe if (*i*) is true and (*ii*) false, then, while we might be unwilling to enforce a reversal of the gamble's outcome, we might also be unwilling to enforce the outcome itself.[30] Or, with respect to rights of bequest, it might matter whether a given lump of cash was or was not acquired by gambling. If it was the fruit of a fair gamble, then you might have less right to bequeath it than if it was the product of your labor,[31] and, correspondingly, we might think that the proceeds of gambling are more legitimately taxable than some other types of income. It is simply untrue—see the second sentence of this section—that I shall treat winning and losing gamblers the same regardless of my judgments of justice here: in this and other contexts, and/or with other premises in play, the (*i*)/(*ii*) distinction *can* make a practical difference.

Here is an example of how a view as to whether the results of a fair gamble are just or unjust (that is, not fully just) might make a difference, at the level of immediate policy. If gambling produces injustice, that is *a* reason for restricting it. If we account its results just, we lose that reason. One of the least popular policies of Tony Blair was the promotion

[30] Compare my comments on "the slavery gamble" in Cohen, *Self-Ownership, Freedom, and Equality*, p. 47.

[31] Compare Nozick's speculation about bequest in Nozick, *The Examined Life*, pp. 30–31.

of gambling: large casinos, of a kind new to Britain, were to be built in Manchester and elsewhere. One of the most popular early decisions of the new prime minister Gordon Brown was to chop the casino-promoting policy. Whether you think the results of deliberate gambles are just might affect how you evaluate that shift of policy.

10. More on the Relationship between These Matters and Luck Egalitarianism

This paper has defended the claim that what recommends an outcome that was achieved by just steps from a just starting point is not, in the general case, *itself* (unqualified) justice, but the different virtue of legitimacy, or, more precisely, the property that no one can legitimately complain about it.

David Miller has claimed that luck egalitarianism is inconsistent with the principal distinction that I try to draw in the paper, because luck egalitarianism says: distribute equally, compensating appropriately for luck-induced deficits, and then whatever arises from people's choices is just. If I am right in what I say in the paper, so Miller's argument goes, luck egalitarians shouldn't call whatever arises "just," but merely "legitimate" (in the technical sense of being something that no one can complain about).

When I embarked upon this paper, it was my thought that patterned and end-state theories of justice do not themselves say what just *steps* are, the latter being an intuitive matter quite separate from such theories of just distribution. But luck egalitarianism's statement, as given in the foregoing paragraph, seems to comprehend a doctrine of just steps and therefore, perhaps, to confer the title of justice itself on the outcomes that it endorses.

Can it be that plain egalitarianism doesn't define what just steps are but that luck egalitarianism does? Can it be that, unlike plain egalitarianism, luck egalitarianism *is* paradoxical,[32] because the use of shares by people is *bound* to lead to a distribution flecked by luck?

Is the following the right way to look at the matter, to wit, that luck egalitarianism is more developed than plain egalitarianism in that it answers the question about *precisely* which forms of chosen action are just steps, whereas plain egalitarianism is silent as to which steps are just? Hence, by virtue of the content of the luck-egalitarian doctrine, the status of justice proper is conferred, in an unqualified way, on the favored upshots. Doesn't the luck egalitarian theory of, precisely, *justice*, fold the steps issue into itself?

[32] See Section 1 of this paper.

Does luck egalitarianism therefore endorse the results of the Chamberlain transaction as not only "legitimate" but just? No, because there are caveats that affect our judgment about the voluntariness of that transaction, which are reviewed in my Chamberlain article. And there is also the deep consideration that Chamberlain benefits from the brute luck of his superior talent, a consideration that I have ignored in this paper. I did so because to have introduced the highly controversial claim that people should not benefit from endowments of special talent would have drawn attention away from the more structural issues that have occupied this paper and that are relatively independent of different views about the precise content of justice.

But what is the answer to the "flecked by luck" paradox question at the end of the paragraph three paragraphs back? Mustn't it be "yes," since one man's choice is another man's luck? Choices both to give and to buy have the property that it is accidental who is favored by them: we both offer a commodity at £10, and it is an accident from whom a purchaser decides to buy, even in the most "perfect" of markets. And the underlying point might be that a luck egalitarian can't allow *any* transactions. Sure, she can allow transactions that preserve absence of luck in distribution, but that won't confer much choice.

Perhaps this démarche shows that we have to interrogate the initial situation/steps/resultant situation structure harder than we have done so far. It is perfectly clear in a model situation like Chamberlain, but how do we apply it to the thick of continuous transacting, that is, more generally, of continuous stepping?

So: back to the drawing board, later! I would still be there now, but *Festschrifts* have deadlines, and this one's has come. I am therefore constrained to offer Hillel, and you, an inconclusive, and also unconcluding, piece, but I hope that it raises some good questions that have received too little attention in the literature to which our honorand has contributed so substantially.[33]

[33]I thank Chris Brooke, Dan Butt, Simon Caney, Cécile Fabre, Keith Hyams, David Miller, Mike Otsuka, Zosia Stemplowska, Larry Temkin, and Peter Vallentyne for excellent criticisms of an earlier draft of this paper, and Arnold Zuboff for stimulating the production of the paper in the first place: see n. 18 above.

PART TWO

Freedom and Property

Chapter Seven

CAPITALISM, FREEDOM, AND THE PROLETARIAT

1. IN CAPITALIST SOCIETIES everyone owns something, be it only his own labor power, and each is free to sell what he owns, and to buy whatever the sale of what he owns enables him to buy. Many claims made on capitalism's behalf are questionable, but here is a freedom which it certainly provides.

It is easy to show that under capitalism everyone has some of this freedom, especially if being free to sell something is compatible with not being free not to sell it, two conditions whose consistency I would defend. Australians are free to vote, even though they are not free not to vote, since voting is mandatory in Australia. One could say that Australians are forced to vote, but that proves that they are free to vote, as follows: one cannot be forced to do what one cannot do, and one cannot do what one is not free to do. Hence one is free to do what one is forced to do. Resistance to this odd-sounding but demonstrable conclusion comes from failure to distinguish the idea of being free to do something from other ideas, such as the idea of doing something freely.

Look at it this way: before you are forced to do *A*, you are, except in unusual cases, free to do *A* and free not to do *A*. The force removes the second freedom, not the first. It puts no obstacle in the path of your doing *A*, so you are still free to. Note, too, that you could frustrate someone who sought to force you to do *A* by making yourself not free to do it.

I labor this truth—that one is free to do what one is forced to do—because it, and failure to perceive it, help to explain the character and persistence of a certain ideological disagreement. Marxists say that working-class people are forced to sell their labor power, a thesis we shall look at later. Bourgeois thinkers celebrate the freedom of contract manifest not only in the capitalist's purchase of labor power but in the worker's sale of it. If Marxists are right, then workers, being forced to sell their labor

Originally published as "Capitalism, Freedom, and the Proletariat," in *The Idea of Freedom* (1979). The present extensively revised version draws heavily on two of Cohen's later papers: "Illusions about Private Property and Freedom" and "The Structure of Proletarian Unfreedom."

Editor's note: The Appendix and the quoted passage in n. 11, which have been added by the editor, are reprinted in part from "Illusions about Private Property and Freedom," in Steven Cahn, ed. *Philosophy for the 21st Century: A Comprehensive Reader*, Oxford: Oxford University Press, 2002. By permission of Oxford University Press.

power, are, in an important way, unfree. But it must remain true that (unlike chattel slaves) they are free to sell their labor power. Accordingly, the unfreedom asserted by Marxists is compatible with the freedom asserted by bourgeois thinkers. Indeed: if the Marxists are right, the bourgeois thinkers are right, unless they also think, as characteristically they do, that the truth they emphasize refutes the Marxist claim. The bourgeois thinkers go wrong not when they say that the worker is free to sell his labor power, but when they infer that the Marxist cannot therefore be right in his claim that the worker is forced to. And Marxists[1] share the bourgeois thinkers' error when they think it necessary to deny what the bourgeois thinkers say. If the worker is not free to sell his labor power, of what freedom is a foreigner whose work permit is removed deprived? Would not the Marxists who wrongly deny that workers are free to sell their labor power nevertheless protest, inconsistently, that such disfranchised foreigners have been deprived of a freedom?[2]

2. Freedom to buy and sell is one freedom of which in capitalism there is a great deal. It belongs to capitalism's essential nature. But many think that capitalism is, quite as essentially, a more comprehensively free society. They believe that, *if* what you value is freedom, as opposed, for example, to equality, then you should be in favor of an unmixed capitalist economy without a welfare sector. In the opinion I am describing, one may or may not favor such a purely capitalist society, but, if one disfavors it, then one's reason for doing so must be an attachment to values other than freedom, since, from the point of view of freedom, there is little to be said against pure capitalism. It is in virtue of the prevalence of this opinion that so many English-speaking philosophers and economists now call the doctrine which recommends a purely capitalist society "libertarianism."

It is not only those who call themselves "libertarians" who believe that that is the right name for their party. Many who reject their aim endorse their name: they do not support unmodified capitalism, but they agree that it maximizes freedom. This applies to *some* of those who call themselves "liberals," and Thomas Nagel is one of them. Nagel says that

[1] Such as Ziyad Husami, if he is a Marxist, who says of the wage-worker: "Deprived of the ownership of means of production and means of livelihood he is forced (not free) to sell his labor power to the capitalist" ("Marx on Distributive Justice," pp. 51–52). I contend that the phrase in parentheses introduces a falsehood into Husami's sentence, a falsehood which Karl Marx avoided when he said of the worker that "the period of time for which he is free to sell his labour power is the period of time for which he is forced to sell it" (*Capital*, vol. 1, p. 415; cf. p. 932: "the wage-labourer . . . is compelled to sell himself of his own free will").

[2] For a more developed account of the relations between force and freedom, see *History, Labour, and Freedom*, pp. 239–47.

"libertarianism exalts the claim of individual freedom of action," and he believes that it does so too much. He believes that it goes too far toward the liberty end of a spectrum on which he believes leftists go too far toward the equality end.[3]

Nagel-like liberals—and henceforth, by 'liberals,' I shall mean ones of the Nagel kind—assert, plausibly, that liberty is a good thing, but they say that it is not the only good thing. So far, libertarians will agree. But liberals also believe that libertarians wrongly sacrifice other good things in too total defense of the one good of liberty. They agree with libertarians that pure capitalism is liberty pure and simple, or anyway *economic* liberty pure and simple, but they think the various good things lost when liberty pure and simple is the rule justify restraints on liberty. They want a capitalism modified by welfare legislation and state intervention in the market. They advocate, they say, not unrestrained liberty, but liberty restrained by the demands of social and economic equality. They think that what they call a free economy is too damaging to those who, by nature or circumstance, are ill placed to achieve a minimally proper standard of life within it, so they favor, within limits, taxing the better off for the sake of the worse off, although they believe that such taxation interferes with liberty. They also think that what they call a free economy is subject to fluctuations in productive activity and misallocations of resources which are potentially damaging to everyone, so they favor measures of interference in the market, although, again, they believe that such interventions diminish liberty. They do not question the libertarian description of capitalism as the (economically) free society, the society whose economic agents are not, or only minimally, interfered with by the state. But they believe that economic freedom may rightly and reasonably be abridged. They believe in a compromise between liberty and other values, and that what is known as the welfare state mixed economy approaches the right sort of compromise.

3. I shall argue that libertarians, and liberals of the kind described, misuse the concept of freedom. That is not, as it stands, a comment on the attractiveness of the institutions they severally favor, but on the rhetoric they use to describe those institutions. If, however, and as I contend, they misdescribe those institutions, then a correct description of them might

[3] "Libertarianism . . . fastens on one of the two elements [that is, freedom and equality—G. A. Cohen] of the liberal ideal and asks why its realization should be inhibited by the demands of the other. Instead of embracing the ideal of equality and the general welfare, libertarianism exalts the claim of individual freedom of action and asks why state power should be permitted even the interference represented by progressive taxation and public provision of health care, education and a minimum standard of living" ("Libertarianism without Foundations," p. 192).

make them appear less attractive, and then my critique of the defensive rhetoric would indirectly be a critique of the institutions the rhetoric defends.

My principal contention is that, while liberals and libertarians see the freedom which is intrinsic to capitalism, they overlook the unfreedom which necessarily accompanies capitalist freedom.

To expose this failure of perception, I shall begin by criticizing a description of the libertarian position provided by the libertarian philosopher Antony Flew in his *Dictionary of Philosophy*. Flew defines 'libertarianism' as "whole-hearted political and economic liberalism, opposed to any social or legal constraints on individual freedom." Liberals of the Nagel kind would avow themselves *un*wholehearted in the terms of Flew's definition. For they would say that they support certain (at any rate) legal constraints on individual freedom. Indeed, after laying down his definition of 'libertarianism,' Flew adds that "the term was introduced in this sense by people who believe that, especially but not only in the United States, those who pass as liberals are often much more sympathetic to socialism than to classical liberalism."[4]

Now a society in which there are *no* "social and legal constraints on individual freedom" is perhaps imaginable, at any rate by people who have highly anarchic imaginations. But, be that as it may, the Flew definition misdescribes libertarians, since it does not apply to defenders of capitalism, which is what libertarians profess to be, and are. For consider: If the state prevents me from doing something I want to do, it evidently places a constraint on my freedom. Suppose, then, that I want to perform an action which involves a legally prohibited use of your property. I want, let us say, to pitch a tent in your large back garden, perhaps just in order to annoy you, or perhaps for the more substantial reason that I have nowhere to live and no land of my own, but I have got hold of a tent, legitimately or otherwise. If I now try to do this thing I want to do, the chances are that the state will intervene on your behalf. If it does, I shall suffer a constraint on my freedom. The same goes for all unpermitted uses of a piece of private property by those who do not own it, and there are always those who do not own it, since "private ownership by one person presupposes non-ownership on the part of other persons."[5] But the free enterprise economy advocated by libertarians and described as the "free" economy by liberals rests upon private property: you can sell and buy only what you respectively own and come to own. It follows that the Flew definition is untrue to its *definiendum*, and that the term 'liber-

[4] *A Dictionary of Philosophy*, p. 188.
[5] Marx, *Capital*, vol. 3, p. 812.

tarianism' is a gross misnomer for the position it now standardly denotes among philosophers and economists.

4. How could Flew have brought himself to publish the definition I have criticized? I do not think that he was being dishonest. I would not accuse him of appreciating the truth of this particular matter and deliberately falsifying it. Why then is it that Flew, and libertarians like him, *and* liberals of the kind I described, see the unfreedom in state interference with a person's use of his property, but fail to note the unfreedom in the standing intervention against anyone else's use of it entailed by the fact that it is that person's private property? What explains their monocular vision? (By that question, I do not mean: what motive do they have for seeing things that way? I mean: how is it possible for them to see things that way? What intellectual mechanism or mechanisms operate to sustain their view of the matter?)

Notice that we can ask similar questions about how antilibertarian liberals are able to entertain the description which they favor of *modified* capitalism. According to Nagel, "progressive taxation" entails "interference" with individual freedom.[6] He regards the absence of such interference as a value, but one which needs to be compromised for the sake of greater economic and social equality, as what he calls the "formidable challenge to liberalism . . . from the left" maintains.[7] Yet it is quite unclear that social democratic restriction on the sway of private property, through devices like progressive taxation and the welfare minimum, represents *any* enhancement of governmental interference with freedom. The government certainly interferes with a landowner's freedom when it establishes public rights of way and the right of others to pitch tents on his land. But it also interferes with the freedom of a would-be walker or tent-pitcher when it prevents them from indulging *their* individual inclinations. The general point is that incursions against private property which *reduce* owners' freedom and transfer rights over resources to nonowners thereby *increase* the latter's freedom. The net effect on freedom of the resource transfer is, therefore, in advance of further information and argument, a moot point.

Libertarians are against what they describe as an "interventionist" policy in which the state engages in "interference." Nagel is not, but he agrees that such a policy "intervenes" and "interferes." In my view, the use of words like 'interventionist' to designate the stated policy is an ideological distortion detrimental to clear thinking and friendly to the libertarian

[6] See n. 3 above.

[7] "Libertarianism without Foundations," p. 191.

point of view. It is, though friendly to that point of view, consistent with rejecting it, and Nagel does reject it, vigorously. But, by acquiescing in the libertarian use of 'intervention,' he casts libertarianism in a better light than it deserves. The standard use of 'intervention' esteems the private property component in the liberal or social democratic settlement too highly, by associating that component too closely with freedom.

5. I now offer a two-part explanation of the tendency of libertarians and liberals to overlook the interference in people's lives induced by private property. The two parts of the explanation are independent of each other. The first part emerges when we remind ourselves that "social and legal constraints on freedom" (see p. 150 above) are not the only source of restriction on human action. It restricts my possibilities of action that I lack wings, and therefore cannot fly without major mechanical assistance, but that is not a social or legal constraint on my freedom. Now I suggest that one explanation of our theorists' failure to note that private property constrains freedom is a tendency to take as part of the structure of human existence in general, and therefore as no social or legal constraint on freedom, any structure around which, *merely as things are*, much of our activity is organized. A structure which is not a permanent part of the human condition can be misperceived as being just that, and the institution of private property is a case in point. It is treated as so given that the obstacles it puts on freedom are not perceived, while any impingement on private property itself is immediately noticed. Yet private property, like any system of rights, pretty well *is* a particular way of distributing freedom *and unfreedom*. It is necessarily associated with the liberty of private owners to do as they wish with what they own, but it no less necessarily withdraws liberty from those who do not own it. To think of capitalism as a realm of freedom is to overlook half of its nature.

I am aware that the tendency to the failure of perception which I have described and tried to explain is stronger, other things being equal, the more private property a person has. I do not think really poor people need to have their eyes opened to the simple conceptual truth I emphasize. I also do not claim that anyone of sound mind will for long deny that private property places restrictions on freedom, once the point has been made. What is striking is that the point so often needs to be made, against what should be *obvious* absurdities, such as Flew's definition of 'libertarianism.'

6. But there is a further and independent and conceptually more subtle explanation of how people[8] are able to believe that there is no restriction,

[8] This part of the explanation applies more readily to libertarian than to liberal ideological perception. It does also apply to the latter, but by a route too complex to set out here.

or only minimal restriction, of freedom under capitalism, which I now want to expound.

You will notice that I have supposed that to prevent someone from doing something he wants to do is to make him, in that respect, unfree; I am *pro tanto* unfree *whenever* someone interferes with my actions, whether *or not I have a right to perform them, and whether or not my obstructor has a right to interfere with me*. But there is a definition of freedom which informs much libertarian writing and which entails that interference is not a sufficient condition of unfreedom. On that definition, which may be called the rights definition of freedom, I am unfree only when someone prevents me from doing what I have a right to do, so that he, consequently, has no right to prevent me from doing it. Thus Robert Nozick says: "Other people's actions place limits on one's available opportunities. Whether this makes one's resulting action non-voluntary depends upon whether these others had the right to act as they did."[9]

Now, if one combines this rights definition of freedom with a moral endorsement of private property, with a claim that, in standard cases, people have a moral right to the property they legally own, then one reaches the result that the protection of legitimate private property cannot restrict anyone's freedom. It will follow from the moral endorsement of private property that you and the police are justified in preventing me from pitching my tent on your land, and, because of the rights definition of freedom, it will then further follow that you and the police do not thereby restrict my freedom. So here we have a further explanation of how intelligent philosophers are able to say what they do about capitalism, private property, and freedom. But the characterization of freedom which figures in the explanation is unacceptable. For it entails that a properly convicted murderer is not rendered unfree when he is justifiably imprisoned.

Even justified interference reduces freedom. But suppose for a moment that, as libertarians say or imply, it does not. On that supposition one cannot argue, without further ado, that interference with private property is wrong *because* it reduces freedom. For one can no longer take it for granted, what is evident on a normatively neutral account of freedom, that interference with private property *does* reduce freedom. On a rights account of what freedom is one must abstain from that assertion until one has shown that people have moral rights to their private property. Yet libertarians tend *both* to use a rights definition of freedom *and* to take it for granted that interference with his private property diminishes the owner's freedom. But they can take that for granted only on the normatively neutral account of freedom, on which, however, it

[9] *Anarchy, State, and Utopia*, p. 262.

is equally obvious that the protection of private property diminishes the freedom of *non*owners, to avoid which consequence they adopt a rights definition of the concept. And so they go, back and forth, between inconsistent definitions of freedom, not because they cannot make up their minds which one they like better, but under the propulsion of their desire to occupy what is in fact an untenable position. Libertarians want to say that interferences with people's use of their private property are unacceptable because they are, quite obviously, abridgments of freedom, and that the reason why protection of private property does not similarly abridge the freedom of nonowners is that owners have a right to exclude others from their property and nonowners consequently have no right to use it. But they can say all that only if they define freedom in two inconsistent ways.

7. Now, I have wanted to show that private property, and therefore capitalist society, limit liberty, but I have not said that they do so more than communal property and socialist society. Each form of society is by its nature congenial and hostile to various sorts of liberty, for variously placed people. And concrete societies exemplifying either form will offer and withhold additional liberties whose presence or absence may not be inferred from the nature of the form itself. Which form is better for liberty, all things considered, is a question which may have no answer in the abstract. Which form is better for liberty may depend on the historical circumstances.[10]

I say that capitalism and socialism offer different sets of freedoms, but I emphatically do not say that they provide freedom in two different senses of that term. To the claim that capitalism gives people freedom some socialists respond that what they get is *merely bourgeois* freedom. Good things can be meant by that response: that there are important particular liberties which capitalism does not confer; and/or that I do not have freedom, but only a necessary condition of it, when a course of action (for example, skiing) is, though not *itself* against the law, unavailable to me anyway, because other laws (for example, those of private property, which prevent a poor man from using a rich man's unused skis) forbid me the means to perform it. But when socialists suggest that there is no "real" freedom under capitalism, at any rate for the workers, or that socialism promises freedom of a higher and as yet unrealized kind, then, so I think, their line is theoretically incorrect and politically disastrous. For there is freedom under capitalism, in a plain, good sense, and if socialism will not give us more of it, we shall rightly be disappointed.

[10] For further discussion of that question, see "Illusions about Private Property and Freedom," pp. 232–35. [This discussion is included as an Appendix to this chapter.—Ed.]

If the socialist says he is offering a new variety of freedom, the advocate of capitalism will carry the day with his reply that he prefers freedom of the known variety to an unexplained and unexemplified rival. But if, as I would recommend, the socialist argues that capitalism is, all things considered, inimical to freedom *in the very sense* of 'freedom' in which, as he should concede, a person's freedom is diminished when his private property is tampered with, then he presents a challenge which the advocate of capitalism, by virtue of his own commitment, cannot ignore.

For it is a contention of socialist thought that capitalism does not live up to its own professions. A fundamental socialist challenge to the libertarian is that pure capitalism does not protect liberty in general, but rather those liberties which are built into private property, an institution which also limits liberty. And a fundamental socialist challenge to the liberal is that the modifications of modified capitalism modify not liberty, but private property, often in the interest of liberty itself. Consequently, transformations far more revolutionary than a liberal would contemplate might be justified on grounds similar to those which support liberal reform.

A homespun example shows how communal property offers a differently shaped liberty, in no different sense of that term, and, in certain circumstances, more liberty than the private property alternative. Neighbors *A* and *B* own sets of household tools. Each has some tools which the other lacks. If *A* needs a tool of a kind which only *B* has, then, private property being what it is, he is not free to take *B*'s one for a while, even if *B* does not need it during that while. Now imagine that the following rule is imposed, bringing the tools into partly common ownership: each may take and use a tool belonging to the other without permission provided that the other is not using it and that he returns it when he no longer needs it, or when the other needs it, whichever comes first. *Things being what they are* (a substantive qualification: we are talking, as often we should, about the real world, not about remote possibilities) the communizing rule would, I contend, increase tool-using freedom, on any reasonable view. To be sure, some freedoms are removed by the new rule. Neither neighbor is as assured of the same easy access as before to the tools that were wholly his. Sometimes he has to go next door to retrieve one of them. Nor can either now charge the other for use of a tool he himself does not then require. But these restrictions probably count for less than the increase in the range of tools available. No one is as sovereign as before over any tool, so the privateness of the property is reduced. But freedom is probably expanded.

It is true that each would have more freedom still if he were the sovereign owner of *all* the tools. But that is not the relevant comparison. I do not deny that full ownership of a thing gives greater freedom than shared ownership of that thing. But no one did own all the tools before the modest measure of communism was introduced. The kind of comparison we need to make is between, for example, sharing ownership with ninety-nine others in a hundred things and fully owning just one of them. I submit that which arrangement nets more freedom is a matter of cases. There is little sense in one hundred people sharing control over one hundred toothbrushes. There is an overwhelming case, from the point of view of freedom, in favor of our actual practice of public ownership of street pavements. Denationalizing the pavements in favor of private ownership of each piece by the residents adjacent to it would be bad for freedom of movement.[11]

8. Sensible neighbors who make no self-defeating fetish of private property might contract into a communism of household tools. But that way of achieving communism cannot be generalized. We could not by contract bring into fully mutual ownership those nonhousehold tools and resources which Marxists call means of production. They will never be won for socialism by contract, since they belong to a small minority, to whom the rest can offer no quid pro quo.[12] Most of the rest must hire out

[11] Editor's note: Cohen offered the following further remarks on pp. 237–38 of "Illusions about Private Property and Freedom":

> But someone will say: ownership of private property is the only example of *full* freedom. Our practice with pavements may be a good one, but no one has full freedom with respect to any part of the pavement, since he cannot, for instance, break it up and put the results to a new use, and he cannot prevent others from using it (except, perhaps, by the costly means of indefinitely standing on it himself, and he cannot even do that when laws against obstruction are enforced). The same holds for any communal possessions. No one is fully free with respect to anything in which he enjoys a merely shared ownership. Hence even if private property entails unfreedom, and even if there is freedom without private property, *there is no case of full freedom which is not a case of private property*. . . .
>
> The [italicized] thesis. . . . is a piece of bourgeois ideology masquerading as a conceptual insight. The argument for the thesis treats freedom fetishistically, as control over *material things*. But freedom, in the central sense of the term with which we have been occupied, is freedom to *act*, and if there is a concept of full freedom in that central sense, then it is inappropriate, if we want to identify it, to focus, from the start, on control over *things*. I can be fully free to walk to your home when and because the pavement is communally owned, even though I am not free to destroy or to sell a single square inch of that pavement. To be sure, action requires the use of matter, or at least space, but it does not follow that to be fully free to perform an action with certain pieces of matter in a certain portion of space I need full control over the matter and the space, since some forms of control will be unnecessary to the action in question. The rights I need over things to perform a given action depend on the nature of that action.

[12] Unless the last act of this scenario qualifies as a contract: in the course of a general strike a united working class demands that private property in major means of production

their labor power to members of that minority, in exchange for the right to some of the proceeds of their labor on facilities in whose ownership they do not share.

So we reach, at length, the third item in the title of this paper, and an important charge, with respect to liberty, which Marxists lay against capitalism. It is that in capitalist society the great majority of people are forced to sell their labor power, because they do not own any means of production. The rest of this paper addresses a powerful objection to that Marxist charge.

To lay the ground for the objection, I must explain how the predicate 'is forced to sell his labor power' is used in the Marxist charge. Marxism characterizes classes by reference to social relations of production, and the claim that workers are forced to sell their labor power is intended to satisfy that condition: it purports to say something about the proletarian's position in capitalist relations of production. But relations of production are, for Marxism, *objective*: what relations of production a person is in does not turn on his consciousness. It follows that if the proletarian is forced to sell his labor power in the relevant Marxist sense, then this must be because of his objective situation, and not merely because of his attitude to himself, his level of self-confidence, his cultural attainment, and so on. It is in any case doubtful that limitations in those subjective endowments can be sources of what interests us: unfreedom, as opposed to something similar to it but also rather different: incapacity. But even if diffidence and the like could be said to force a person to sell his labor power, that would be an irrelevant case here.[13]

9. Under the stated interpretation of 'is forced to sell his labor power,' a serious problem arises for the thesis under examination. For if there are persons whose objective position is standardly proletarian but who are not forced to sell their labor power, then the thesis is false. And there do seem to be such persons.

I have in mind those proletarians who, initially possessed of no greater resources than most, secure positions in the petty bourgeoisie and elsewhere, thereby rising above the proletariat. Striking cases in Britain are members of certain immigrant groups, who arrive penniless, and without good connections, but who propel themselves up the class hierarchy with effort, skill, and luck. One thinks—it is a contemporary example—of

be socialized, as a condition of their return to work, and a demoralized capitalist class meets the demand. (How, by the way, could libertarians object to such a revolution? For hints, see Nozick, "Coercion.")

[13] Except, perhaps, where personal subjective limitations are explained by capitalist relations of production: see *History, Labour, and Freedom*, pp. 278–79.

those who are willing to work very long hours in shops bought from native British petty bourgeois, shops which used to close early. Their initial capital is typically an amalgam of savings, which they accumulated, perhaps painfully, while still in the proletarian condition, and some form of external finance. *Objectively speaking*, most[14] British proletarians are in a position to obtain these. Therefore most British proletarians are not forced to sell their labor power.

10. I now refute two predictable objections to the above argument.

The first says that the recently mentioned persons were, *while they were proletarians*, forced to sell their labor power. Their cases do not show that proletarians are not forced to sell their labor power. They show something different: that proletarians are not forced to remain proletarians.

This objection illegitimately contracts the scope of the Marxist claim that workers are forced to sell their labor power. But before I say what Marxists intend by that statement, I must defend this general claim about freedom and constraint: *fully explicit attributions of freedom and constraint contain two temporal indexes*. To illustrate: I may now be in a position truly to say that I am free to attend a concert tomorrow night, since nothing has occurred, up to now, to prevent my doing so. If so, I am *now* free to attend a concert *tomorrow night*. In similar fashion, the time when I am constrained to perform an action need not be identical with the time of the action: I might *already* be forced to attend a concert *tomorrow night* (since you might already have ensured that if I do not, I shall suffer some great loss).

Now when Marxists say that proletarians are forced to sell their labor power, they mean more than 'X is a proletarian at time t only if X is at t forced to sell his labor power at t'; for that would be compatible with his not being forced to at time $t + n$, no matter how small n is. X might be forced on Tuesday to sell his labor power on Tuesday, but if he is not forced on Tuesday to sell his labor power on Wednesday (if, for example, actions open to him on Tuesday would bring it about that on Wednesday he need not do so), then, though still a proletarian on Tuesday, he is not then someone who is forced to sell his labor power in the relevant Marxist sense. The manifest intent of the Marxist claim is that the proletarian is forced at t to *continue* to sell his labor power, throughout a period from t to $t + n$, for some considerable n. It follows that because there is a route out of the proletariat, which our counterexamples traveled, reach-

[14] At least most: it could be argued that *all* British proletarians are in such a position, but I stay with "most" lest some ingenious person discover objective proletarian circumstances worse than the worst one suffered by now prospering immigrants. But see also n. 15 below.

ing their destination in, as I would argue, an amount of time less than *n*,[15] they were, though proletarians, not forced to sell their labor power in the required Marxist sense.

Proletarians who have the option of class ascent are not forced to continue to sell their labor power, just because they do have that option. Most proletarians have it as much as our counterexamples did. Therefore most proletarians are not forced to sell their labor power.

11. But now I face a second objection. It is that necessarily not more than a few proletarians can exercise the option of upward movement. For capitalism requires a substantial hired labor force, which would not exist if more than just a few workers rose.[16] Put differently, there are necessarily only enough petty bourgeois and other nonproletarian positions for a small number of the proletariat to leave their estate.

I agree with the premise, but does it defeat the argument against which it is directed? Does it refute the claim that most proletarians are not forced to sell their labor power? I think not.

An analogy will indicate why I do not think so. Ten people are placed in a room, the only exit from which is a huge and heavy locked door. At various distances from each lies a single heavy key. Whoever picks up this key—and each is physically able, with varying degrees of effort, to do so—and takes it to the door will find, after considerable self-application, a way to open the door and leave the room. But if he does so he alone will be able to leave it. Photoelectric devices installed by a jailer ensure that it will open only just enough to permit one exit. Then it will close, and no one inside the room will be able to open it again.

It follows that, whatever happens, at least nine people will remain in the room.

Now suppose that not one of the people is inclined to try to obtain the key and leave the room. Perhaps the room is no bad place, and they

[15] This might well be challenged, since the size of *n* is a matter of judgment. I would defend mine by reference to the naturalness of saying to a worker that he is not forced to (continue to) sell his labor power, since he can take steps to set himself up as a shopkeeper. Those who judge otherwise might be able, at a pinch, to deny that most proletarians are not forced to sell their labor power, but they cannot dispose of the counterexamples to the generalization that all are forced to. For our prospective petty bourgeois is a proletarian on the eve of his ascent when, unless, absurdly, we take *n* as 0, he is not forced to sell his labor power.

[16] "The truth is this, that in this bourgeois society every workman, if he is an exceedingly clever and shrewd fellow, and gifted with bourgeois instincts and favoured by an exceptional fortune, can possibly convert himself into an *exploiteur du travail d'autrui*. But if there were no *travail* to be *exploité*, there would be no capitalist nor capitalist production" (Marx, "Results of the Immediate Process of Production," in *Capital*, vol. 1, p. 1079). For commentary on similar texts, see my *Karl Marx's Theory of History*, p. 243.

do not want to leave it. Or perhaps it is pretty bad, but they are too lazy to undertake the effort needed to escape. Or perhaps no one believes he would be able to secure the key in face of the capacity of the others to intervene (though no one would in fact intervene, since, being so diffident, each also believes that he would be unable to remove the key from anyone else). Suppose that, whatever may be their reasons, they are all so indisposed to leave the room that if, counterfactually, one of them were to try to leave, the rest would not interfere. The universal inaction is relevant to my argument, but the explanation of it is not.

Then whomever we select, it is true of the other nine that not one of them is going to try to get the key. Therefore it is true of the selected person that he is free to obtain the key, and to use it.[17] He is therefore not forced to remain in the room. But all that is true of whomever we select. Therefore it is true of each person that he is not forced to remain in the room, even though necessarily at least nine will remain in the room, and in fact all will.

Consider now a slightly different example, a modified version of the situation just described. In the new case there are two doors and two keys. Again, there are ten people, but this time one of them does try to get out, and succeeds, while the rest behave as before. Now necessarily eight will remain in the room, but it is true of each of the nine who do stay that he or she is free to leave it. The pertinent general feature, present in both cases, is that there is at least one means of egress which none will attempt to use, and which each is free to use, since, *ex hypothesi*, no one would block his way.

By now the application of the analogy may be obvious. The number of exits from the proletariat is, as a matter of objective circumstance, small. But most proletarians are not trying to escape, and, as a result, *it is false that each exit is being actively attempted by some proletarian*. Therefore for most[18] proletarians there exists a means of escape. So even though necessarily most proletarians will remain proletarians, and will sell their labor power, perhaps none, and at most a minority, are forced to do so.

In reaching this conclusion, which is about the proletariat's *objective* position, I used some facts of consciousness, regarding workers' aspira-

[17] For whatever may be the correct analysis of '*X* is free to do *A*,' it is clear that *X* is free to do *A* if *X* would do *A* if he tried to do *A*, and that sufficient condition of freedom is all that we need here. (Some have objected that the stated condition is not sufficient: a person, they say, may do something he is not free to do, since he may do something he is not legally, or morally, free to do. Those who agree with that unhelpful remark can take it that I am interested in the nonnormative use of 'free,' which is distinguished by the sufficient condition just stated.)

[18] See nn. 14, 15 above.

tions and intentions. That is legitimate. For if workers are objectively forced to sell their labor power, then they are forced to do so whatever their subjective situation may be. But their actual subjective situation brings it about that they are not forced to sell their labor power. Hence they are not objectively forced to sell their labor power.

12. One could say, speaking rather broadly, that we have found more freedom in the proletariat's situation than classical Marxism asserts. But if we return to the basis on which we affirmed that most proletarians are not forced to sell their labor power, we shall arrive at a more refined description of the objective position with respect to force and freedom. What was said will not be withdrawn, but we shall add significantly to it.

That basis was the reasoning originally applied to the case of the people in the locked room. Each is free to seize the key and leave. But note the conditional nature of his freedom. He is free not only *because* none of the others tries to get the key, but *on condition* that they do not (a condition which, in the story, is fulfilled). Then *each is free only on condition that the others do not exercise their similarly conditional freedom.* Not more than one can exercise the liberty they all have. If, moreover, any one were to exercise it, then, because of the structure of the situation, all the others would lose it.

Since the freedom of each is contingent on the others not exercising their similarly contingent freedom, we can say that there is a great deal of unfreedom in their situation. Though each is individually free to leave, he suffers with the rest from what I shall call *collective unfreedom.*

In defense of that description, let us reconsider the question why the people do not try to leave. None of the reasons suggested earlier—lack of desire, laziness, diffidence—go beyond what a person wants and fears for himself alone. But sometimes people care about the fate of others, and they sometimes have that concern when they share a common oppression. Suppose, then, not so wildly, that there is a sentiment of solidarity in that room. A fourth possible explanation of the absence of attempt to leave now suggests itself. It is that no one will be satisfied with a personal escape which is not part of a general liberation.

The new supposition does not upset the claim that each is free to leave, for we may assume that it remains true of each person that he would suffer no interference if, counterfactually, he sought to use the key (assume that the others would have contempt for him, but not try to stop him). So each remains free to leave. Yet we can envisage members of the group communicating to their jailer a demand for freedom, to which he could hardly reply that they are free already (even though, individually, they are). The hypothesis of solidarity makes the collective unfreedom evident. But unless we say, absurdly, that the solidarity creates the unfreedom to which it is a response, we must say that there is collective unfreedom whether or not solidarity obtains.

Returning to the proletariat, we can conclude, by parity of reasoning, that although most proletarians are free to escape the proletariat, and, indeed, even if everyone is, the proletariat is collectively unfree, an imprisoned class.

Marx often maintained that the worker is forced to sell his labor power not to any particular capitalist, but just to some capitalist or other, and he emphasized the ideological value of that distinction.[19] The present point is that although, in a collective sense, workers are forced to sell their labor power, scarcely any particular proletarian is forced to sell himself even to some capitalist or other. And this, too, has ideological value. It is part of the genius of capitalist exploitation that, by contrast with exploitation which proceeds by "extra-economic compulsion,"[20] it does not require the unfreedom of specified individuals. There is an ideologically valuable anonymity on *both* sides of the relationship of exploitation.

13. It was part of the argument for affirming the freedom to escape of proletarians, taken individually, that not every exit from the proletariat is crowded with would-be escapees. Why should this be so? Here are some of the reasons.

i. It is possible to escape, but it is not easy, and often people do not attempt what is possible but hard.

ii. There is also the fact that long occupancy, for example from birth, of a subordinate class position nurtures the illusion, which is as important for the stability of the system as the myth of easy escape, that one's class position is natural and inescapable.

iii. Finally, there is the fact that not all workers would like to be petty or trans-petty bourgeois. Eugene Debs said, "I do not want to rise above the working class, I want to rise with them,"[21] thereby evincing an attitude like the one lately attributed to the people in the locked room. It is sometimes true of the worker that, in Brecht's words,

> He wants no servants under him
> And no boss over his head.[22]

[19] See *Karl Marx's Theory of History*, p. 223, for exposition and references.

[20] Marx, *Capital*, vol. 3, p. 926.

[21] And Tawney remarked that it is not "the noblest use of exceptional powers . . . to scramble to shore, undeterred by the thought of drowning companions" (*Equality*, p. 106).

[22] From his "Song of the United Front."

Those lines envisage a better liberation: not just from the working class, but from class society.[23]

Appendix on Whether Socialism or Capitalism Is Better for Freedom[24]

I am here separating two questions about capitalism, socialism, and freedom. The first, or *abstract* question, is which form of society is, just as such, better for freedom, not, and this is the second, and *concrete* question, which form is better for freedom in the conditions of a particular place and time.[25] The first question is interesting, but difficult and somewhat obscure. I shall try to clarify it presently. I shall then indicate that two distinct ranges of consideration bear on the second question, about freedom in a particular case, considerations which must be distinguished not only for theoretical but also for political reasons.

Though confident that the abstract interpretation of the question, which form, if any, offers more liberty, is meaningful, I am not at all sure what its meaning is. I do not think we get an answer to it favoring one form if and only if that form would in all circumstances provide more freedom than the other. For I can understand the claim that socialism is by nature a freer society than capitalism even though it would be a less free society under certain conditions.

Consider a possible analogy. It will be agreed that sports cars are faster than Jeeps, even though Jeeps are faster on certain kinds of terrain. Does the abstract comparison, in which sports cars outclass Jeeps, mean, therefore, that sports cars are faster on *most* terrains? I think not. It seems sufficient for sports cars to be faster in the abstract that there is some

[23] See *History, Labour, and Freedom*, chapter 13 [entitled "The Structure of Proletarian Unfreedom"—Ed.], for a fuller and more nuanced presentation of Sections 8–13 of this paper. See, too, Gray, "Against Cohen on Proletarian Unfreedom," which criticizes the material presented above. What Gray says against the claims developed in Sections 1–7 strikes me as feeble, but his critique of the idea of collective proletarian unfreedom demands a response, which I hope in due course to provide.

[24] [See n. 10 above.—Ed.]

[25] One may also distinguish not, as above, between the capitalist form of society and a particular capitalist society, but between the capitalist form in general and specific forms of capitalism, such as competitive capitalism, monopoly capitalism, and so on (I provide a systematic means of generating specific forms in *Karl Marx's Theory of History*, chapter 3, sections 6 and 8). This further distinction is *at* the abstract level, rather than between abstract and concrete. I prescind from it here to keep my discussion relatively uncomplicated. The distinction would have to be acknowledged, and employed, in any treatment which pretended to be definitive.

unbizarre terrain on which their maximum speed exceeds the maximum speed of Jeeps on any terrain. Applying the analogy, if socialism is said to be freer than capitalism in the abstract, this would mean that there are realistic concrete conditions under which a socialist society would be freer than *any* concrete capitalist society would be. This, perhaps, is what some socialists mean when they say that socialism is a freer society, for some who say that would acknowledge that in some conditions socialism, or what would pass for it,[26] would be less free than at any rate some varieties of capitalism.

There are no doubt other interesting abstract questions, which do not yield to the analysis just given. Perhaps, for example, the following intractably rough prescription could be made more usable: consider, with respect to each form of society, the sum of liberty which remains when the liberties it withholds by its very nature are subtracted from the liberties it guarantees by its very nature. The society which is freer in the abstract is the one where that sum is larger.

So much for the abstract issue. I said that two kinds of consideration bear on the answer to concrete questions, about which form of society would provide more freedom in a particular here and now. We may look upon each form of society as a set of rules which generates, in particular cases, particular enjoyments and deprivations of freedom. Now the effect of the rules in a particular case will depend, in the first place, on the resources and traditions which prevail in the society in question. But secondly, and distinctly, it will also depend on the ideological and political views of the people concerned. (This distinction is not always easy to make, but it is never impossible to make it.) To illustrate the distinction, it could be that in a given case collectivization of agriculture would provide more freedom on the whole for rural producers, were it not for the fact that they do not *believe* it would, and would therefore resist collectivization so strongly that it could be introduced only at the cost of enormous repression. It could be that though socialism might distribute more liberty in Britain now, capitalist ideology is now here so powerful, and the belief that socialism would reduce liberty is, accordingly, so strong, that conditions *otherwise* propitious for realizing a socialism with a great deal of liberty are not favorable in the final reckoning, since the final reckoning must take account of the present views of people about how free a socialist society would be.

[26]Which way they would put it depends on how they would define socialism. If it is defined as public ownership of the means of production, and this is taken in a narrowly juridical sense, then it is compatible with severe restrictions on freedom. But if, to go to other extreme, it is defined as a condition in which the free development of each promotes, and is promoted by, the free development of all, then only the attempt to institute socialism, not socialism, could have negative consequences for freedom.

I think it is theoretically and politically important to attempt a reckoning independent of that final reckoning.

It is theoretically important because there exists a clear question about whether a socialist revolution would expand freedom whose answer is not determined by people's beliefs about what its answer is. *Its* answer might be "yes," even though most people think its answer is "no," and even though, as a result, "no" is the correct answer to the further, "final reckoning" question, for whose separateness I am arguing. Unless one separates the questions, one cannot coherently evaluate the ideological answers to the penultimate question which help to cause the ultimate question to have the answer it does.

It is also politically necessary to separate the questions, because it suits our rulers not to distinguish the two levels of assessment. The Right can often truly say that, all things considered, socialism would diminish liberty, where, however, the chief reason why this is so is that the Right, with its powerful ideological arsenal, have convinced enough people that it is so. Hence one needs to argue for an answer which does not take people's conviction into account, partly, of course, in order to combat and transform those convictions. If, on the other hand, you want to defend the status quo, then I recommend that you confuse the questions I have distinguished.

The distinction between concrete questions enables me to make a further point about the abstract question, which *form* of society provides more freedom. We saw above that a plausible strategy for answering it involves asking concrete questions about particular cases. We may now add that the concrete questions relevant to the abstract one are those which prescind from people's beliefs about their answers.

I should add, finally, that people's beliefs about socialism and freedom affect not only how free an achieved socialist society would be, but also how much restriction on freedom would attend the process of achieving it. (Note that there is a somewhat analogous distinction between how much freedom we have in virtue of the currently maintained capitalist arrangements, and how much we have, or lose, because of the increasingly repressive measures used to maintain them.) Refutation of bourgeois ideology is an imperative task for socialists, not as an alternative to the struggle for socialism, but as part of the struggle for a socialism which will justify the struggle which led to it.

Chapter Eight

FREEDOM AND MONEY

In grateful memory of Isaiah Berlin

> . . . . when ideas are neglected by those who ought to attend to them—that is to say, those who have been trained to think critically about ideas—they sometimes acquire an unchecked momentum and an irresistible power. . . .
>
> —*Isaiah Berlin, "Two Concepts of Liberty," p. 119*

I HAVE NEVER DEDICATED an article to a person before. I have considered it to be a pretentious thing to do. Whole books are big things: they are manifestly big enough to warrant the device of a dedication. But to dedicate a mere article seems to imply an immodest belief on the author's part that the intellectual value of his little piece is pretty special.

For all that, I have dedicated this article to the memory of my sadly late[1] but imperishably present teacher and friend, Isaiah Berlin. I have been impelled to this departure from normal practice not because I think that what you are reading is truly wonderful, but by my feelings of loss, and of consequent desolation. This article's theme, freedom, was at the heart of Isaiah's contribution to our understanding of humanity and of the social world, and, in the wake of his recent death, the dedication of the article to him seemed to me so entirely fitting as to be unavoidable.

Although I was devoted to Isaiah, and although he was bountifully kind to me, we were not of one mind on political questions, and we were also not of one mind on those academic questions that mattered, to each of us, because of the political questions on which they bear. I have elsewhere set out our disagreements, as I understand them, about the thought, and the personality, of Karl Marx.[2] Here, I explain a disagreement that we had about freedom, and, more particularly, about the relationship between freedom and money.

My principal contention, one that contradicts very influential things that Isaiah wrote, is that lack of money, poverty, carries with it lack of

Editor's note: All Berlin quotations in this chapter are from his *Four Essays on Liberty* unless otherwise indicated.

[1] Isaiah Berlin died on November 5, 1997.

[2] See "Isaiah's Marx and Mine."

freedom. I regard that as an overwhelmingly obvious truth,[3] one that is worth defending only because it has been so influentially denied. Lack of money, poverty, is not, of course, the *only* circumstance that restricts a person's freedom, but it is, in my view, one of them, and one of the most important of them. To put the point more precisely—there are lots of things that, *because* they are poor, poor people are not free to do, things that nonpoor people *are*, by contrast, indeed free to do.

Now, you might think that few poor people need to be persuaded of that proposition, that their daily life experience offers ample enough evidence for it; and my own casual observation suggests that it is a truth which is indeed pretty obvious to them. But, however that may be, many nonpoor intellectuals have strenuously denied that lack of money means lack of freedom, perhaps because it is a comfort for well-off people to think that poor people, whatever their other sufferings may be, are not deprived of *freedom*: that false thought might reduce the guilt that some well-off people feel when they face folk who are much less fortunate than they are themselves. Or maybe the relevant intellectuals, being subtler than the relevant poor people, notice something that the poor people don't. A poor person might say that she feels no longer free to visit her sister in a distant town, when the special bus service has been withdrawn. Maybe the intellectual can show that that is *just* a feeling: that she may *feel* less free than she was before, but that *actually* she *isn't*. But I disagree with the relevant intellectuals: I believe that the feeling that the poor woman expresses represents a correct judgment.

The issue that I raise here asserts itself within the frame of a standard political debate, which runs as follows. Right-wing people celebrate the freedom enjoyed by all in liberal capitalist society. Left-wing people respond that the freedom which the Right celebrate is merely formal, that, while the poor are *formally* free to do all kinds of things that the state does not forbid anyone to do, their parlous situation means that they are not *really* free to do very many of them, since they cannot afford to do them, and they are, therefore, in the end, prevented from doing them. But the Right now rejoin that, in saying all that, the Left confuse freedom with resources. You are *free* to do anything that no one will interfere with, say the Right. If you cannot *afford* to do something, that does not mean that you lack the *freedom* to do it, but just that you lack the *means*, and, therefore, the *ability* to do it. The problem the poor face is

[3] Utterly obvious truths can subvert grand claims, and I think this one does so. Wittgenstein said that (good) philosophy "consists in assembling reminders for a particular purpose." *Philosophical Investigations*, para. 127, p. 50e. Reminders affirm what we already know, not new insights. That is how I understand my effort here, the particular purpose being to deny the nonobvious, and, in my view, false claim that the poor lack not freedom but only the ability to use it.

not that they lack *freedom*, but that they are not always able to *exercise* the freedom that they undoubtedly have. When the Left say that the poor, by virtue of being poor, lack freedom *itself*, the Left, so the Right claim, indulge in a tendentious use of language.

Let me set out the full right-wing position on this matter in the form of an argument, with separately indicated steps. In effect, the right-wing reasoning contains two movements, the first being conceptual, and the second normative. For my part, I reject both movements. Berlin, by contrast, accepted the first movement: indeed, he did more than anyone else ever has to persuade philosophers, and others, of the soundness of the first movement, even though his compassion for suffering people led him to reject, without reservation, the second movement.

The first movement of the right-wing argument runs as follows:

(1) Freedom is compromised by (liability to) interference[4] (by other people),[5] but not by lack of means.
(2) To lack money is to suffer not (liability to) interference, but lack of means.
∴ (3) Poverty (lack of money) does not carry with it lack of freedom.

The conclusion of the first movement of the argument, proposition (3), is a conceptual claim, a claim about how certain concepts are connected with one another. But, in the Right's hands, that conceptual conclusion is used to support a normative claim, a claim about what ought to be done, which is reached as follows, in the second movement of the argument:

(3) Poverty (lack of money) does not carry with it lack of freedom.
(4) The primary task of government is to protect freedom.
∴ (5) Relief of poverty is not part of the primary task of government.

[4] See n. 7 below.

[5] 'Interference' will always mean, here, 'interference by other people.' Thus, for example, her limp will not here constitute an interference with a person's attempt to negotiate difficult terrain (whether or not it compromises her freedom to negotiate that terrain, which matter is discussed in the Addendum to this paper advertised at n. 8 below).

A further significant stipulation. Interference is often understood to be merely one form of prevention: something interferes when it prevents a person from *continuing* on a course of action on which she has embarked, or, at any rate, when it prevents a person from continuing on a course of action without hindrance. Interference, thus understood, does not occur where prevention (of another form) does, when, that is, a person is prevented from *embarking* on a course of action. But I shall here also call that form of prevention "interference," since such prevention by other people is also considered freedom-reducing by the Right. (For the importance of the distinction between interference in particular and prevention in general with respect to theories of appropriation of private property, see my "Once More into the Breach of Self-Ownership," pp. 62ff.)

The conclusion of this argument follows from its three premises, to wit, (1), (2), and (4). There are, accordingly, only three ways of resisting the argument. A familiar form of left-wing resistance to it challenges proposition (1), by asking how a person can reasonably be said to be *free* to do what she is *unable* to do? Another left-wing way of resisting the argument, also employed, as we have seen, by Berlin and Rawls, is to deny (4), by saying: even if lack of money *is* just lack of means, lack of means is just as confining as lack of freedom, and, therefore, just as important a thing for the state to rectify. I shall not resist the argument in either of those ways in the body of this paper, which is not to say that I disagree with those who resist either premise (1) or premise (4). I am not disagreeing with them, or agreeing with them, in the present paper, but simply shelving challenges to (1) and (4) here.[6] Instead, I shall reject premise (2), a premise which, so far as I know, has not been resisted in the relevant literature. I believe that the nonstandard resistance to the argument that I deploy here is more powerful, because it meets the Right on their own conceptual ground.

The rest of this article has seven sections. In Section 1, I show that the conceptual part of the right-wing argument has penetrated academic thought which cannot be described as right-wing. Isaiah Berlin and John Rawls, in particular, and their many followers, have advocated the conceptual part of the right-wing argument, which culminates in (3), even though, because they do not accept (4), they have not endorsed the Right's normative conclusion, (5).

In Section 2, I attempt a refutation of proposition (2). I argue that to lack money is indeed to be prey to interference. If that argument is sound, then proposition (3) is false, if, as the Right insist, proposition (1) is true, since, if (1) is true, then the falsehood of (2) entails that (3) is false. I believe, moreover, that my argument, if sound, also establishes that proposition (3) is false whether or not (1) is true, since I cannot imagine how anyone who does not think that (2) is true could think that (3) is true. That's a complicated statement, but it boils down to this: I shall argue that the poor lack freedom, even in the Right's, and Berlin's and Rawls's, preferred sense of freedom, where freedom is identified with lack of interference,[7] and whether or not that identification of freedom is too restrictive.

[6] I deal with (1) in the Addendum advertised at n. 8 below.

[7] Or, strictly, with lack of interference and of liability to interference: my freedom to do *A* is restricted if I *would* be interfered with if I were to try to do *A*, and not merely if I am *actually* interfered with. I may be unfree although I suffer no actual interference, because, knowing that I am likely to be interfered with, I refrain from trying to do *A*. 'Lack of interference' will include lack of liability to interference throughout this paper.

Section 3 applies the Section 2 argument, to, and against, a number of Berlin's formulations.

In Section 4, I seek to fortify, but also to nuance, my argument, by presenting some analogies and disanalogies between the freedom conferred by money and (directly) state-regulated freedom.

In Section 5, I discuss the bearing of certain Marxian theses about the difference between bourgeois and prebourgeois society on the widespread failure to perceive that money confers freedom and that its lack restricts it.

I close (Section 6) with a few words about the importance of the semantic tangle that I believe I am unraveling here. (An Appendix responds to the objection, as it is formulated by Jonathan Wolff, that what I say about *freedom* does not hold for *liberty*.)[8]

1. The most celebrated twentieth-century Anglophone political philosophers are Isaiah Berlin and John Rawls. As I have said, both reject[9] the conclusion of the right-wing argument: Berlin was a social democrat, in the broad sense, and Rawls is a liberal, in the American sense, and, within those political positions, relief of poverty is at the top of the political agenda. Accordingly, Berlin and Rawls both deplore the Right's comparative unconcern about what they would call the ability to *use* freedom, which, in their view, is what the poor lack. But, in my opinion regrettably, they both fully accept the right-wing contrast between freedom and money. They agree with the Right's *conceptual* claim, even though (not at all inconsistently) they reject the Right's *normative* conclusion.

In the following passage, Berlin shows at one and the same time agreement with the Right's conceptualization of freedom[10] and forthright rejection of the normative conclusion which the Right build upon that conceptualization:

[8] In an unpublished Addendum on "Freedom and Ability" [now published as an Addendum to this chapter—Ed.], I discuss the relationships that obtain among freedom, means, and ability. I show that the latter two have a much stronger bearing on freedom than is recognized by those against whose views this lecture is directed, and I thereby refute proposition (1): I show that freedom *is* compromised by lack of means.

[9] It is somewhat zeugmatic to employ the present tense with respect to Rawls and Berlin jointly, since, in its second employment, it is merely (alas) historic. I hope that the reader will forgive this infelicity, which reduces the number of sentences or clauses that I must enter to fix attributions like the one above.

[10] To be sure, Berlin speaks of "liberty" rather than of "freedom," but I do not believe that this makes a substantial difference: as he later expressly said (see *The First and the Last*, p. 58), he used those words interchangeably, and he would certainly never have said, as his (semi)defender Jonathan Wolff does, that what holds for liberty does not hold for freedom: see, further, the Appendix below.

> It is important to discriminate between liberty and the conditions of its exercise. If a man is too poor or too ignorant or too feeble to make use of his *legal rights*, the liberty that these rights confer upon him is nothing to him, but it is not thereby annihilated. The obligation to promote education, health, justice, to raise standards of living, to provide opportunity for the growth of the arts and the sciences, to prevent reactionary political or social or legal policies or arbitrary inequalities, is not made less stringent because it is not necessarily directed to the promotion of *liberty itself*, but to conditions in which alone its possession is of value, or to values which may be independent of it.[11]

That Berlin agreed with the conceptual side of the right-wing claim is also revealed in his phrasing of a certain commendation which he offered in 1949 of the Franklin Roosevelt presidency.[12] Berlin described Roosevelt's New Deal as a "great liberal enterprise" which was "certainly the most constructive compromise between individual liberty and economic security which our own time has witnessed."[13] The Berlin commendation of Roosevelt implies that individual liberty and economic security are competing desiderata, that, at least sometimes, more of the one means less of the other, and that, in Roosevelt's "constructive compromise," there was some loss of one of them, or, perhaps, of each, for the sake of the other. One may safely say, moreover, that, in Berlin's view, there was, in the New Deal "compromise," more sacrifice of individual liberty than of economic security, that, broadly speaking, the New Deal reduced the first for the sake of increasing the second. Within the terms introduced earlier, the New Deal, according to Berlin, reduced freedom itself in the

[11] *Four Essays*, p. liii, emphases added.

While I am confident that the quoted text agrees and disagrees with the right-wing view precisely as I have just claimed that it does, I do not say that Berlin's discourse in this region was consistent, or free of problems. His work on liberty was as profoundly original as it was influential, and it is common, in groundbreaking work, for distinctions to be missed and for different distinctions to be confused with one another. See n. 30 below, for a demonstration of some relevant lapses in Berlin's text.

[12] I was privileged to see a great deal of Isaiah during his final months, when he was at home, chair-ridden. Just a few days before his death, he encouraged me (I don't know why he thought I had this kind of influence: he was perhaps harking back to a day when our college, All Souls, was influential in the real world) to encourage the present Labour government to imitate his political hero, Franklin Roosevelt, by instituting a great program of public works which would reduce unemployment and enthuse young people. He confessed himself unable to see why there had been a turn away, in our time, from the use of the state for progressive purposes, even by a Labour government. He was entirely hostile to total state control—he thought that the claims of socialist planning were illusory—but he was passionately against Thatcherism: he knew that "free" markets destroy people's lives.

[13] "Political Ideas in the Twentieth Century," p. 31.

interest of rendering the freedom that then remained more valuable. Berlin was commending Roosevelt for having rendered American society less *laissez-faire* and more social-democratic than it had been. Roosevelt introduced union-supporting legislation that restricted the freedom attached to ownership of productive assets, social security legislation that removed free disposal over part of earned income, and state enterprises such as the Tennessee Valley Authority, which blocked free exercise of private property in certain domains.

Policies of that kind, so Berlin believed, enhance the security of those who suffer not lack of freedom but exposure to disaster in less regulated, more Herbert Hoover- (or Margaret Thatcher-) like, economies. In Berlin's conception of the New Deal, comparatively poor and powerless people gained security and resources, while wealthy people lost some resources, and everyone lost some freedoms. In the net result of the New Deal, on Berlin's view, security was enhanced, and certain freedoms were rendered more *valuable*, at the (justifiable) expense of freedom itself.

Although I am happy to join Berlin in applauding the New Deal, I disagree with the terms in which he chose to commend it. In Berlin's discourse, freedom and economic security are distinct values which humane politicians must trade off against each other, and the Roosevelt administration achieved a most intelligent trade-off, in which realization of the first was restricted, for the sake of greater realization of the second. I do not doubt that, like virtually all distinct values, freedom and economic security *can* conflict, but I do not agree with Berlin that, in the net effect of the New Deal, economic security was enhanced at the expense of freedom.

I defend that disagreement in Sections 2 through 4, but, before I do so, let me show that, like Berlin, John Rawls also accedes to the right-wing conceptualization of freedom:

> The inability to take advantage of one's rights and opportunities as a result of poverty and ignorance, and a lack of means generally, is sometimes counted among the constraints definitive of liberty. I shall not, however, say this, but rather I shall think of these things as affecting the worth of liberty . . . the worth of liberty is not the same for everyone. Some have greater authority and wealth, and therefore greater means to achieve their aims.[14]

Although his language is characteristically cautious and the second sentence in the passage might make it seem that he is merely laying down an innocent stipulation, Rawls here denies, in effect, that poverty constrains liberty. For he could not have resolved (as he puts it) to "think

[14] *A Theory of Justice*, p. 204, and cf. *Political Liberalism*, pp. 325–26.

of" poverty as affecting (only) the *worth* of liberty if he had believed that it affects liberty itself, and the view that poverty does not affect liberty itself is the unambiguous message conveyed by the Rawls paragraph as a whole (only part of which is presented above).[15]

Given the position struck in the foregoing quotation, it is curious, it seems to generate an inconsistency, that, at a later point, Rawls argues as follows for "the rule of law":

> . . . the connection of the rule of law with liberty is clear enough . . . if the precept of no crime without a law is violated, say by statutes being vague and imprecise, what we are at liberty to do is likewise vague and imprecise. The boundaries of our liberty are uncertain. And to the extent that this is so, liberty is restricted by reasonable fear of its exercise.[16]

It is hard to see why liberty (*itself*) is restricted by mere *fear* of its exercise yet not at all restricted by the *impossibility* of its exercise that (Rawls thinks) poverty ensures.[17]

2. The right-wing position to which Berlin and Rawls regrettably accede says that poverty is lack of means, and that it therefore entails lack of ability rather than lack of freedom. I shall challenge that position without questioning the contrast it proposes between means and ability, on the one hand, and freedom on the other: I argue that a certain lack of freedom accompanies lack of money, whatever the relationships among ability, means, and freedom may be, and I am happy to assume, here, with

[15] I do not believe that my comments on the *Theory* paragraph are inconsistent with the *Political Liberalism* remark (p. 326) that it offers "merely a definition and settles no substantive question." "Substantive question" surely means, there, 'substantive normative question': the conceptual claim that I pin on Rawls sticks.

[16] *A Theory of Justice*, p. 239.

[17] It has been objected to my use of the passage on p. 204 of *Theory* that it concerns *political liberty* alone, and not also the liberty of access to goods and services that is the focus of the present article.

But this objection lacks purchase. Rawls is not saying that poverty fails to restrict political liberty, while leaving it open that it may restrict some *non*political kind of liberty: nothing in his text suggests that he might countenance the relationship between poverty and nonpolitical liberty as a separate issue. There is, for example, no reason to take the "rights and opportunities" of the first sentence in the quotation from p. 204, or the "aims" of its last sentence, as, respectively, *political* rights and opportunities, and *political* aims. Rawls is referring to all the rights and opportunities, and all the aims, that obtain or come to obtain when political liberty, as he understands the latter, prevails. (Note, further, that the people with whom Rawls parts company, because they treat poverty as a constraint on liberty [itself], do not regard poverty as a constraint on political liberty alone; and poverty is, indeed, more evidently [on the view Rawls opposes] a constraint on freedom of access to goods and services than it is a constraint on political freedom proper.)

the Right, and with Berlin and Rawls, that freedom is identical with lack of interference. (In the Addendum advertised in n. 8 I challenge the right-wing [and Berlin/Rawls] position from another direction, by arguing that the contrast it employs between means and ability on the one hand and freedom on the other is [anyhow] unsustainable.)

Let me state a further assumption that will govern our discussion, an assumption that matches the intentions of those who propound the argument under scrutiny here. I shall assume that, in the examples that we shall have occasion to consider, the law of the relevant land is fully enforced, that people, therefore, are prevented from doing all and only those things that are illegal, and that they suffer interference when and only when they would otherwise behave illegally. The assumption is legitimate, and required, because, when the authors whom I oppose affirm the freedom of the poor, they are not speaking of a legal freedom which might lack effective force (such as the legal freedom of a person of the wrong color to enter a restaurant to which vigilantes forbid his entry), or of a freedom which is effective but illegal (such as the freedom of the said vigilantes to bar the entry to that restaurant of people of the wrong color). We shall consider only the central case, in which the law prevails, and where legal freedom therefore runs alongside what we may call *effective* freedom.[18]

Now, in my view, the Berlin position depends upon a *reified* view of money: that is, it wrongly treats money as a *thing*, in a sufficiently narrow sense of 'thing' that, as I shall labor to show, money is *not*, in fact, a thing. The Berlin view is false, because money is unlike intelligence or strength,[19] poor endowments of which do not always,[20] indeed, prejudice freedom, as long as freedom is identified with absence of interference. The difference between money and those endowments implies, I shall argue, that lack of money induces lack of freedom, *even if we accept*

[18] Note that what a person is *effectively* free to do, in the present sense, is not identical with what a person is *able* to do, all things considered. Suppose that someone is unable to do *A*, which, to fix ideas, is to walk across the square: the person in question is paralyzed. Then he may nevertheless possess what is here defined as the effective freedom to cross the square: he has that freedom if, were he not paralyzed, and he tried to cross the square, no one would prevent him from doing so. The question whether, as the Left is inclined to affirm and the Right is inclined to deny, incapacity reduces unfreedom is here set aside: I address it in the Addendum advertised in n. 8. According to the Right, a person may be free to do what he is unable to do, and no objection to that will be raised here.

[19] Berlin's "too poor or too ignorant or too feeble" disjunction (see p. 171 of this chapter above) is, therefore, malconstructed.

[20] I say "do not always," rather than "do not (ever)," because of complexities explored in the Addendum advertised in n. 8. In a word: freedom-removing interference entails a relevant inability on the part of its victim, the inability, that is, to overcome that interference, but inabilities do not in *general* imply unfreedoms, on an interference-centered view.

the identification of freedom with absence of interference. Even *if* incapacities like illness and ignorance do not restrict freedom, because no interference need obtain where they are present, poverty demonstrably implies liability to interference, and people on the center-left, such as Berlin and Rawls, accede needlessly to the Right's misrepresentation of the relationship between poverty and freedom when they treat poverty (as a Labour-leaning think tank[21] recently did) as restricting not *freedom* itself but only "what [people] can *do* with their freedom."[22]

Now, before I develop my argument, let me make clear what it is *not* supposed to show. My argument overturns the claim that a liberal capitalist society is, by its very nature, a *free* society, a society in which there are no significant constraints on freedom, but that does not mean, and I do not claim it does, that a capitalist society is therefore inferior, all things considered, or even in respect of freedom, to other social forms. All forms of society grant freedoms to, and impose unfreedoms on, people, and no society, therefore, can be condemned just because certain people lack certain freedoms in it. But societies have structurally different ways of inducing distributions of freedom, and, in a society like ours, where freedom is to a massive extent granted and withheld through the distribution of money, that fact, that money structures freedom, is often not appreciated in its full significance, and an illusion develops that freedom in a society like ours is not restricted by the distribution of money. This lecture exposes that illusion. But that money *is*, contrary to the illusion, and to what others claim, a way of structuring freedom, does not imply that a money society is inferior, in general, or even in respect of freedom, to other forms of society. That may be true, but it is no part of what I am here claiming.

Here, then, is my argument for the proposition that poverty betokens an absence of freedom itself, in the sense of 'freedom' favored by my opponents, in which lack of freedom entails presence of interference.

[21] That is, the Labour-leaning Institute for Public Policy Research (IPPR) in London.

[22] Commission on Social Justice, *The Justice Gap*, p. 8, my emphasis: "People are likely to be restricted in what they can do with their freedom and their rights if they are poor, or ill, or lack . . . education. . . . "

For a critical assessment of that text, and related ones, see my "Back to Socialist Basics," which is reprinted in Jane Franklin, ed., *Equality* (London: IPPR, 1997), where it is followed by a sharp reply ("Forward to Basics") by Bernard Williams, one which has not caused me to change my view. ["Back to Socialist Basics" is reprinted as Chapter 10 of this volume.—Ed.]

The argument at pp. 176ff. of this chapter below is an extended and (I hope) improved version of the argument linking money and freedom in the Appendix of "Back to Socialist Basics." [Since it has been superseded by this chapter, that Appendix has not been reproduced in this volume.—Ed.]

Consider those goods and services, be they privately or publicly provided, which are not provided without charge to all comers. Some of the public ones depend on special access rules (you won't get a state hospital bed if you are judged to be healthy, or a place in secondary school if you are forty years old). But the private ones, and many of the public ones, are inaccessible save through money: giving money is both necessary for getting them, and, indeed, sufficient for getting them, if they are on sale.[23] If you attempt access to them in the absence of money, then you will be prey to interference.

A property distribution just *is*, as I have argued at length elsewhere,[24] a distribution of rights of interference.[25] If *A* owns *P* and *B* does not, then *A* may use *P* without interference and *B* will, standardly, suffer interference if he attempts to use *P*. *But money serves, in a variety of circumstances (and, notably, when A puts P up for rent or sale), to remove that latter interference. Therefore money confers freedom, rather than merely the ability to use it*, even if freedom is equated with absence of interference.

Suppose that an able-bodied woman is too poor to visit her sister in Glasgow. She cannot save enough, from week to week, to buy her way there. If she attempts to board the train, she is consequently without the means to overcome the conductor's prospective interference. Whether or not this woman should be said to have the *ability* to go to Glasgow, there is no deficiency in her ability to do so which restricts her *independently* of the interference that she faces. She is entirely capable of boarding the underground and of traversing the space that she must cross to reach the train. But she will be physically prevented from crossing that space, or physically ejected from the train. Or consider a moneyless woman who wants to pick up, and take home, a sweater on the counter at Selfridge's. If she contrives to do so, she will be physically stopped outside Selfridge's

[23] More precisely, money is an *inus* condition of the said getting: see pp. 177–78 of this chapter below.

[24] The private property argument first appeared at pp. 11–15 of "Capitalism, Freedom, and the Proletariat," in Alan Ryan, ed., *The Idea of Freedom: Essays in Honour of Isaiah Berlin* (Oxford: Oxford University Press, 1979), which was reprinted, with extensive revisions, in David Miller, ed., *Liberty* (Oxford: Oxford University Press, 1991), the private property argument appearing, there, at pp. 167–72 [and also at pp. 150–54 of Chapter 7 of this volume—Ed.]. The argument has been criticized by, among others, Gray, at pp. 169–70 of "Marxian Freedom, Individual Liberty, and the End of Alienation," and throughout his "Against Cohen on Proletarian Unfreedom"; by Reeve, *Property*, pp. 109–10; and by Brenkert, at pp. 29–39 of "Self-Ownership, Freedom, and Autonomy." I reply to Gray at pp. 62–65 of *Self-Ownership, Freedom, and Equality*, and to Reeve and Brenkert at pp. 79–82 of "Once More into the Breach of Self-Ownership."

[25] That is a point about property in general, one that I am making as prelude to a distinct point about money, which is a very special form of property, some truths about which do not hold for property in general.

and the sweater will be removed. The only way you won't be prevented from getting and using things that cost money in our society—which is to say: most things—is by offering money for them.

So to lack money *is* to be liable to interference, and the assimilation of money to physical, or even mental, resources is a piece of unthinking fetishism, in the good old Marxist sense that it misrepresents *social relations of constraint* as *people lacking things*. In a word: money is no object.

The value of money is that it gives you freedom, and that is so even though (a) you may not want to exercise (all the) freedom in question, and (b) money alone never suffices, by itself, to supply the freedom its seekers seek.

(a) is true because a person may desire money other than in order to spend it.[26] She may, for example, desire it because of the *power* that possessing the freedoms in question bestows upon her: she can, for example, threaten to sue others in circumstances where a like threat from a poor person would not be credible. She may also desire money because of the *prestige* that it brings: many people admire the rich. But the claim that money provides freedom is not prejudiced by these motivational complexities.

(b) is true because, in order to buy something, conditions other than possession of the required money are necessary: you need to have appropriate information, the seller must want to sell, you need to be of an age where you can contract, etc. Money, then, is an *inus* condition of the freedom to acquire, an insufficient but necessary part of an unnecessary but sufficient condition.[27] But the key point is that the other conditions apply to rich and poor alike, yet the poor, *as such*, are far less free than the rich are, *as such*, because in their case the relevant *inus* condition is widely unsatisfied, and this makes that condition worthy of special focus. The key truth is that, if you are poor, you are *pro tanto* less free than if you are rich. To be sure, it is as true of the rich person as it is of the poor one that he is unfree to take the sweater *without* paying money: no one is free to take the sweater without paying money. But, uniquely for the poor person, this means that he is not free to take the sweater, whereas the rich person *is* free to take the sweater, by paying money for it.

Things other than lack of money can prevent you from overcoming interference: things like ignorance, or stupidity, or ugliness. They constitute lack of freedom, they are *inus* conditions of unfreedom, in particular

[26] See my *Karl Marx's Theory of History*, pp. 300–301.

[27] The concept of an *inus* condition was introduced by Mackie in an attempt to illuminate singular causal claims. [See Mackie, *The Cement of the Universe*, chapter 3.—Ed.] My appropriation of his concept here does not imply that I endorse the use to which Mackie put it.

circumstances. But they don't distinguish the poor from the rich, and they are not, as poverty is, a pervasive *inus* condition of unfreedom. Unlike intelligence and beauty, which may or may not serve to extinguish interference under particular circumstances, the whole point of money is to extinguish interference: that is its defining function, even if further conditions are required for it to perform it. Compare: the defining function of a knife is to cut, but that is not to say that any knife can cut any block of stone.

A final point needs to be made. It is sometimes said, by way of objection to the position I have defended here, that their riches can bring *un*freedoms for the rich from which the poor do not suffer: so, for example, their investments may require laborious attention, they are more prey to begging letters, and even, sometimes, to being kidnapped. But my claim is not that, all things considered, the poor are less free than the rich, though that is undoubtedly true, but that what makes the poor count as poor, their lack of money, makes them thus far unfree, whatever other unfreedoms—or indeed, freedoms—that may vagariously cause. It is undoubtedly true that freedom can generate unfreedom, and that unfreedom can generate freedom. You cannot, for example, be forced to do what you are not free to do,[28] and, since being forced to do something is a form of unfreedom, it is a form of *un*freedom that *requires* freedom.

But these complexities, too, are beside the point, which concerns what money, in and of itself, immediately *does*. Despite the indicated complexities, money confers freedom, and those who deny that, those who affirm that the poor as such are no less free than the rich as such, do not, after all, do so on the ground that wealth frequently carries freedom-compromising burdens with it.

3. Let us now return to Berlin.

For Berlin, the favored freedom, freedom from interference, the freedom that he famously called *negative*, the freedom that he distinguished from the ability to use it, is "opportunity for action" (p. xlii), "the absence of obstacles to possible choices and activities" (p. xxxix). And the "absence" of said "freedom is due to the closing of . . . doors or failure to open them, as a result, intended or unintended, of alterable human practices, of the operation of human agencies" (p. xl and cf. p. xlviii). Yet it seems evident, in contradiction of the contrast between freedom and money on which Berlin insisted, that lack of money implies lack of

[28] For the deep bearing of this (for many, surprising) truth on debates about market freedom, see pp. 241–44 of my "Are Disadvantaged Workers Who Take Hazardous Jobs Forced to Take Hazardous Jobs?" (For a briefer exposition, see my "Capitalism, Freedom, and the Proletariat," in Miller, ed., pp. 163–65 [pp. 147–48 of Chapter 7 of this volume—Ed.]).

freedom in just that sense. The woman prevented by her poverty from traveling to Glasgow faces just such a closed door. (Under a "smart-card" technology for controlling access to the train, that will be literally true, in a physical sense).

Now, it might be claimed that I have misused a looseness in Berlin's characterization of negative freedom; that, although he several times said that it was a matter of unclosed doors, his more considered view was that it was to be understood more narrowly than that, as a matter of doors that are not closed by *government*, in particular. For he says, at p. xliii, that my negative liberty is determined by the answer to the question: "[h]ow much am I governed?" One might then suggest that, in the passages that I have quoted from pp. xlii, xxxix, and xl (and in the supremely important footnote 1 on p. 130), Berlin misdescribes his own position when he identifies absence of freedom with *any* closure of an avenue, rather than, in line with p. xliii, with only those avenue-closures that are due to government.

Yet it was surely the pressure of truth that produced the wider formulations: a person who blocks my way need not be wearing a government uniform to deprive me, thereby, of freedom.[29] And blockages by anyone, whether in or out of uniform, standardly succeed, in a law-abiding society, only by virtue of the state's disposition to support them. So the contrast between doors that are closed by government and doors that are closed by others lacks relevant application: it makes a difference only when a certain illegality obtains, and it is absurd to suppose that those who wish to resist the left-wing claim that the poor suffer an extensive lack of freedom will be content to do so by pointing out that the poor can, after all, break the law.

Berlin offers a curious prognosis regarding "those who are obsessed by the truth that negative freedom is worth little without sufficient conditions for its active exercise." He says that they "are liable to minimize its importance, to deny it the very title of freedom . . . and finally to forget that without it human life . . . withers away" (pp. lviii–lix). Or, again: "in their zeal to create social and economic conditions in which alone freedom is of genuine value, men tend to forget freedom itself" (p. liv). But how could this be so, given that, on Berlin's own reckoning, what they are obsessed by precisely *are* (certain forms of) valuable *freedom*? Berlin's diagnosis of the supposed error of the Left, namely, that they are so concerned with the ability to *use* freedom that they confuse it with freedom itself, is inconsistent with his *prognosis* that they will

[29] Suppose that two people are prevented from boarding a plane, one because she lacks a passport and the other because she lacks a ticket. Was only the first unfree to board it? What the airline does to the ticketless passenger is exactly what the state does to the passportless one: block her way.

tend to forget that freedom itself is an essential value. Why should the Left insist that freedom be capable of use if they do not, in the end, *care* about freedom?

I believe that Berlin here misdescribes the object of his anxiety, which is rather that these champions of the poor come to care so much about the freedoms specifically associated with the defeat of poverty, the freedoms associated with having money (whether one thinks, here, that money is required for freedom of access to goods itself *or* only for the value of that freedom: in what *really* bothers Berlin, *here*, that distinction is quite secondary), as opposed to civil and political freedoms (such as freedom of speech, of association, of assembly, and so forth),[30] that they come to care too little about the latter. It is a large mistake, made not only by Berlin but also (by implication) by Rawls, to describe the Left as willing to sacrifice freedom, as such, to the conditions that make it valuable. The distinction between political freedom and money freedom is an entirely different distinction from the distinction between freedom itself and the conditions that make it valuable.

We can now reassess Berlin's description of Roosevelt's New Deal (see pp. 171–72 above). We can confidently insist that, when a person's economic security is enhanced, there typically are, *as a result*, fewer "obstacles to possible choices and activities" for him (p. xxxix), and that he therefore typically has more individual liberty, on Berlin's own liberty-equals-no-obstacles-posed-or-left-by-others conception of liberty. Per-

[30]The alert reader will note that these are not freedoms with which the New Deal (see pp. 171–72 above) could plausibly be regarded as a compromise. But that is a *further* décalage in Berlin's position, and not, I am sure, a reason for claiming that my gloss on what he means *here* is incorrect. (Roosevelt, so Berlin surely thought, restricted *property rights*, yet he cannot mean to include just such rights among the "legal rights" with which he identifies "liberty itself" in the text to n. 11 above: that would make nonsense of the (putative) contrast in that text, since being poor just *means* having few property rights.)

There are other important lapses in Berlin's text. Consider, for example, his defense, at pp. liii–liv of the introduction to his *Four Essays*, of publicly provided education. Among its recommendations, he says, is that it satisfies "the need to provide the maximum number of children with opportunities for free choice," and he presumably means to reiterate that desideratum when he speaks, a little later, of "the need to create conditions in which those who lack them will be provided with opportunities to exercise those rights (freedom to choose) which they legally possess, but cannot, without such opportunities, put to use."

Now, I take it that, if you have "opportunities for free choice," you *have* free choice, or you have it effectively, you have it at will: all you need do, in order to have it, is *take* the opportunities in question. So, within the terms of the first quoted excerpt, education provides free choice itself. But that can't be what education provides according to the second excerpt, which implies that poorly educated children do *have* "freedom to choose," but that they lack the opportunity to *exercise* that freedom. (Unless, to stretch things to their limits, 'legally possess' doesn't, here, entail 'possess,' but means 'possess [merely] legally'—but then Berlin would be abandoning the distinction between [truly] *having* liberty and being able to use it.)

haps the individual liberty of already economically secure people was reduced by the New Deal, but, given his own characterization of liberty, Berlin had no right to the conclusion, implied by his talk of "compromise" between liberty and economic security, that individual liberty as such (and not just that of members of certain classes) was reduced.[31]

4. Money provides freedom because it extinguishes interference with access to goods and services: it functions as an entry ticket to them. I shall now fortify, but also qualify, my argument, by comparing and contrasting money with access tickets to goods and services in a moneyless society.

Imagine, then, a society without money, in which, in the first instance, the state owns everything, and in which courses of action available to people, courses they are free to follow without interference, are laid down by the law. The law says what each sort of person, or even each particular person, may and may not do without interference, and each person is endowed with a set of tickets detailing what she is allowed to do. So I may have a ticket which says that I am free to plow and sow this land, and to reap what comes as a result; another one which says that I am free to go to that opera, or to walk across that field, while you have different tickets, with different freedoms inscribed on them. (We could suppose, further, that tickets are tradable, so that I can swap some of my freedoms for some of yours.)

Further uncertainties occur in the "Two Concepts" essay itself. Thus, at pp. 124–25, Berlin appears to conflate human desiderata (such as not starving, being clothed, etc.) that are so urgent that they are needs *greater* than the need for freedom with "conditions for the use of freedom," which are another matter.

[31](1) I do not think the quoted characterization of the New Deal is compatible with Berlin's later acknowledgment, at p. xlvi of *Four Essays*, that "the case for social legislation or planning, for the welfare state and socialism" can be based on considerations of liberty.

(2) It might be thought that Berlin strongly qualifies his denial that poverty represents an unfreedom when he says, at pp. 122–23 of "Two Concepts," that, consistently with the conception of freedom as noninterference, I may indeed "think myself a victim of coercion or slavery," *if* I hold a "theory about the causes of my poverty" according to which it is "due to the fact that other human beings ["with or without the intention of doing so"] have made arrangements whereby I am, whereas others are not, prevented from having enough money with which to pay for [things]." That theory is so weak in its claims as to be, so it seems to me, undeniable, and Berlin himself implies that it is "plausible" (p. 122). Yet Berlin, so one might infer, must deny it to sustain his claim that poverty affects not liberty but only the conditions of its exercise.

The asserted inference is, however, erroneous. The pp. 122–23 passage shows a recognition not that, as I insist, *lack of money*, however it may be explained, represents lack of freedom, but that *lack of access to money* represents lack of freedom, when it has a certain explanation (which, I have just suggested, always is its explanation).

My reading of the pp. 122–23 passage is comprehensively confirmed by a statement which appears at pp. 61–62 of *The First and the Last*: "A poor man . . . is . . . free to rent

Imagine, now, that the structure of the options written on the tickets is more complex than it was above. Now each ticket lays out a disjunction of conjunctions of courses of action that I may perform. That is, I may do *A* and *B* and *C* and *D* OR *B* and *C* and *D* and *E* OR *E* and *F* and *G* and *A*, and so on. If I try to do something not licensed by my ticket or tickets, armed force intervenes.

By hypothesis, these tickets say what a person's freedoms (and, consequently, her unfreedoms) are. But a sum of money is, *in effect*, a highly generalized form of such a ticket. My statement emphasizes "in effect" because money differs from a state ticket in that, as we have seen, it is an *inus* condition of freedom of access to goods, rather than, as the ticket is, both necessary and sufficient for such freedom of access, in all circumstances. The effect of money for a person's freedom, is, nevertheless, in standard circumstances, exactly the same as that of owning the sort of ticket I described. A sum of money is *tantamount* to (≠ is) a license to perform a disjunction of conjunctions of actions, actions like, for example, visiting one's sister in Glasgow, or taking home, and wearing, the sweater on the counter at Selfridge's. (As far as her freedom to go to Glasgow is concerned, the woman who is too poor to take the train is like someone whose tickets in the imagined nonmonetary economy do not have "trip to Glasgow" printed on them). That money's effect is that of a freedom ticket is perhaps more clear when physical money is replaced by credit cards, or by credit accounts that have no compact physical realization. To improve the parallel, suppose that no physical tickets are issued in the state economy, but that people's authorizations with respect to their freedom to use goods are available only on computer screens. It makes no difference to a person's freedoms whether the screen records his ticket collection or how much money he has.

Having drawn this analogy, I now note its limits, and, then, how modest they are.

First, the limits, which reflect the fact, already acknowledged here, that money is an *inus* condition of freedom.

Whereas it is the government that restricts a person's freedom in the moneyless society, it is not, standardly, the government, but the owner of the good to which a person desires access, who, in the first instance, restricts her freedom in the money case. What the government in a money economy does is to enforce the asset-holder's will, *inter alia* when that

---

a room" "in an expensive hotel," "but has not the means of using this freedom. He has not the means, perhaps, because he has been prevented from earning more than he does by a man-made economic system—but that is a deprivation of freedom to earn money, not of freedom to rent the room. This may sound a pedantic distinction, but it is central to discussions of economic versus political freedom."

will is a will to deny access except in return for money. And the strategic role of the asset-holder's will means both that money does not absolutely ensure access (as a state-issued freedom ticket does), and that lack of money does not absolutely ensure lack of access (as lack of a state ticket does). If Selfridge's are, for whatever reason, determined not to sell the sweater that is on display, then an offer of money will not wrest it from them. And if, contrariwise, Selfridge's are minded to give the sweater away, then the government, far from preventing the (possibly penniless) beneficiary of Selfridge's largesse from picking up the sweater *gratis*, will, instead, protect that gift transaction. Money is not always necessary for freedom of access to a good, since a generous seller need not demand it, and it is not always sufficient either, because the seller is not obliged to sell.

Yet the size of the indicated difference between money and state tickets should not be exaggerated. To take its proper measure, let us enter a complexity into the specification of the state ticket society that matches, to a certain required extent, the complexity in monetary economies exposed above.[32]

Imagine, then, that, like money, the state tickets are neither always necessary nor always sufficient to secure goods, because state-appointed asset administrators are free, to some small extent, to grant access to ticketless people and to withhold it from people with tickets: this is an officially recognized perk of office. The administrators, let us further suppose, exercise bias in favor of some citizens and against others to precisely the same extent that private asset-holders do in the money economy. So, in parallel with the complexity in the money society noted above, tickets no longer absolutely ensure access and ticketlessness no longer absolutely ensures nonaccess, in the nonmoney economy. But it remains true that the ticket distribution strongly affects freedom; tickets establish what you are free and not free to do, not, now, to be sure, as we originally supposed, *tout court*, but within the feasible set established by asset administrators' spheres of discretion, and their particular intentions. And the size of those spheres of discretion enables us to say that freedom of access is *largely* established by tickets, in the revised state economy.

Now, private asset-holders have full discretion over their holdings,[33] and asset administrators only a partial one,[34] but that persisting disanalogy makes no difference to the freedoms that others enjoy, under the

[32] Arnold Zuboff suggested the rudiments of the complexity that I introduce here.

[33] From the point of view of nonowners, legal property owners are, in a sense, ununiformed state agents with wide personal discretion.

[34] The state in my story has, of course, the full discretion that Selfridge's have, and its administrators may be compared to fictive Selfridge's sales assistants who (most unusually!) enjoy a comparable discretion. But that completion of the analogy has no bearing here.

stated assumptions. For, in typical real money economies, there is not much disposition either to give things away *gratis* or to withhold things that are (otherwise) on sale from selected moneyed customers,[35] and, in our parallel state case, the discretion afforded to and used by the administrators is, by stipulation, comparably modest in size. But freedom of access is, we saw, largely established by tickets in the modified state economy. And we can say, in proper parallel, that freedom of access to goods is largely established by money in our form of economy.[36] We can therefore say that, in the *normal* case, lack of money carries with it lack of freedom. The prospect of freedom to travel to Glasgow for the woman too poor to buy the ticket is not much enhanced by the possibility that Richard Branson's Virgin Trains might give her a free ride, since the probability of that is negligibly small. And the discrepancy, in general, between money and freedom, is comparably negligible.

5. The feature of capitalism that makes money partly different from state tickets is the separation, in capitalist civilization, between the state and civil society. Freedom of access to goods in a market society is not, indeed, decided by the state, but by asset-holders whose decisions the state supports. But a market society is nevertheless one in which freedom of access to goods is substantially a function of money, even if the multipersonal agency which grants and denies that freedom in a market society is more complexly structured than is its counterpart agency (that is, the state and its administrators) in the ticket society. In both the state ticket society and the money society, (private and/or state) owners decide what I am free to do in respect of goods and services; and owners deciding what I'm free to do in market society is pretty well equivalent to my money deciding that, because of the (systematically)[37] typical dispositions of owners.

Money, and its lack, imply social relations of freedom and unfreedom. Money is, of course, a resource, but it is not a resource like strength or brains. It is, as Karl Marx said, "*social* power in the form of a thing,"[38] but it is not, like a screwdriver or a cigarette lighter, *itself* a thing (mean-

[35] Indeed, as Hillel Steiner has pointed out to me, a too extensive disposition to withhold from selected would-be customers would derogate from money's status as a general medium of exchange: money is *by definition* generally acceptable, and—see the following footnote—it is compulsorily acceptable as *legal tender* in fully formed capitalist systems.

[36] Note that, when private asset-holders are *forbidden* not to sell to whoever has the money to buy what they offer for sale, then money becomes more like a ticket in the first form of ticket economy (the one without administrators' discretion) precisely because there's a certain guarantee of civil rights: you can't, now, discriminate oppressively.

[37] See n. 36 above.

[38] Marx's statement appears in this passage, which I have discussed at pp. 124–25 of my *Karl Marx's Theory of History*: "The less social power the medium of exchange possesses

ing, here, by a "thing," a physical object), for social power is not a thing. If you swap your ten one-pound coins for a ten-pound note, you've got a different thing from what you had before, but the very same money. You've got the same license to travel, to acquire goods and services and so on, the same social entitlement, the same prospects of noninterference that you had before (or nearly the same: the bus conductor who is happy to accept your pound-coin may refuse to change your ten-pound note, and kick you off the bus).

Money is a social power in a sense in which muscles, for example, are not. What you can do with your muscles depends, of course, on social rules and on socially created material structures—such as roads and doors and staircases. But money (as opposed to gold) is not something material, like muscles (and gold), whose practical significance society *affects*, but social in its very essence. Money doesn't even have to be three-dimensionally embodied: it can take the form of entries on a computer (see Section 4 above), and it could, in principle, be less material still. If people all had wonderful memories and were all law-abiding, and information flowed rapidly from person to person, money could take the form of nothing more than common knowledge of people's entitlements.[39] The *raison d'être* of money is to overcome the interference in access to goods that prevails when money is not forthcoming: that is not true of, for example, muscles, even though big ones may provide access to goods when social order breaks down.

That the tickets establish a social structuring of freedom is manifest in the state economy. My claim is that money does so quite as much in the private property economy, albeit less manifestly, since a five-pound note, unlike an equivalent ticket, does not actually have the freedoms that it confers written on it. One purpose of the present lecture is to make it manifest that money confers freedom quite as much as such a ticket does. It is only deficits in knowledge and in cognitive capacity that disable me from knowing what freedoms a five-pound note represents. Minds more powerful than ours could look at such a note and say what disjunction of conjunctions of actions it frees us to perform.

. . . the greater must be the power of the community which binds the individuals together, the patriarchal relation, the community of antiquity, feudalism and the guild system. [In market society] each individual possesses social power in the form of a thing. Rob the thing of this social power and you must give it to persons to exercise over persons" (*The Grundrisse*, pp. 157–58).

[39] I therefore disagree with John Searle's claim (*The Construction of Social Reality*, p. 35) that "money must come in some physical form or other," unless, what I doubt, he was resting it on limitations in human cognitive and/or moral powers. (Note that even if mental states are brain [and, therefore, physical] states, money does not *take the form* of brain states in the fantasy sketched in the sentence to which this footnote is attached.)

Notice that I have not claimed that either economy is more attractive than the other. Many will prefer the private property money economy in which my freedom does not depend so immediately on the state, but on the decisions of other people that the state endorses.[40] But that does not touch the present point, which is that what depends on those decisions in the money economy precisely *is* my freedom.[41]

The message, then, is that the Left's protest against poverty *is*[42] a plea on behalf of freedom, and, more particularly, a protest against the extreme unfreedom of the poor in capitalist society, and in favor of a much more equal distribution of freedom.[43]

6. The arguments and the conclusions of this article are conceptual in character. No normative claim has been defended, or even asserted, although I have allowed myself to deliver certain conceptual claims in a distinctly normative tone of voice.

Some people respond to such work by complaining that, in virtue of its purely conceptual character, it establishes no normative conclusions. Why, then, they ask, is it important?

The answer is that conceptual claims are sometimes key premises in arguments with normative conclusions, and the right-wing movement from (1) through to (5) is a case in point. That important normative argument is defeated when its critical conceptual subconclusion, (3), is shown to be false, as it has been here. And this way of countering normative arguments is often more effective than a properly normative confrontation with them, which so often leads to impasse.

Some who have heard this paper make the correct point that it does not prove that the Right must abandon their political preferences, since

[40] Capitalist economies are often thought superior to state-controlled economies, from the point of view of freedom, *just* in that there is a wider dispersion of property in the former. But, by that token, a market socialist society, with far wider dispersion of property, and, consequently, of the freedom that goes with it, is even better. To be sure, there is much more to be said on both sides of this argument: these are just *prima facie* considerations. But, for balance, I enter the pro-market-socialist anticapitalist point, which deserves to be set beside the wearisomely familiar pro-capitalist anti-state-control point.

[41] It is perhaps curious that, whereas liberals regard distribution through money as liberating, by contrast with distribution through status, or political power, they are nevertheless concerned to deny, as we have seen, that money is a form of freedom.

[42] Contrary to what Berlin says in texts presented at pp. 171 and 179 above.

[43] I believe that H.L.A. Hart was mistaken when he spoke of "the Marxists whose *identification* of poverty with lack of freedom confuses two different evils" ("Are There Any Natural Rights?" p. 77, emphasis in original). A contrast between poverty and lack of freedom follows from stipulative restrictions on the uses of 'freedom' and 'liberty' which Hart introduces in the relevant paragraph, and which nicely suit his perfectly legitimate intellectual purposes. But he had no good reason to apply those restrictions against Marxist uses of the contested terms.

they can always reformulate them without using the language of freedom. That is indeed so, but the Right lose, if my line is sound, not, indeed, the capacity to stick to the policies that they favor, but an *argument* for those policies rooted in the value of freedom. The counterargument that I have provided will not detach hard-core "libertarians" from their political position, *but that is precisely because, despite their rhetoric, they do not care about liberty or freedom as such*.[44] But others, who are not hard-core "libertarians," do care about liberty, and are attracted to the right-wing position because it appears to have liberty on its side. It is those "floating voters," rather than either the committed Left or the committed Right, who represent the constituency whose political opinion is most likely to be affected by this paper.

Let me now offer some more general remarks about the Right's attitude to interference, not, now, in relation to money in particular, but in relation to private property in general.

The Right profess to be hostile to interference, *as such*, but they do not really oppose interference *as such*. They oppose interference with the rights of private property, but they support interference with access by the poor to that same private property, and they consequently cannot defend property rights by invoking the value of freedom, in the sense of noninterference.[45] They cannot, on the basis of a principled aversion to interference, defend private property against the grievance that poverty represents by recourse to the familiar tactic that I have sought to discredit here.

Some readers may be perplexed, and some incensed, by what they may think to be a strange, or even a brazen, assimilation of *illegal* interference with private property (such as trespass) and *legally justified* interference with those who would trespass on it or otherwise violate it. But the immediate point, once again, is not a normative one: nothing is here being said, directly, about the comparative moralities of protecting and violating private property.

Philosophers have construed the words 'freedom,' 'free,' and so forth in two contrasting ways. As some, including the present author, construe them, one may say that *A* is (*pro tanto*) unfree so long as *B* successfully interferes with his action, and, therefore, irrespective of the moral rights enjoyed and lacked by *A* and *B*. On that latter understanding of 'freedom,' it is as clear as noonday that an arresting police officer renders a

[44] I do not doubt that they believe that they care about freedom, but that is because they confuse freedom with self-ownership: see my *Self-Ownership, Freedom, and Equality*, pp. 67–68, and chapter 10.

[45] See n. 24 above. (To be sure, the Right often also oppose other interferences, such as with security of the person, with freedom of speech, and so on, but these optional extras in right-wing thought are outside our present focus.)

trespasser unfree, whether or not the officer is morally justified in doing so. Alternatively, and flying in the face of ordinary language, others construe *B*'s interference with *A* as freedom-reducing only where *A* has the moral right to do what he is doing and/or *B* has no moral right to stop him.[46] But such a rights-laden understanding of freedom, whether or not it is otherwise acceptable,[47] renders impossible a defense of the legitimacy of private property by reference to freedom, since, on the rights-laden view of it, one cannot say what freedom (so much as) *is* until one has decided (on, perforce, grounds other than freedom) whether or not private property is morally legitimate.

Accordingly, neither the rights-laden nor the rights-free understanding of freedom allows private property to be vindicated through a conceptual connection between private property and freedom. More empirically based vindications of private property that make crucial reference to freedom (rights-independently defined) are not therefore excluded. But no one has, in my view, succeeded in presenting such an empirical vindication, which is one reason why the bad conceptual argument that connects private property with freedom is so popular among defenders of the capitalist system.[48]

In effect if not in intention, the argument criticized in the present paper illicitly short-circuits complex empirical questions. It is altogether too swift, and it discredits the defenders of the capitalist market who use it. But its very weakness restricts the size of the victory that its defeat represents for critics of market capitalism, since it is an unlikely supposition that nothing more than what the argument says can be said on behalf of a connection between market capitalism and freedom.

To see where the real discussion must be situated, return to the point made in n. 29, that the airline company withholds freedom from the ticketless aspiring traveler no less than the government does from the passportless aspiring traveler. There is no reason to modify or qualify that judgment, but there is nevertheless a difference between state-originating and business-originating preventions, which a soberly circumstantial as-

[46] Note that the distinction between morally freighted and morally unfreighted conceptions of freedom is not the same distinction as that between legal freedom and effective freedom, which was made at p. 174 above.

[47] I imply that it is not acceptable when I say, above, that it violates ordinary language, but the issue of its acceptability, on that or any other basis, is entirely incidental here: Cf. *Self-Ownership*, chapter 2, section 3e.

[48] There is also an argument, favored by the Right, and articulated by Jan Narveson in his "Libertarianism vs. Marxism," pp. 3ff., according to which the regime of private property may be defended not as *constituting* a realm of freedom but as *resulting* from exercises of freedom in a pre-private-property state of nature. I refute that argument in my "Once More into the Breach of Self-Ownership," which shows, at pp. 60–67, that it fails to consider the unfreedom suffered by nonappropriators of private property.

sessment of capitalism and freedom must observe. And the difference is that when the government grants freedom to travel to *A*, there is no *B* who loses a significant freedom as a result: the distribution of passports is not the distribution of a scarce good. When the government provides a passport, it removes a barrier to one person other than at the cost of erecting one for another.

What holds for the government and the traveler vis-à-vis passports contrasts, thereby, with what holds for the airline company (be it privately owned or not) and the traveler vis-à-vis tickets. Airplane seats being in finite supply, providing a seat to one person means not providing a seat to countless other persons. Or, if everyone is crazy about flying, then providing seats for all means nevertheless denying freedom of access to other goods for them, because of finite overall resources. This does not make it false that the person who cannot afford a ticket lacks a freedom. But it does mean that partisans of freedom cannot propose the abolition of airline tickets in the way that they might propose abolition of passports.

So the real issue, which is illicitly circumvented by the right-wing argument, and as was suggested in the fourth paragraph of Section 2 above, is how freedom is to be distributed where resource finitude makes limitations on freedom unavoidable. The claim that, in the face of resource finitude, market capitalism is optimal for freedom, has not been proved. But the case against that claim is not made by the defeat of the short-circuiting argument that has been refuted here.

Appendix on Jonathan Wolff on Freedom and Liberty

In "Freedom, Liberty, and Property," Jonathan Wolff proposes that both Left and Right overreach themselves in the claims that they lodge regarding freedom and/or liberty. To a first approximation, so he contends, the Left is right about freedom but wrong about liberty, while the Right is right about liberty but wrong about freedom. That is merely to a first approximation, however, since 'freedom' and 'liberty,' in ordinary usage, do not always comply with the partly stipulative definitions of those terms that Wolff offers in pursuit of his claim. For his clarifying purposes, 'freedom' may be understood as 'real possibility,' while 'liberty' may be understood as 'permissibility.' The Left is interested in real possibility, and correctly denies that permissibility delivers it. The Right is interested in permissibility, and correctly denies that it entails real possibility. These denials are logically equivalent, so Left and Right are right about the same thing. But the Left is wrong when it assimilates everything important that can be meant by 'liberty' to its plausible conception of freedom as real possibility. And the Right is wrong when it assimilates everything important that can be meant by 'freedom' to its plausible conception of liberty as permissibility.

I do not accept Wolff's contention that, in common with other philosophers on the left, I neglect conceptual truths about what he calls "liberty." I believe that the conceptual part of Wolff's critique of the Left is multiply flawed. But there is no space to go into that here, and anyway, it isn't the most important question.[49] This question is more important: why should we *care* about (what Wolff calls) *liberty* where it isn't matched by (what Wolff calls) *freedom*? Why might the woman of my example care that she is, as Wolff would say, at liberty to go to Glasgow (simply because the activity of going to Glasgow is not, as such, legally impermissible), when she is not, as Wolff would acknowledge, free to do so (when it is not a "real possibility" for her)?

Wolff states three supposed reasons[50] for my caring about a liberty[51] that I cannot use, a liberty, that is, which I have but which is not accompanied by a corresponding freedom. Most revealingly, however, each reason for caring about such a liberty that Wolff gives is a reason for caring about it *entirely* because of a freedom that is in one way or another associated with it. None is a reason for caring about liberty *other* than because of a freedom that is connected with it, and none is, moreover, a reason for caring about the liberty that *I* have *now*. Each is a reason for caring about liberty entirely because of freedom, but merely not because of the freedom it grants (1) *me* (2) *now*.

Wolff's first reason is that I may "enjoy living in a society of diversity and tolerance, where a wide range of behavior is permitted." But that desirable diversity supervenes only if others *are* able to use the relevant liberty, only, that is, if liberty indeed generates freedom, albeit not for me. In this first reason, I care about a liberty that I lack the freedom to exercise because others who have that liberty *do* have that freedom, and society therefore exhibits a desirable diversity. Given why I am said to care about this liberty, I would care the same about it even if *I* did not have it: I care about *my* liberty only because it is a *sign* that others have it (since everyone has the same liberties, in a society governed by the rule of law) and what's good about that is that some of them will have the corresponding freedom, which is good because a desirable diversity ensues.

Wolff's second reason is that I "may welcome the fact that" "people [I care] about" find certain behavior "permissible and possible." But, once

[49] Those who happen to be interested in my exposition of Wolff's specifically conceptual errors can get it from me on demand.

[50] [These three reasons are stated on p. 356 of "Freedom, Liberty, and Property."—Ed.]

[51] Across the course of this Appendix, I use 'liberty' and 'freedom' as Wolff defines those terms.

again, the value I am glad they enjoy is the freedom that, in their case (though not in mine), the liberty gives them. In Wolff's second reason, then, even more directly than in his first, I care about a liberty-without-freedom that I have because others also have that liberty and *they* enjoy an associated freedom (whatever further good consequences, such as diversity, this may or may not have). And, once again, I would care the same about this liberty even if *I* did not have it.

Finally, Wolff says, I may value my freedomless liberty even if I cannot at present use it, because I may come to be able to use it. But that is no reason for valuing my liberty *now*: it is a reason for valuing it later, on the assumption that it will persist. And, as before, and, therefore, with respect to all three of Wolff's reasons, liberty matters here because of freedom. In Wolff's third reason, I care about my liberty now, despite not having a corresponding freedom now, because I may want—and have—a corresponding freedom later. But then I care about *present* liberty only because it is a *sign* of (likely) future liberty (just as, in the other two cases, I care about *my* liberty only because it is a sign that relevant others have the *same* liberty). I care nothing, so far as this goes, about present liberty as such. And I care about the indicated future liberty solely because I may hope that it will be associated with a future freedom.

So Wolff's reasons for caring about a liberty that *I* cannot (now) use are, none of them, reasons for caring about liberty in the absence of freedom. In all three cases, I care about liberty *because* of freedom. On Wolff's own showing, liberty turns out to matter wholly because of the freedoms to which, in particular circumstances, it leads.

I believe, however, that Wolffian liberty does have an independent importance, which has nothing *directly* to do with Wolffian, or any other, freedom, and nothing to do with what we should *naturally* (as opposed to Wolffianly) say we are *at* liberty to do.[52] Wolffian liberty matters, in my view, apart from its promise of Wolffian freedom, in that it is an *insult to the status of persons* when certain acts are forbidden to them, whether or not the permissibility of those acts would generate a corresponding freedom for those persons.[53] Thus, for example, suppose that I have, and will continue to have, no desire to travel to Australia, and suppose, further, that I lack and always will lack the money to do so. I would nevertheless consider it an insult if I were forbidden by a state to travel to Australia (whether it be by Canada or by Australia—though the insults might be of different significance and/or weight in the two cases). Accordingly, my Wolffian liberty to travel to Australia matters to me

[52] We naturally say, "the escaped convicts are still at liberty": that contradicts Wolff's stipulations.

[53] Cf. Pogge, *World Poverty and Human Rights*, p. 59. [Cohen added this reference after this paper was published online in 2001 in the *Revista Argentina de Teoria Juridica*.—Ed.]

independently of whether or not I am Wolffianly free to do so. If I were free to do so, through, for example, undetectable passport fraud, I might nevertheless regret that what I was thereby free to do was something that I was not (officially) at liberty to do. ("Officially" needs to be added because of the discrepancy between Wolff's definition of 'liberty' and its use in ordinary discourse. Someone might say: despite the state prohibition, you are at liberty to travel to Australia, since I can forge a visa for you).

So the *real* reason for caring about liberty when no freedom goes with it is that lack of liberty then (still) means an insult to my dignity, a diminution of my status. But that has *nothing* to do with caring about freedom, as such. (It has to do, instead, with caring about who presumes to restrict my freedom, and why they seek to do so.)

So why is it worse for the state to forbid me access to, say, Glasgow, than for the railway company to do so? Because the former involves a judgment on my status, and the latter doesn't. That is why state-legislated impermissibility matters *distinctively* to me, whether or not it removes my freedom. When the state forbids me to do something that it should forbid no one to do, it seeks to make me unfree in a respect in which no one need be unfree. And it thereby insults my status, in a way that a business that will not give its wares to me *gratis* does not.[54]

[54] For comments on earlier drafts of "Freedom and Money," I thank Talia Bettcher, Allen Buchanan, Myles Burnyeat, Ian Carter, Paula Casal, Emiliano Catán, Bill Child, Ronald Dworkin, Eyjolfur Emilsson, David Estlund, Cécile Fabre, Harry Frankfurt, John Gardner, Olav Gjelsvik, Alvin Goldman, Keith Graham, Henry Hardy, Natalie Jacottet, Mark Johnston, Jeroen Knijff, Matthew Kramer, David Lewis, Eduardo Lopez, Stephen Menn, David Miller, Thomas Nagel, Bertell Ollman, Michael Otsuka, Derek Parfit, Peter Rosner, Michael Rustin, Horacio Spector, Arvi Sreenivasan, Hillel Steiner, Adam Swift, Larry Temkin, Peter Vallentyne, Frank Vandenbroucke, and Jo Wolff, and especially Arnold Zuboff, who rescued me at a number of critical points. A precursor of this article was delivered as the first Isaiah Berlin Memorial Lecture in May 1998 in Haifa. I benefited from searching criticisms by the audience on that occasion.

TWO ADDENDA TO "FREEDOM AND MONEY"

1. Freedom and Ability

a. I here take up the issue suspended in the course of "Freedom and Money," that of the relationship between freedom and ability, or, equivalently, the question whether the first premise of the right-wing argument is true. It is customary for the Left to deny that premise, but the Left overestimates the significance of doing so. The Left says: since the Right cherish freedom, and, contrary to what they say, inability *is* a form of lack of freedom, the Right cannot dispute the Left view that inability requires attention as much as (other forms of) freedom do.

The reason why, so I say, this move overestimates the significance of affirming that ability is required for freedom is that the Right need not resist it. They can accept that conceptualization: they can give up premise (1) and insist that the freedom that matters *politically* is lack of interference by other people. That is not an *ad hoc* move, since there is an important difference between freedom that is secured by removal of interference by others and freedom, if such it be, that is secured by assistance to the unable. Preventing people from preventing others from doing things carries a stronger intuitive license than forcing people to assist others. By contrast, my demonstration that the Right perforce endorses interference, in endorsing a money civilization, is less readily set aside.

The question is nevertheless of some conceptual interest, and I therefore address it in this Addendum.

Consider then, once again, the conceptual movement of the right-wing argument:

(1) Freedom is compromised by (liability) to interference, but not by lack of means.
(2) To lack money is to suffer not (liability to) interference, but lack of means.
∴ (3) Poverty (lack of money) does not carry with it lack of freedom.

In "Freedom and Money" I disprove, or so I believe, the second premise of that argument, by showing that to lack money *is* to be subject to widespread interference. But I do not (expressly) challenge the first premise of the argument in that paper, and I now proceed to do so.

We can safely suppose,[55] here, that all candidates for the office of compromisers of freedom may be reduced to some form of interference or some form of lack of means. On that assumption, proposition (1) is equivalent to the quartet of claims presented at (6) through (9) below, and (6) and (7), and (8) and (9), are, respectively, equivalent to each other, on the stated safe supposition (together with the even safer one that there is such a thing as lack of freedom!):

(6) Interference is sufficient for unfreedom.
(7) Lack of means is unnecessary for unfreedom.
(8) Interference is necessary for unfreedom.
(9) Lack of means is insufficient for unfreedom.

In Section *b* I show that (7), and, therefore, (6), are false. In Section *c* I target, and refute, the (8)/(9) pair, but the latter result, so it will be seen, is, conceptually speaking, less interesting, and less important, ideologically and politically, than the former.

b. In my treatment of (7), I show, first, that, at least in certain cases, lack of means is indeed necessary for unfreedom. I then generalize the result, to show that lack of means is always necessary for unfreedom.

Now money clearly is a means: if money isn't a means, what *is*? Yet, as we have seen, lack of money ensures lack of freedom in almost all cases[56] in which something is up for sale. In almost all such cases, the seller's disposition to interfere, with state backing, against access to the relevant good or service, is extinguished (only) by the offer of money. In such cases, then, lack of money is necessary for unfreedom, because money removes (prospective) interference.

Now, it might be thought that money represents a counterexample to (7) because, although it is a paradigm case of a means, it is, as I argued in Section 5 of "Freedom and Money," a very different kind of means from material means like screwdrivers or cigarette lighters: it is not a material but a social means. Its very *raison d'être*, unlike theirs, is to remove interference.[57]

Money is indeed very special. Its deeply social character distinguishes it from means like muscles, or good looks, or a fine brain. But material

[55] *Safely* suppose: the supposition may be, strictly speaking, false, for subtle and/or complicated reasons, but that would not, I believe, affect the substance of what follows.

[56] Lack of money is, more precisely, an *inus* condition of lack of freedom: see pp. 177–78 of this chapter.

[57] That is why money serves as a counterexample both to (1) and to (2): it is a means whose point is to remove interference. It therefore destroys the lack-of-means/presence-of-interference contrast: when *this* means is lacking, interference is present. Both (1) and (2) are false, because they both turn on a contrast that the case of money proves to be false.

and other asocial means also provide counterexamples to (6) and (7). Reflection on those means shows that *interference is never sufficient for unfreedom because lack of means is always necessary for it.*

That is so because, absolutely generally, *an interference restricts my freedom to do x only if I lack the means to overcome that interference, and, therefore, the ability to do x despite that interference.*[58] If I have that ability, if I am able to overcome the interference, then I am free to do *A* even in the face of the interference. So interference is insufficient for lack of freedom. An appropriate inability is also required.[59]

For an illustration of this point, consider a convict who is not free to leave a prison cell. Notice that he is unfree because he is not strong enough, and is therefore unable, to bend the bars with which interfering agents of the law have surrounded him. His inability to do that is a necessary condition of his unfreedom: if his ability were to grow, miraculously, to a sufficient extent, then he would, as a result, be free to leave.

That illustration of the falsehood of (6) and (7) violates the assumption imposed on the proceedings in "Freedom and Money" (see p. 174), to wit, that society is fully law-abiding, since *either* a prisoner who broke the bars of his cell would be engaged in illegal activity *or* his imprisonment would have itself been illegal. But there are counterexamples to (6) and (7) which respect the "Freedom and Money" assumption: I began with a case that violates the assumption merely because of its special vividness.

Consider, then, two women with whom the law interferes because it imposes on each of them an injunction against entering a certain territory. Our "Freedom and Money" assumption being back in force, neither can simply flout the injunction and escape punishment. But, so we may suppose, one of them is able, by virtue of money or kinship or charm, to retain a lawyer who can successfully fight the injunction, while the other cannot do so. The interference in question therefore succeeds in limiting the freedom of only one of these women, precisely because the other enjoys the (perfectly legal) ability to overcome it.

[58] I owe this pregnant point to Arnold Zuboff.

[59] (1) It has been suggested to me that, although *A*'s *interference* may not suffice to remove *B*'s freedom, *A*'s *constraint* suffices to do so. But, if that is true, it is true only because *A*'s constraint entails *B*'s inability to nullify whatever action(s) of *A* constitute that constraint. The substantial point, which is that *A* cannot remove *B*'s freedom unless *B* has a relevant inability, stands.

(2) It might be charged that there is an inconsistency between my earlier claim that the poor are unfree because they are subject to interference and my present claim that interference does not suffice for unfreedom. But the charge is easy to deflect. The claim that the poor are unfree because they are subject to interference stands because they lack the ability required to overcome the interference they face, when, as I legitimately assumed (see p. 174 of this chapter), the law of the land is successfully enforced.

It follows from the foregoing considerations that the Left's reply to Berlin's distinction between freedom and ability should be not, as the Left sometimes say, that ability is as important as freedom or, as they also sometimes say, that Berlin's conception of freedom is too narrow, and that we need to cobble up a wider conception of freedom but, rather, that inability is integral to what Berlin himself would regard as paradigm cases of lack of freedom. For a necessary condition of *successful* (i.e., freedom-removing) interference[60] is that its victim lacks the ability to overcome the interference. You are free to do a given thing when you are interfered with, as long as you are able to overcome that interference.

c. I do not see how anyone can deny the conclusion that, in cases of interference, inability helps to generate unfreedom, and that (6) and (7) are, therefore, false. But the Right, and Berlin and Rawls, might nevertheless insist that inability betokens no unfreedom where there is no interference in the offing. They might say that you are not unfree to walk merely because your legs are broken, where no one would stop you from walking if they were not broken. They might say that interference, if not, indeed, sufficient for unfreedom, remains necessary for it: the refutation of (6)/(7) leaves (8)/(9) intact.

But they can say that only by riding roughshod over what appear to me to be banal truths. For we readily and unproblematically say: now he's out of his cast, he's once again free to take a walk in the park. Or consider a car, which, it will be agreed, is a means of transport, and, unlike a sum of money or an entitlement to travel, a physical means at that. Who could deny, other than someone in the grip of an ill-considered philosophical theory, that having a car at my disposal that I know how to drive enhances my freedom to get around London, and that lacking one, or lacking the ability to drive one, diminishes it? (When mortal Billy Watson of the Marvel Comics of my childhood shouted "Shazam," and thereby turned himself into superpowered Captain Marvel, he had at his immediate disposal a vast number of freedoms.) Lack of ability is, accordingly, sufficient for unfreedom:[61] when I am *disabled* from driving,

[60] Note that unsuccessful interference is not an attempt to interfere that fails to constitute an interference, but an attempt to interfere that fails of its object, which is, typically, to prevent someone from doing something (we can ignore, here, untypical cases, where the point of interference is not to prevent, but, for example, to annoy, or to ruffle). If I try to block your path, but don't actually get in your way, then, indeed, I try to interfere and fail to interfere. But if I do get in your way, and you push me aside, then I undoubtedly interfere, unsuccessfully.

[61] I thereby abandon a contrast between inability and lack of freedom that I have affirmed elsewhere: see my *History, Labour, and Freedom*, p. 242; "Capitalism, Freedom,

because I come to lose a *means* (a car, or sound legs) needed to perform that action, I lose a freedom.

Many think that losing a means means losing a freedom only if a *person* causes the deprivation of that means. If you take away the key to my car, I am deprived of a freedom, but, if I just *lose* my key, I do not, on this view, lose a freedom. So even if interference is not sufficient for unfreedom, it remains necessary: (8) and (9) are true. But the distinction mooted here is *wildly* implausible. If you despair of finding your key you won't refrain from saying that you're no longer free to drive it unless and until you've discovered that the key was stolen or purloined.

So the contrast between means and ability, in general, on the one hand, and freedom on the other, is a right-wing myth (even though its most salient proponent was the centrist Isaiah Berlin). Whether or not the Left sometimes strain against ordinary language (see pp. 189–90 of this chapter), the Right, and those who accede to their insistences, twist the ordinary meanings of words, in this domain.

(It has been objected that the usages that I invoke above in refutation of (8) and (9) are "loose," and that, "strictly speaking," lack of a car [for example] diminishes ability only, and not also freedom. But I do not know what criterion of "loose usage" condemns as "loose" so widespread a use of 'free,' 'freedom,' etc.

Of course, even if the objection is correct, and disability means no unfreedom in the absence of human intervention, my principal thesis, that poverty restricts freedom, stands: my argument for that thesis in "Freedom and Money" does not challenge (8) and (9), and I made clear at the outset of this Addendum that the truth or falsehood of premise (1) [which is equivalent to the conjunction of (6) through (9)] is in any case a matter of little political or ideological consequence.)

2. More on Goods, Services, and Interference[62]

Here is an objection to my claim that lack of money betokens liability to interference with access to goods and services. The examples that I use in illustration of my claim, to wit, the train ride and the Selfridge's sweater, are, respectively, a service and a good which are, as it were, there for the

---

and the Proletariat," in David Miller, ed., *Liberty*, p. 175 [p. 157 of Chapter 7 of this volume—Ed.]. [See also p. 223 of "Illusions about Private Property and Freedom," where Cohen writes: "I may be unable to do something not because I am unfree to, but because I lack the relevant capacity. Thus I am no doubt free to swim across the English Channel, but I am nevertheless unable to."—Ed.]

[62] I thank Michèle Cohen and David Lewis for suggestions regarding the topic of this second Addendum.

taking (or there for the nontaking, if interference will supervene). But other goods and services do not so much as *exist* if money is not given or promised for them: an example of such a good is a garment, to be made to my measurements, which I order by mail; an example of such a service is my house being painted by a decorator. Where, it may be asked, does interference obtain for the moneyless in these cases? If, being moneyless, I ask the painter to paint my house, I don't, indeed, get my house painted, but, so it seems, no interference obtains: the painter simply refuses to paint it.[63]

To take the measure of this objection, let us return to the state ticket society. If, in that society, I lack a ticket that provides access to *n* hours of painter *P*'s labor, then I am not free to avail myself of that labor. And, so I would maintain, resting my case on the ticket analogy, it is equally true that, if I lack the right amount of money, then I am not free to avail myself of the painter's labor in a market society.

But this might just show that the ticket analogy argument is independent of, and more reliable than, the "interference" argument. Perhaps, by virtue of the ticket argument, the claim that money confers freedom (itself) stands, but the unfreedom that lack of money therefore betokens does not in all cases manifest itself as a liability to interference.

Well, notwithstanding whatever strength should be conceded to the ticket analogy argument, am I *interfered with* if, being moneyless, I wish to avail myself of the painter's labor? Am I in any sense *prevented*[64] from availing myself of it? If I ask him for his labor, does his will, conveyed by his negative answer, count as preventing me from availing myself of it? Not unless we abrogate the distinction between hindering someone and not helping her, and I have no wish to do that. But we *can* discern prospective interferences and absences thereof, in this context, ones that distinguish the poor from the rich: if I try to get the unpaid painter to paint, by nagging him, and so forth, he can take out an injunction against me, and that interference won't obtain in the case of a paid painter; if I promise to pay on receipt of the garment I ordered, and don't, then, once again, interference will supervene.

[63] If painters were constantly in painting motion, and engaging them involved transporting them to the relevant wall, then they would be relevantly like train rides and sweaters on counters: but painters aren't like that.

It might be thought that conditions less extreme than nonexistence, such as great distance, produce counterexamples to similar effect. Think, for example, of goods in faraway warehouses. Moneyed people do not access those goods by walking to them, so they do not get them by virtue of the absence of an interference to their activity that the poor would face. But we must also consider relevant noninterferences with clerks, truck drivers, and so on who act, in effect, on the moneyed person's behalf.

[64] See n. 5 above on prevention.

Someone might say: you are giving too much shrift to the present objection. It could have been answered more briefly, by reference to the "*inus* condition" discussion at the end of Section 2 of "Freedom and Money": the purpose of a knife is to cut, even if it turns out to cut fewer things than might originally have been supposed. But it might also be thought, in contradiction of the *inus* recourse, that, *if* money confers freedom, then it does so no differently in the painter case from how it does in the railway ride case. So it remains a desideratum to produce a *general* truth, and perhaps the right general truth is this: where the good or service exists, money removes the interference with access to it, and, where it does not exist, money both induces its creation *and* removes interference with access to it. (The final conjunct in that statement is justified by considerations adduced at the end of the immediately preceding paragraph.)

PART THREE

Ideal Theory and Political Practice

Chapter Nine

MIND THE GAP

THOMAS NAGEL ARGUES, in *Equality and Partiality*, that the task of political philosophy is to reconcile the opposed deliverances of two standpoints. In the personal point of view, everything gets its value from my distinctive interests, relationships, and commitments. But I can also look at things impersonally, and then I realize that the interests and projects of others are just as important as mine are, that my life is no more important than anyone else's is.

Since we occupy both the personal and the impersonal standpoints, "we are simultaneously partial to ourselves, impartial among everyone, and respectful of everyone else's partiality." We see both that "1. everyone's life is equally important," and that "2. everyone has his own life to live." 2. means that organizing people's lives entirely in order to suit the egalitarian dictate of 1. is inadmissible. But 1. "implies some limit to the license given by" 2. to live a life unencumbered by social obligation.

A political system is legitimate if—and only if—it honors both truths. It is then *unanimously acceptable*, which is not to say that everyone would in fact accept it, but that no one could *reasonably reject* it: equivalently, a system enjoys legitimacy if and only if whoever rejects it does so unreasonably. And, corresponding to the two numbered truths, there are two grounds of reasonable rejection: "What makes it reasonable for someone to reject a system, and therefore makes it illegitimate, is either that it leaves him too badly-off by comparison with others (which corresponds to a failure with respect to impartiality), or that it demands too much of him by way of sacrifice of his interests or commitments by comparison with some feasible alternatives (which corresponds to failure with respect to reasonable partiality)."

And so, in a general way, we know what conditions a legitimate society must meet, but Nagel is confident that, in our current state of understanding, we do not know how to satisfy them together. We do not know how to do "justice to the equal importance of all persons, without

Reprinted in part from "Mind the Gap," *London Review of Books*, Vol. 14, No. 9, May 14, 1992, pp. 15–17. By kind permission of the *London Review of Books*.

Editor's note: This is an abridged version of a review of Nagel's *Equality and Partiality*.

making unacceptable demands on individuals"; and, what is worse, such justice may be inherently inconceivable, for "the two conditions pull in contrary directions," and an acceptable compromise between them might not be possible, even in theory.

The problem is not (in the first instance) that actual systems fail to realize an ideal but that "we do not *possess* an acceptable political ideal" (my emphasis), and there might actually be none. And whether or not an ideal solution is possible in situations different from our own, no policy for modern society that sufficiently respects both standpoints can now be designed, and even the inadequate best that we could design would have no chance of being realized. Nagel's gloomy "conclusion" is "that a strongly egalitarian society [one that is egalitarian enough to satisfy condition 1.] populated by reasonably normal people is difficult to imagine and in any case psychologically and politically out of reach."

Our present situation is such that "any standards of individual conduct which try to accommodate both [personal and impartial] reasons will be either too demanding in terms of the first or not demanding enough in terms of the second." In our unequal world the rich should sacrifice to help the poor. But how much should they give up? There is a level of sacrifice so modest that the rich could not reasonably refuse it, and a level so high that the poor could not reasonably demand it. If those levels were adjacent, then a coherent ideal could be stated; and, if they were not adjacent but near one another, then something resembling an ideal could be aimed at. In fact, however, there is between the two thresholds of reasonableness a substantial "gap, within which fall all those levels of sacrifice which the poor would have sufficient reason to impose if they could and which the rich have sufficient reason to resist if they can." Note that, by 'sufficient reason,' Nagel means, not 'self-interested reason,' but 'good reason,' or 'justification': the rich plainly have a self-interested reason to resist what he thinks they could not reasonably (that is, with good reason) resist and the poor a self-interested reason to demand what he thinks they could not reasonably demand.

The diachronic implication of the impasse is that "the poor can refuse to accept a policy of gradual change and the rich can refuse to accept a policy of revolutionary change, and neither of them is being unreasonable in this. The difference for each of the parties between the alternatives is just too great." Three places where this gap occurs are mentioned: in Mexico, in India, and in the world as a whole. Obviously, many more nation-states might have been singled out.

I shall argue that, in this description of the current position, Nagel defers more than he should to the exigencies of the status quo. But notice that he is not offering a simple defense of it. For he is clear that the rich could not reasonably reject an amount of transfer which is much greater than their political spokespersons now envisage. And, even with that much transfer continually occurring, while the rich could reasonably refuse more, the poor, so Nagel also says, could reasonably fight for more: no one could blame them for swarming toward the Western shores, even though no one could blame the rich for putting them back in their boats once they got there.

Nagel's distinction between the impersonal and personal standpoints is profound and unavoidable. He has given us a novel and intriguing apparatus, but many of the judgments he uses it to frame are highly contestable, and some strike me as just dogmatic. Much of the trouble lies in Nagel's overconfident use of the idea of what no one could reasonably reject. For the notion of reasonableness is fuzzy, not, to be sure, through and through, but at the edges, and some way in. When we try to say what it would be unreasonable not to accept, the question can appear nebulous, and there is a temptation to get a handle on it by grasping and sticking to customary judgment ("custom" being the name Nagel himself suggests for one of the forces that spoil the innocence of intuition). For my part, I find Nagel's intuitive renderings of unreasonable too easy to associate with a particular historical and social emplacement to grant them authority as markers for philosophy.

It is undoubtedly true "that the freedom to arrange one's own personal and family life . . . has an importance for almost every individual that can hardly be exaggerated." Yet, while Nagel acknowledges that such freedom must be restricted in deference to the legitimate demands of others, he is also certain with respect to some controversial uses of it that it would be wrong to criticize them, and his confidence puzzles me.

Consider, for example, the "modern liberals" who buy exclusive education for their children while claiming to support state promotion of equality of opportunity. Nagel insists, plausibly enough, that a liberal is not a hypocrite merely because she favors her own child in her private choices: but where does he get his certainty about how far such favor can go before a charge of hypocrisy begins to stick? Think of the liberals who buy superior education not to protect their children from a blackboard jungle but to give them what Nagel calls a "competitive edge." How can he be so sure that "scorn" for their particular double act is "quite unwarranted, for it is simply another example of the partition of motives which pervades morality"? Criticizing their private choice just because it is self- or family-serving is indeed misguided, but what about criticizing it because it is insufficiently sensitive to the requirement of "ensuring everyone a fair start in life"? Does Nagel think that well-to-do progressive people who insist on sending their children to state schools because they don't believe in giving them a "competitive edge" display a "pathological inhibition of natural family sentiment"?[1]

Pathology is out of bounds since, as we saw, the problem is how to legislate for "reasonably normal people," a set that includes "almost every individual." But it is not fussy, in the present context, to ask what kind of qualification the words 'reasonably normal' impose here. If the truth of the sentence ("a strongly egalitarian society populated by *reasonably normal* people is difficult to imagine") in which the phrase occurs depends on its presence, then, with suitably abnormal people, an egalitarian society would be possible. So who is abnormal? Mother Teresa? Dedicated Oxfam activists? Do such people lack the personal point of view? Do they not feel their *own* hunger with special urgency, dote on their *own* hopes, care especially about their *own* parents and children? Of course they do, and, far from being universally considered to be freaks, they are widely regarded as models that put the rest of us to shame. A suspicion arises that the metaphysical distinction between subjective and objective standpoints lacks the fertility for moral philosophy that Nagel expects to find in it. Even Mother Teresa is not *metaphysically* abnormal, and when Nagel exercises his intuition on the question of how much right we have to pursue our own interests in a miserable world he may be using an instrument unfitted to the issue at hand. He would think it a parochial mistake to regard bat sonar as a not quite genuine form of sensory consciousness. Maybe it is a partly similar mistake to rule exceptional forms of motivational consciousness out of court in a philosophical discussion of ideal societies.

Whether or not such skepticism about Nagel's approach to political philosophy is finally right, I shall now argue that various of his statements about reasonable rejection generate an inconsistency at a politically sensitive point.

Nagel is aware that his endorsement of rich people's opposition to radical redistribution "may seem to authorize pure selfishness," but, he says, "that is too harsh a word for resistance to a radical drop in the standard of living of oneself and one's family." That word might be too harsh, but Nagel's verdict that the rich need accept only a moderate (that is, nonradical) drop in their wealth is too soft. Officially, and, in my view, rightly, he depreciates the moral weight of the status quo, but the status quo seems, in the end, to preponderate in his judgment.

[1] Persons to Nagel's right will wonder about other certainties he displays: that a social democratic solution which ensures a high basic minimum but also allows large inequalities is an inadequate "response to the impartial attitude which is the first manifestation of the impersonal standpoint," and that swingeing inheritance and gift taxes do not violate its second "manifestation," which respects the individual's desire to benefit his family.

The restriction Nagel lays down on the role of the status quo in political morality is related to his affirmation of a principle of negative responsibility at the societal level: "we are responsible, through the institutions which require our support, for the things they could have prevented as well as for the things they actively cause." Accordingly, the status quo is just one system among others, the one that happens to have been chosen up to now, and, in the problem of social choice, "all systems of allocation" are "prima facie equally eligible." It is a crucial consequence of this doctrine that, when we ask how much sacrifice people could reasonably reject, we measure "by comparison with possible alternatives rather than by comparison with the status quo." There is no "moral bias in favor of the status quo, except insofar as losing what one has is *somewhat* more reasonable to reject than not getting what one doesn't have. I don't believe that that should be a large element in the calculation" (my emphasis).

In fact, however, the status quo plays a major role in Nagel's assessment of what the rich could reasonably reject. The reasonable demands of the poor mean a "radical *drop*" in the wealth of the rich, and it is only because they are asked to give up what they *have*, and not merely what they *would* have in an allocation that enjoys no particular salience within the set of possible allocations, that the sacrifice facing the rich can seem so tough, and that it can therefore seem reasonable for them to resist it. To see this, suppose that the status quo happened to be an equality in which everyone had 10, and in a possible alternative most would have 5 (which is just about a decent minimum) and some would have 20 (a ratio of wealth to poverty dwarfed by what prevails in the real world). Would we not regard rejection of the equal status quo by those who, like everybody else, have 10, but who would get the 20 while the others go down to 5, as far less reasonable than rejection, by those who have long since actually had 20, of a shift from a 20/5 status quo to a condition where everyone has 10? I am certain that we would, and that, notwithstanding his declaration to the contrary, Nagel's estimate of the size of the gap between the reasonable claims depends, inappropriately, on how hard it is to give up what one has.

If "the main thing is the identification of the feasible alternatives, and the size of the difference a choice among them would make for *each* of the parties," if we cover up the caption saying "status quo" when we train our reasonableness intuitions on the set of alternatives, we will not, when we return to reality, excuse as much resistance of transfer to the poor as Nagel does. For it is much harder to give up what one has than to forgo what one could get, and it is only if our judgment of what constitutes a just distribution wrongly tracks that fact, so that we then regard it as more than "*somewhat* more reasonable" to cling to what one has, that we can agree with Nagel about the rich. But that is an inappropriate basis for agreement, since it allows the status quo to have more influence on our judgment than Nagel (rightly) says it should when he is speaking at the level of principle.

If the status quo lacks moral significance, then we cannot say what Nagel does about the rich who would refuse drastic change, but it does not follow that we must condemn them in Savonarolic terms. We cannot say that, since their resistance to a large drop in their wealth is justifiable, radical redistribution is legitimate, but we can say that, even if it is legitimate, they are not monstrous to be unwilling to give up the riches around which they have built their lives.

I believe that Nagel has misinterpreted a forgivable resistance to a just claim as a reasonable rejection that defeats a would-be claim of justice. In some life-situations that call for self-sacrifice, either you are a moral hero or you are unjust: being averagely just is not an option. That might be the situation of the rich.

Speaking of India, Mexico, and the world as a whole, Nagel says that "inequality can be so extreme that it makes a legitimate solution unattainable, except possibly over a long period by gradual stages each of which lacks legitimacy, or (improbably) over a shorter period by a cataclysmic revolution which also lacks legitimacy." Here inequality has to be the inequality of the status quo, and it is remarkable that Nagel gives Mexico and India as instances, since their inequalities are, by his standards, spectacularly unjust, and there is little reason to think that those who are on top in India and Mexico would occupy even the same ordinal position in the smaller inequalities that would be produced within the framework of legitimate (by Nagel's lights) institutions. Accordingly, it is impossible to see how Nagel's endorsement of the resistance to revolution of the Mexican or Indian rich draws on anything beyond the thought that it is painful to lose what one has. (This is not to deny that there might be reasons other than ones of justice to oppose revolution, of the sort that are hinted at in Nagel's parenthetical "improbably"—which suggests that revolutions fail to achieve their aims—but those are reasons for anyone to be against it: they have nothing to do with the apparatus of reasonable rejection.)

It must be because he thinks that inequality is by pertinent measures larger in the poorer countries that Nagel refers to Mexico and India, and not the United States or Great Britain. The other outsize inequality that he mentions is the wealth difference between rich and poor nation-states. This inequality is, in Nagel's technical sense, a "gaping" one, for he says that "at least on the plausible assumption" that Western wealth is causally unconnected with Southern poverty, "the degree of sacrifice by the rich that it would be reasonable for the poor countries to insist on in some hypothetical collective arrangement is one that it would not be unreasonable for the rich to refuse." Now, Nagel-style negative responsibility operates through "common social institutions," and it would therefore appear to lack worldwide application, since, arguably, global inequality did not develop under common global institutions, and it certainly did not do so if Nagel's "plausible assumption" is correct. This should mean that a stance of refusal by the rich countries becomes reasonable at relatively low levels of sacrifice, if, indeed, there is any sacrifice at all called for by Nagelian justice at the global level. Nagel makes it plain that he favors a lot of immediate ameliorative sacrifice, but I do not know how it would be justified on his principles and factual assumptions.

I have focused on the issue of distributive justice, which is the central topic in Nagel's book, and the one that exercised me politically. This has left no space to report on Nagel's refined discussions of inequality in cultural goods, the foundations of rights, and the grounds of toleration, all of which are characteristically original and compelling.

That is my review of the text of *Equality and Partiality*. But I would also like to review part of its blurb, the bit that says: "Egalitarian communism has clearly failed." It is no accident that both the subject and the predicate of that sentence are ambiguous. Exactly what has failed, and what does it mean to say that it has failed?

If "egalitarian communism" is just a name for the Soviet experiment, then it has failed, in every sense. But one may not infer, as the ambiguities invite us to do, that the social form, egalitarian communism as such, cannot succeed.

The other ambiguity is in the meaning of failure. And in this connection I want to protest against the mix of political malevolence and intellectual fatuity within the horde of *clercs* who show triumphant confidence that no one with any sense can *still* be called a socialist.

Before Mikhail Gorbachev took office in 1985, there was already broad agreement among socialists and antisocialists who read and wrote for papers like this one [i.e., the *London Review of Books*—Ed.] that the Soviet Union had utterly failed to achieve a classless, or even a decent, society. And there was a serious and honorable disagreement about the reasons for that failure, with the Right referring it to the very nature of the social form that the Bolsheviks had set out to realize and the Left assigning failure to some combination of adverse circumstance and human error. Nothing that has happened since 1985 settles that important question. What has happened is that Soviet civilization has failed in a further sense, beyond failing to achieve its objectives, in the further sense, that is, that it has collapsed, disappeared from the scene. Yet the Right, and not only the Right, infers that the debate about why it had failed in the first sense (that is, to achieve a classless society) should now be concluded, in favor of the old right-wing answer. It is understandable that people should want to make that inference, since it would be a relief not to have to think about the matter any more, but the inference remains unjustified. "Egalitarian communism has clearly failed" is a cheating shortcut around a crucial question of our age. The premise that the would-be egalitarian society has collapsed is true, but uncontroversial. The interest of the sentence lies in its cheap insinuation that we now know that an egalitarian society is unachievable. This new conclusion is cheap because it is bought at no extra cost of evidence or argument.

Nagel's own reflection on the matter of the Soviet collapse is decently nuanced (see page 28). If you favor vigorous crudity in political thought, read something else.

Chapter Ten

BACK TO SOCIALIST BASICS

On November 24, 1993, a meeting of Left intellectuals occurred in London, under the auspices of the Institute for Public Policy Research (IPPR), which is a Labour-leaning think tank. A short document was circulated in advance of the said meeting, to clarify its purpose. Among other things, the document declared that the task of the IPPR was "to do what the Right did in the seventies, namely to break through the prevailing parameters of debate and offer a new perspective on contemporary British politics." The explanatory document also said that "our concern is not to engage in a philosophical debate about foundations of socialism."

If this meant that those foundations were not the appropriate thing to talk about at the November 24 meeting, then that might have been right: not everything has to be discussed at every meeting. But if what was meant was that discussion of philosophical foundations is not what the Left now needs, then I disagree, and, if that indeed is what was meant, then I think it curious that the breakthrough by the Right should have been invoked as an achievement for the Left to emulate. For, if there is a lesson for the Left in the Right's breakthrough, it is that the Left must repossess itself of its traditional foundations, on pain of continuing along its present politically feeble reactive course. If the Left turns its back on its foundations, it will be unable to make statements that are truly its own.

1. Theory, Conviction, Practice

An essential ingredient in the Right's breakthrough was an intellectual self-confidence that was grounded in fundamental theoretical work by academics such as Milton Friedman, Friedrich Hayek, and Robert Nozick. In one instructive sense, those authors did not propose new ideas. Instead, they explored, developed, and forthrightly reaffirmed the Right's traditional principles. Those principles are not so traditional to the British *political* Right as they are to the American, but they are traditional nevertheless, in the important sense that they possess a historical

Reprinted in part from "Back to Socialist Basics," *New Left Review*, No. 207, September–October 1994, pp. 3–16. By kind permission of *New Left Review*.

depth which is associated with the conceptual and moral depth at which they are located.

What the Right did is no *proof* of what the Left should do. It is nevertheless extremely suggestive. It tells against looking for "a big new idea." That is anyway a futile endeavor, since you do not land a new idea as a result of angling for one, in the wide sea of intellectual possibility. New ideas standardly come from attempts to solve problems by which old ideas are stumped. Sometimes the new idea turns out to be big, but looking for a big new idea, as such, because it would be impressive to have one, is a ridiculous agendum.

The character of the Right's success suggests that if, as the IPPR document also said, and as I agree, customary inherited socialist rhetoric now turns people off, then the remedy is not to cast about for a different rhetoric, or "buzz"-phrase, irrespective of what its relationship to traditional principles may be, but to restore our own contact with those principles, from which exercise a new rhetoric may indeed emerge. The old rhetoric now sounds "dated" not because everybody knows the content behind it but partly because its content has been forgotten. The Left will not recoup itself ideologically without addressing that foundational content.

The relationship between theory and political practice is more complex than some friends of the Labour Party appear now to suppose. The point of theory is not to generate a comprehensive social design which the politician then seeks to implement. Things don't work that way, because implementing a design requires whole cloth, and nothing in contemporary politics is made out of whole cloth. Politics is an endless struggle, and theory serves as a weapon in that struggle, because it provides a characterization of its direction, and of its controlling purpose.

Considered as practical proposals, the theories of Friedman, Hayek, and Nozick were crazy, crazy in the strict sense that you would have to be crazy to think that such proposals (e.g., abolition of *all* regulation of professional standards and of safety at work, abolition of state money, abolition of *all* welfare provision) might be implemented in the near, medium, or long term.[1] The theories are in that sense crazy precisely because they are uncompromisingly fundamental: they were not devised with one eye on electoral possibility. And, just for that reason, their serviceability in electoral and other political contest is very great. *Politicians and activists can press not-so-crazy right-wing proposals with conviction because they have the strength of conviction that depends upon depth of conviction,*

[1] Profoundly transforming though the Thatcher revolution has been, the distance between British society now and the standards set by right-wing theory remains enormous.

and depth comes from theory that is too fundamental to be practicable in a direct sense.

I said that politicians make nothing out of whole cloth. All change in modern conditions of social differentiation and international integration is perforce incremental, 2 percent here, 5 percent there, accumulating after, say, fifteen years, into a revolution. The large fundamental values help to power (or block) the little changes by nourishing the justificatory rhetoric which is needed to push (or resist) change. Fundamental socialist values which point to a form of society a hundred miles from the horizon of present possibility are needed to defend every half-mile of territory gained and to mount an attempt to regain each bit that has been lost.

Consider Gordon Brown's response to Kenneth Clarke's budget of November 1993. Its central themes were two: the Tories have broken their promise not to raise taxes, and it is they who are responsible for the mess which obliged them to break that promise. That combined charge, important though it is, and important as it was to level it, requires no socialist value, no non-Tory value, to back it up. Consider, too, Michael Portillo's artful maneuver around Brown's charge. He did not have to face it in its own terms because he could say with conviction to Brown that Brown proposed no solution to the £50 billion deficit (to which Brown's criticisms of betrayal and incompetence and Brown's policy of long-term greater investment indeed represented no solution). Brown centered his attack on the misdemeanors of economic mismanagement and political promise breaking, instead of on the crime of depressing the conditions of life of poor people, and on the crime of not loading more burden on the better off, including the not stupendously well off. I do not say that Brown did not mention the sheer inegalitarianism of the budget's profile. But he did not and could not make that point with conviction as a central point, because he thinks about who votes for what and because he has lost touch with foundational values.

The Brown response was relatively ineffectual partly because it presupposed for its effect that people are dumber than they actually are. People already knew that the Tories made the mess, though it was no doubt useful to remind them of it, to keep it at the forefront of their consciousness. But they are not so dumb that they think it follows from the fact that the Tories made the mess that Labour would be better at getting the country out of it. Labour will win the politics of competence only if people have confidence in its competence. That requires that Labour itself be confident in its own superior competence, and that in turn requires that it be confident in itself, *tout court*, which it can be only if it transcends its furtive relationship to its traditional values. Electoral success is to a large extent a by-product of commitment to something other than electoral success.

Success in a particular election can, moreover, be bought at the cost of an ideological backslide which has lasting deleterious effect. It is one thing to point out that the Tories have failed by their own standards. It is quite another, in the course of making that good point, to endorse those standards yourself. Labour is now so beguiled by the prospect of exposing the Tories as tax-raisers that it is beginning to treat tax restraint not merely as a Tory goal but as an intrinsic desideratum. Therewith traditional pledges to reinforce and extend welfare provision are being seriously compromised.[2]

2. Principle and Politics

In its ideologically self-confident phase, when its relationship to its values was forthright rather than furtive, the Labour Party affirmed a principle of community and a principle of equality. ('Community' and 'equality' can be defined in different ways, and I shall say what I mean by them, as names of traditional mainstream Labour values, in the following sections.) Each principle was regarded as authoritative in its own right, but also as justified through its connection with the other. Each value supported the other, and each was strengthened by the fact that it was supported by the other. And these values were not only central to the Labour Party and to the wider Labour movement surrounding it. They were also the values that distinguished Labour from other parties at Westminster. They were, indeed, the only values which *the Left affirmed as a matter of principle and which the Center and Right reject as a matter of principle.*[3]

The values of community and equality were articulated in books and pamphlets. But they were also carried by, and they expressed the sentiments of, a broad movement that no longer exists and that will never

[2] Cf. the excellent article by David McKie on p. 18 of the *Guardian* for January 31, 1994, one paragraph of which runs as follows: "Unless it is handled with extreme deftness, Labour's present campaign is in danger of shoring up the classic Thatcherite picture of taxation as something inherently undesirable, even wicked; something that shackles opportunity rather than, as Labour once taught, expanding it by building the public services on which the great majority of voters and their families will always need to depend: safeguarding *your* health, *your* welfare, *your* children's education."

[3] 'X rejects V as a matter of principle' means, here, 'X rejects V when it is put as a matter of principle,' and *not* 'It is a matter of principle, for X, to reject V.' You could disagree with the italicized claim in either of two ways. You might think that one or both of the values I've identified don't fit the italicized description, or you might think that some value which I've

be re-created. It will never be re-created because technological change means that the class base of that movement is gone, forever. Socialist values have lost their mooring in capitalist social structure. Partly because of that, but also partly because of right-wing ideological successes, community and equality have lost the quite extensive ideological hegemony that they once enjoyed. If I had to hazard a causal story, I'd say that right-wing values filled a space vacated by left-wing values which went on vacation because their class base was eroded. Because I think that a likely causal story, I should not be accused of accusing Labour's leaders of gratuitous betrayal, in their abandonment of traditional values. "Betrayal" is the wrong name for abandonment which has a hard underlying social cause. But the hardness of the cause does not mean that there is no alternative but to allow wholesale abandonment of values to be its effect.

The struggle for community and equality is perforce more difficult when the calculus of class interest reduces the constituency that would gain from them, in an immediate sense of 'gain.' But there remain two reasons for insisting on their authority. The first, which is decisive on its own, is a self-standing moral-cum-intellectual reason. The second, more contingent and debatable, is a reason related to the identity and survival of the Labour Party, and it is contingent partly because it is not a necessary truth that the Labour Party should continue to exist.

The decisive reason for not abandoning community and equality is that the moral force of those values never depended on the social force supporting them that is now disappearing. No one who believed in the values could have said that she believed in them *because* they expressed the sentiments of a social movement. Anyone who believed in them believed in them because she thought them inherently authoritative, and the withering of the social force that backed them cannot justify ceasing to think them authoritative. And the second reason for not abandoning the values is that, once they are dropped, then there is no reason of principle, as opposed to of history, for Labour not to merge with the Liberal Democrats. Labour cannot cherish its independence as a party, believe in a politics of principle, and affirm nothing but the "four principles of social justice" affirmed in *The Justice Gap* and *Social Justice in*

---

not identified does. I'll be more surprised if you're able to disagree in the second way, not, that is, by challenging the distinguishing role of the values I've identified, but by claiming that a value not identified here also enjoyed such a role. (Perhaps a third such value, as suggested to me by Danny Goldstick, is equality of power, in a political sense, as opposed to equality in the economic-distributive sense which occupies me here. This value was indeed affirmed by the Left. But I doubt that it was rejected by *both* the Right and the Center.)

a Changing World.[4] No Liberal Democrat or progressive Tory need reject those principles.[5]

A different response to the present predicament is to think the values afresh in a spirit of loyalty to them and in order to see how one can sustain commitment to them in an inhospitable time, and what new modes of advocacy of them are possible. But that partly practical task requires foundational reflection of just the sort that the IPPR (see p. 211 of this chapter above) might have meant us to eschew.

You can ask what our principles are, what, that is, we believe with passion, and you can ask what is the best way to win the next election. But you cannot ask what principles we should have, what we should believe with passion, as a *means* of winning the next election.[6] For the answer won't be principles you can really believe in, and you might therefore not even help yourself electorally, since electors are not so unperceptive that they can be relied upon not to notice that you are dissembling.

The two IPPR documents bow before the success of pro-market and antiegalitarian ideology that has helped to precipitate Labour's present ideological crisis. There is, as I have said, nothing in their four "core ideas" (see n. 5 above) that any Liberal Democrat or left-wing Tory need reject. To be sure, the Tories in particular do not in practice respect the core ideas as much as a Labour government might, but that does not justify flourishing forth pale principles to define the direction of Labour's renewal.

After each of Labour's four electoral failures, the Labour Right said: we did not win because we looked too socialist; and the Labour Left said: we did not win because we did not look socialist enough. I do not think either side knows that what it claims to be true is true, and,

[4] Both documents, which I shall henceforth call *JG* and *SJCW*, emanated from the Commission on Social Justice and were published by the IPPR in 1993. The present essay was prompted by the consternation and, sometimes, shock that I experienced when reading the two documents.

[5] The four "principles" (*JG*, pp. i, 16) or "key ideas" (*SJCW*, p. i) or "core ideas" (*SJCW*, p. 4): "1. The foundation of a free society is the equal worth of all citizens. 2. All citizens should be able as a right of citizenship to meet their basic needs for income, shelter, education, nutrition and health care. 3. Self-respect and personal autonomy depend on the widest possible spread of opportunities and life-chances. 4. Inequalities are not necessarily unjust but unjustified inequalities should be reduced and where possible eliminated" (*SJCW*, p. 4). In a somewhat different formulation of principle 4, given at *JG*, p. i, it reads: "4. Inequalities are not necessarily unjust—but those which are should be reduced and where possible eliminated."

[6] My own claim that reaffirmation of traditional values would have electoral force is not put as an answer to that counterfeit question. My view that the old principles can be electorally supportive does not imply the (incoherent) recommendation that we should believe in them *because* they can be supportive, even though it does imply rejection of an electorally inspired case for abandoning them.

if one side is right, then I do not know which is.[7] Certainly there exists an aversion to increases in taxation, and although that is no doubt partly because no truly principled defense of greater redistribution is confidently projected, I admit that I do not know how large a part of the explanation of the unpopularity of greater taxation is associated with failure to project its justification. I am therefore not contending that a principled defense of community and equality is a sure route to electoral success in 1996 or '97. But failure to secure acceptance of the principles of community and equality[8] is not a reason to modify one's *belief* in the principles themselves, even if it is indeed a reason, politics being what it is, not to thrust them forward publicly in their unvarnished form.[9] To massage one's beliefs for the sake of electoral gain can, moreover, be electorally counterproductive. It can be inexpedient to abandon principle for expediency, because it is hard to hide the fact that you are doing so, and everyone, Neil Kinnock included, knew that the Tories were right when, to powerful electoral effect, they accused Kinnock of that unprincipled abandonment. The Commission on Social Justice should not pretend to run an exercise in the examination of principle whose real focus is not principle but electoral success, because it will then certainly betray principle and possibly contribute to electoral failure.

3. Community versus Market

I mean, here, by 'community,' the antimarket principle according to which I serve you not because of what I can get out of doing so but because you need my service.[10] That is antimarket because the market motivates productive contribution not on the basis of commitment to one's fellow human beings and a desire to serve them while being served *by* them, but on the basis of impersonal cash reward. The immediate motive

[7] Has there been a postelectoral survey of potential Labour voters who did not vote Labour to determine how many voted otherwise, or abstained, for each of the stated opposite reasons? (Not that what people say in such a survey is conclusive with respect to what their response to a different campaign would have been.)

[8] And, some might add, especially a failure which followed hardly any attempt to defend them.

[9] Politics (again) being what it is, *a* gap between belief and public statement is often unavoidable. But there is a limit to how big that gap can be, without compromising both principle and political effectiveness, and when the gap approaches that limit, principle forbids adjusting belief, as opposed to public statement.

[10] That is by no means the only thing that 'community' can mean. Nor do I regard it as a particularly good name for what I use it to name here: I simply haven't been able to think of a better one.

to productive activity in a market society is typically[11] some mixture of greed and fear, in proportions that vary with the details of a person's market position and personal character. In greed, other people are seen as possible sources of enrichment, and in fear they are seen as threats. These are horrible ways of seeing other people, however much we have become habituated and inured to them, as a result of centuries of capitalist development.[12]

I said that, in community motivation, I produce because of my commitment to my fellow human beings and with a desire to serve them while being served by them.[13] In such motivation, there is indeed an expectation of reciprocation, but it nevertheless differs critically from market motivation. The marketeer is willing to serve, but only in order to be served. He does not desire the conjunction (serve-and-be-served) as such, for he would not serve if doing so were not a means to get service. The difference is expressed in the lack of fine tuning that attends nonmarket motivation. Contrast taking turns in a loose way with respect to who buys the drinks with keeping a record of who has paid what for them. The former procedure is in line with community, the latter with the market.

Now, the history of the twentieth century encourages the thought that the easiest way to generate productivity in a modern society is by nourishing the motives of greed and fear, in a hierarchy of unequal income. That does not make them attractive motives. Who would propose running a society on such motives, and thereby promoting the psychology to which they belong, if they were not known to be effective, did they not have the instrumental value which is the only value that they have? In the famous statement in which Adam Smith justified market relations, he pointed out that we place our faith not in the butcher's generosity but in his self-interest when we rely on him to provision us. Smith thereby

[11] People can operate under a sense of service even in a market society, but, insofar as they do so, what makes the market work is not what makes them work. Their discipline is not market discipline. (Some think that the very success of the market depends on the tempering leaven within it of noncapitalist motivation: for present purposes, there is no need to form a judgment about that complex claim.)

[12] Capitalism did not, of course, invent greed and fear: they are deep in human nature, related as they are to elementary infantile structures. But capitalism has undoubtedly magnified the role of greed in particular in ordinary life, and, unlike its predecessor feudal civilization, which had the (Christian) grace to condemn greed, capitalism celebrates it.

[13] Under its most abstract description, the motivation in question might be consistent with hierarchy: Prince Charles's motto is "*Ich dien*," and serfs and lords alike who buy feudal ideology wholesale can describe themselves as being motivated thus. If community motivation is indeed consistent with hierarchy, then the principle of equality informs the principle of community, in its socialist form.

propounded a wholly extrinsic justification of market motivation, in face of what he acknowledged to be its unattractive intrinsic character. Traditional socialists have often ignored Smith's point, in a moralistic condemnation of market motivation which fails to address its extrinsic justification. Certain contemporary overenthusiastic market socialists tend, contrariwise, to forget that the market is intrinsically repugnant, because they are blinded by their belated discovery of the market's extrinsic value. The genius of the market is that it recruits shabby motives to desirable ends, and, in a balanced view, both sides of that proposition must be kept in focus.

Generosity *and* self-interest exist in everyone. We know how to make an economic system work on the basis of self-interest. We do not know how to make it work on the basis of generosity. But that does not mean that we should forget generosity: we should still confine the sway of self-interest as much as we can. We do that, for example, when we tax, redistributively, the unequalizing results of market activity. The extent to which we can do that without defeating our aim (of making the badly off better off) varies inversely with the extent to which self-interest has been allowed to triumph in private and public consciousness.[14] (To the extent that self-interest has indeed triumphed, heavily progressive taxation drives high earners abroad, or causes them to decide to reduce their labor input, or induces in them a morose attitude which makes their previous input hard or impossible to sustain.)

The market, any market, contradicts the principle which not only Marx but his socialist predecessors proclaimed for the good society, the principle embodied in the slogan "From each according to his ability, to each according to his needs." One might ask what it means for each to give according to his ability, and what it means for each to get according to his needs. But for present purposes, the unambiguous message of the slogan is that what you get is *not* a function of what you give, that contribution and benefit are separate matters. Here the relationship between people is not the instrumental one in which I give because I get, but the wholly noninstrumental one in which I give because you need. You do not get more because you produce more, and you do not get less because you are not

[14] My views on this matter run alongside those of John Stuart Mill, who averred that "[e]verybody has selfish and unselfish interests, and a selfish man has cultivated the habit of caring for the former, and not caring for the latter." And one thing that contributes to the direction in which a person's habits develop is the ambient social ethos, which is influenced by the stance of political leaders. (The Mill quotation is from his *Considerations on Representative Government*, p. 444. For sapient commentary on this and other relevant passages in Mill, see Ashcraft, "Class Conflict and Constitutionalism in J. S. Mill's Thought," pp. 117–18.)

good at producing. Accordingly, the ideal in the primeval socialist slogan constitutes a complete rejection of the logic of the market.

The socialist aspiration was to extend community to the whole of our economic life. We now know that we do not now know how to do that, and many think that we now know that it is impossible to do that. But community conquests in certain domains, such as health care and education, have sustained viable forms of production and distribution in the past, and it is consequently a matter for regret that the IPPR documents do not invoke community as a core value, when it is a value that is currently under aggressive threat from the market principle, and when there is even immediate political mileage to be got from reasserting community in the mentioned particular domains.

4. Justice and Equality

The principle of equality says that the amount of amenity and burden in one person's life should be roughly comparable to that in any other's. That principle is not mentioned in the documents; or, to be more precise, it is mentioned only in parody, in the statement that "few people believe in arithmetical equality."[15] Perhaps no one believes in the unlimited sway of the principle of equality, as I defined it above,[16] where, that is, equality is rough similarity of amenity and burden. But I, and many others, certainly believe in it as a value to be traded off against others, and this value is rejected, as such, in the commission's documents. Instead, we have an arrestingly weak proposition—strangely said to be a "radical one" (*JG*, p. i)—in the fourth "core idea" of social justice, which reads as follows: "Inequalities are not necessarily unjust—but those which are should be reduced and where possible eliminated" (*JG*, p. i). Those who are eager to declare their support for unjust inequalities will oppose the fourth core idea.

Proposition 3 on social justice[17] reads, in part, as follows:

> Redistribution of income is a means to social justice and not an end in itself; social justice demands sufficient revenue to meet basic needs and extend opportunities, but there are limits of principle as well as practice to levels of taxation. (*SJCW*, p. 24)

[15] *JG*, p. ii.

[16] For a more precise definition of the principle, see my "On the Currency of Egalitarian Justice" [reprinted as Chapter 1 of this volume—Ed.].

[17] *SJCW*, p. 24 (cf. *JG*, p. 13). This is not one of the "four principles of social justice" listed in n. 5 above, but one of "ten propositions on social justice" which are more specific and more circumstantial than the four principles are.

To say that (an equalizing) redistribution of income is not an end in itself but only a means to fulfill basic needs and extend opportunities is, once again, to abandon equality as a principle.[18]

The fourth core idea and the third proposition on social justice raise two questions: first, what is the difference between a just and an unjust inequality? And, second, what are the "limits of principle" to taxation, beyond which taxation counts as "punitive" (*SJCW*, p. 25)?

An answer to the first question is given at p. 43 of *JG*. The inequalities that "are indeed justified"[19] are, it says there, justified by "need, merit, or reward" (cf., too, ibid., p. 15). I find that list curious, and I want to examine it in a little detail.

"Inequalities" justified in terms of need are not ones that even the most radical egalitarian has ever opposed. *JG* does not say what needs it contemplates here, but there are only two kinds that appear relevant. First, some people need more resources to achieve the same level of well-being as others. But to unequalize resources on that basis is consistent with egalitarianism of a most radical kind. Second, some people need more means of production than others do to carry out their social function. But producer need is out of place in a roll call of justified inequalities which is intended to challenge an uncompromising egalitarianism. No egalitarian thinks that brain surgeons should be denied expensive equipment.

The other supposed ways of justifying inequalities are, first, in terms of merit and, second, in terms of reward. But the phrase "inequality justified in terms of reward" conveys no clear thought, especially when it is, as here, contrasted with "inequality justified in terms of merit." I suppose that the phrase was a piece of innocent carelessness, yet it is symptomatic of the altogether casual treatment of equality in these proceedings that such carelessness should have got by the eyes of what must have been quite a few readers. I presume we can take it that what was intended by "inequality justified in terms of reward" is inequality justified in terms of reward for merit and/or effort. So let me address merit and effort, as grounds of inequality.

If one person produces more than others that is because he is more talented or because he expends more effort or because he is lucky in his circumstances of production, which is to say that he is lucky with respect to whom and what he produces *with*. The last reason for greater productivity, lucky circumstance, is morally (as opposed to economically)

[18] Notice that to say that equalizing redistribution of income *is* an end in itself is not to say that the equality to be achieved thereby is of income, as opposed to, for example, of what Amartya Sen calls "capability."

[19] And, therefore, in conformity with justice, since—see the end of n. 5 above—'just' and 'justified,' which *can* convey different ideas, are used interchangeably in the IPPR documents.

unintelligible as a reason for greater reward. And whereas rewarding productivity which is due to greater inherent talent is indeed morally intelligible, from certain ethical standpoints, it is nevertheless a profoundly antisocialist idea, correctly stigmatized by J. S. Mill as an instance of "giving to those who have,"[20] since greater talent is itself a piece of fortune that calls for no further reward.

Effort might be a different matter. I say that it *might* be different, because it can be contended that unusual effort (largely) reflects unusual capacity for effort, which is but a further form of talent and therefore subject to the same skepticism as talent itself is with respect to its relevance to reward. But let us allow, against such skepticism, that effort is indeed *pertinently*[21] subject to the will. That being granted, ask, now, why the effortful person who is supposed to be handsomely rewarded expended the effort she did. Did she do so in order to enrich herself? If so, then why should her special effort command a high reward? Or did she work hard in order to benefit others? If so, then it contradicts her own aim to reward her with extra resources that others would otherwise have, as opposed to with a salute and a handshake and a sense of gratitude.[22] Of course those remarks are only the beginning of a long argument, but it is indicative of the utter conventionality of the disparagement of equality in the IPPR pamphlets that such considerations lie beyond their horizon.[23]

I turn to the question raised by the third proposition on social justice (see p. 220 above), concerning the "limits of principle on taxation." Now, although those "limits of principle" are not defined or explained in

[20] *Principles of Political Economy*, p. 210.

[21] I emphasize "pertinently," because, among those who agree that effort is subject to the will, some ("hard determinists") would deny that that raises a challenge to egalitarian views of distributive justice, and others (e.g., Rawls) issue the same denial, on the nondeterminist basis that it is inscrutable to what extent a person's emission of effort is not due to differential good fortune. (For a critical discussion of Rawls's remarks on effort, see Section 2 of my "On the Currency.")

[22] Or, indeed, with a sum of money, conceived as a gift expressing gratitude, rather than as an *ex ante* motivating reward.

[23] The two most influential Anglophone political philosophy books of recent years are Rawls's *Theory of Justice*, which is left liberal, and Nozick's *Anarchy, State, and Utopia*, which is extreme free-market Right. It conforms to the outlook of these documents that Rawls should be cited critically and Nozick positively, with respect to their teachings about equality. Nozick's discovery that one does not have to deserve one's talent to deserve the fruits of its exercise is heartily commended (*JG*, p. 13), while the egalitarian Rawlsian reminder that talent is but good fortune is disparaged, and, moreover, misrepresented as a premise for the plainly false conclusion, which Rawls does not assert, that "in the last analysis all that anyone's work represents is a site at which society has achieved something" (*JG*, p. 13). The single moderately extended exposition of academic political philosophy in these documents serves to make an antiegalitarian point in a slapdash way.

the two published documents, I conjecture that part[24] of the unstated explanation of them is the one that appears in the unpublished paper "Ideas of Social Justice" that Bernard Williams prepared for the commission. Echoing a chief claim of Robert Nozick's, Williams said that "sustaining an equal distribution of money would involve continuous incursions into liberty."

This summary remark overlooks the conceptual truth that to have money *is* (*pro tanto*) to have liberty. The richer you are, the more courses of action are open to you, which is to say that you are freer than you would otherwise be. Accordingly, whoever receives money as a result of redistribution thereby enjoys an enhancement of her liberty,[25] albeit at the expense of the liberty of the person from whom it is taken, but with the net result for liberty as such entirely moot. Taxation restricts not, as is here misleadingly suggested, liberty as such, but private property rights, both in external things and in one's own labor power. Whether or not such rights are deeply founded, it is ideological hocus-pocus to identify them with liberty as such, and it is entirely alien to traditional socialist belief so to construe them.

The stout opposition to equality and redistribution as matters of principle is revealed in this rejection of Tory dogma: "Contrary to the 'trickle-down' theory of the 1980s, making the rich richer does not make the poor richer too. Indeed, because the great majority pay the costs of unemployment, crime and ill-health, making the poor poorer makes us all poorer too. Common interests demand social cohesion rather than polarization."[26]

This appeal sidesteps the politically difficult redistributive issue. By plausible absolute standards, most people in the past were poor, and the target for redistribution could then be a rich minority. Now, by the same absolute standards, the standards in the light of which it is pertinently pointed out that 62 percent of UK households have videos (*JG*, p. 19), only a minority are poor. To appeal to the self-interest of the majority (dressed up as an interest they have in common with the poor) as a central reason for relieving the poverty of that minority may work electorally: that depends on how the electoral majority do the arithmetic the appeal invites them to engage in. It depends, that is, on whether they will

[24] Another part, presumably, is the idea that too much taxation trenches against the claims of "need, merit, and reward": see p. 221 above.

[25] For further demonstration of the connection between money and liberty, see the Appendix to this article. [This Appendix has not been reprinted in—since it has been superseded by "Freedom and Money," which is reprinted as Chapter 8 of—this volume.—Ed.]

[26] *SJCW*, p. 22. The statement is part of the elaboration of the first "proposition on social justice," which reads as follows: "Social justice is about more than poverty—it concerns everyone. The best way to help the minority who are poor is to advance social justice for all."

reckon that higher taxation is a smaller price to pay for their own health and security than what they'd have to shell out on BUPA [private health insurance—Ed.], improved antiburglary systems, a house in the suburbs, and so on. But however they figure those sums, inviting them to consider the issue primarily in that framework,[27] under a pretense of common interest, is a cop-out at the level of principle.[28]

[27] As the amalgam consisting of the first proposition on social justice (see n. 26 above) and its complete elaboration does.

[28] I thank Arnold Zuboff for extended, patient criticism of an earlier draft of this paper. I am also grateful for written comments from Norman Geras, Keith Graham, John McMurtry, John Roemer, Amélie Rorty, Hillel Steiner, and Bernard Williams.

Chapter Eleven

HOW TO DO POLITICAL PHILOSOPHY

1. People like me, who have been trying to do philosophy for more than forty years, do in due course learn, if they're lucky, *how* to do what they've been *trying* to do: that is, they do learn how to do philosophy. But although I've learned how to do philosophy, nobody ever told me how to do it, and, so far as I would guess, nobody will have told you how to do it, or is likely to tell you how to do it in the future. The *most* charitable explanation of that fact, the fact, that is, that nobody tells philosophy students how to do philosophy, is that it is impossible to *explain* to anybody how philosophy is to be done. The only way to teach people how to do it is by letting them watch, and listen, and imitate. The *least* charitable explanation of the self-same fact, the fact that we don't teach you how to do philosophy, is that those of us who have learned how to do it struggled so hard to get where we *now* are that we're now selfishly reluctant to give you some of the fruit of our struggle for free: we think you, too, should suffer. Probably there's some truth in each explanation.

2. But however all that may be, let me now give you some tips about how to do philosophy, in no particular order. After I've given these preliminary tips about how to do philosophy in general, I'll turn to some tips about political philosophy in particular.

3. My first piece of advice is that you should try to be as clear as possible about exactly what you *think* you're achieving when you present an argument. To be more precise: when you present an argument (now see Figure 1), try to be as clear as possible whether you think the argument goes against something your opponent holds, and only in *that* way supports your own position (if you have one), or, instead, whether you think the argument supports your *own* position, without going against that of your opponent (if you have one), except in that *way*, that is, by way of supporting a position that rivals hers (see the difference between the rows in Figure 1). Also, try to be clear about how *decisive* you think the argument in question is, that is, and if it is an argument going against

Editor's note: This chapter is a paper that Cohen would present at the first session of a standing Oxford M.Phil. Seminar on Contemporary Political Philosophy and that he had plans to revise and publish after he retired. This version is dated 2004.

	Decisively	Nondecisively
Supports my position	Proves	Doesn't Prove
Attacks her position	Refutes	Doesn't Refute

Fig. 1. Two-by-two matrix that classifies considerations or arguments

your opponent, whether it *refutes* her position, or *merely challenges* it, or displays a weakness in it. And, analogously, try to be clear whether a consideration that in your opinion favors your own position *merely favors* that position of yours or decisively *establishes* it. (See the difference between the columns in Figure 1.) So we've now got a fourfold classification of types of argument in philosophy, or, for that matter, a classification of types of argument in philosophy and in everything else.

4. Note that I said *try* to be clear about which box contains your argument: not—be clear. If I'd said the latter, then, if you thought you were not quite clear about some matter, but that you could *try* to be, then, if I'd said *be* clear, and you wanted to follow my instruction, you might not *try* to be clear, for fear of violating the instruction to *be* clear. I am not saying that clarity is a necessary condition of anything worthwhile in philosophy. Philosophy is a very hard subject, so hard that it can be very hard to be clear about what I've suggested you *try* to be clear about, that is, *exactly* what you're doing, *exactly* what the force of a consideration that occurs to you is. Sometimes one senses that a consideration has *some* sort of bearing on a controversy, without knowing either to which row or to which column it belongs, and it is nevertheless worthwhile bringing the consideration forward, if only because it may provoke a discussion that leads to a clearer idea of the polemical significance of the consideration, that is, into which box(es) in our matrix it falls. One should aspire to clarity, but one should not avoid possible insight for the sake of avoiding unclarity. A bad way never to make a mistake is to shut up and say nothing.

5. Another tip: When you're doing philosophy, don't be afraid to sound dumb, or simpleminded. If, for example, what somebody says sounds to you so obviously mistaken that you conclude that you must be missing something, keep alive in your mind the alternative conclusion, which is that *they* are missing something, or seeing something that isn't there, even if they are the teacher. Some of the most successful philosophical interventions that I've witnessed have been a matter of pointing out that the emperor's not wearing any clothes. This is a subject in which seasoned

professionals can make huge mistakes, equivalent in size to a chemist forgetting that molecules consist of atoms—which is not, of course, a mistake that any chemist would ever make.

6. Let me now turn to political philosophy, and, in particular, to that form of political philosophy which is an argument about principles, that is, general statements about right and wrong. Here my first tip is that when we discuss principles, as we so often do in political philosophy, and we assess their implications, then there are three questions that we should not confuse with one another, questions that are regularly confused with one another even by advanced practitioners, advanced practitioners such as . . . I can't read what I've written here. There are three questions in political philosophy that are in fact distinct but that are not distinguished as often as they should be, to the detriment of both clarity of statement and rigor of argument within our discipline. The three distinct questions are: (i) What is justice?;[1] (ii) What should the state do?; and (iii) Which social states of affairs ought to be brought about?[2] Some simply confuse two or more of those *questions* with each other. Others see that the *questions* are distinct but they take for granted that the answers to some pair of them, or to all three of them, are identical. They take for granted, for example, that it is constitutive of the normative status of the state that its business is to promote justice.

Let me make some pair-wise contrasts across the three questions. First, question (i) is not the same question as question (ii), if only because not everything that the state should do is something it should do in the service of justice, or, at least, and this weaker claim suffices to establish the distinction between questions (i) and (ii), the very *concept* of justice is not the concept of what the state should do. Conversely, not all justice is to be achieved by the state: or, if you prefer, the very concept of justice does not ensure that all justice is to be achieved by the state. Question (ii) is not, moreover, the same question as question (iii), if only because question (ii) places a restriction, and question (iii) does not, on the agency whereby whatever is to be brought about is to be brought about. And finally question (iii) is not the same question as question (i), since justice is not the only reason why it might be right to bring about this social state of affairs rather than that one. Social states of affairs can have, and lack, virtues other than that of justice.

[1] That is: what are the correct principles of justice—*not*: explain the *concept* of justice, which is a *further question*, to which my discussion of questions (i), (ii), and (iii) is a contribution.

[2] One might add question (iv): Which social states of affairs are better than others, whether or not they should be brought about? But distinguishing (iii) from (iv) would import too much complication into our discussion.

Consider, for example, the view associated especially with Harry Frankfurt, but also, to a degree, with Joseph Raz, which says that equality is a false ideal and that what really matters is that everyone should have *enough*.[3] According to this view, many who are drawn to the ideal of equality are drawn to it because they confuse the false desideratum of equality with the true desideratum of sufficiency. The sufficiency view disparages equality and says that what matters is not that people be equal, but that everyone have *enough*. Enough for what?—well, there is some obscurity here, but it doesn't matter for my present purposes. Never mind for *what* the relevant enough is supposed to be enough. My present complaint is not about *that* vagueness but about this one: are we to take the Frankfurt sufficiency thesis as answering question (i), and therefore as saying that economic *justice* is complete if everyone is assured a decent, and possibly quite high, minimum; or is it an answer to question (ii) which says that the responsibility of the *state* in economic justice ends when everyone has enough; or is it, once again, a slightly different answer to question (ii), one which says, differently, that the responsibility of the state ends with ensuring universal sufficiency, whatever *justice* in particular may or may not be; or is the Frankfurt proposal an answer to question (iii), which asks what distributional states of affairs are normatively *preferable* to each other, an answer which says that certain minima are *all* that count, and that equality is not even normatively *preferable* to inequality?

What justice is, what the state should do, and how social states rank normatively, are, I say, distinct questions, and it is controversial what the relationships among the answers to those questions are. Some would say that the state's sole business is justice, and others might say that its sole business is something that they consider to be the sufficiency *part* of justice, and so on. People proceed as though these distinctions don't have to be made when they counterpose one principle to another without specifying in which of the three contexts that I have distinguished they are setting the competition between competing principles. Great masses of literature ranging from the discussion of luck egalitarianism across to the trolley problem fail to make the needed distinctions at pertinent points.

Take another example, the so-called leveling-down objection to egalitarianism. The leveling-down objection says that it is a mistake to favor equality, because favoring equality commits you to leveling down when the alternative to equality is a Pareto-superior inequality.

The objection is characteristically stated as flatly as that, with no specification of who *you* are or of any wider frame in which the question is

[3] [See Frankfurt, "Equality as a Moral Ideal," and Raz, *The Morality of Freedom*, chapter 9.—Ed.]

	Equal Distribution	Unequal Distribution
A has	5	8
B has	5	6

Fig. 2. The Leveling-Down Objection

set. But it makes a difference whether we are in question (i)-territory or in question (ii)-territory or in question (iii)-territory here. For while it might well be grotesque for the *state* to mandate a leveling down in circumstances where the equal 5/5 distribution and the unequal 8/6 distribution in Figure 2 exhaust the feasible set, whereas, that is, it may be grotesque for the *state* to make everybody worse off, it does not follow that there is no *injustice* in the 8/6 inequality, and, partly for that reason, it does not follow that no one should seek to bring the 5/5 world about.

Let me try to give some color of plausibility to those judgments. Imagine a peaceful anarchy, a state of nature with no state, in which manna falls from heaven and gets shared equally because the sharers think that's the right way to deal with manna from heaven.[4] Now suppose that an extra piece of irremovable and unredistributable but destructible manna falls on Jane's plot. Jane says: "Like, I don't want this extra manna, I'm going to make a big bonfire with it to which you're all invited, because it's not fair, it really *sucks*, for me to have more than you guys do." If you think Jane is being *merely* foolish, then you might well claim that the leveling-down objection applies not only against the proposal that the state should *enforce* equality but also against the claim that *justice* favors equality. But I for one would not think that Jane is being foolish. I would think that she is simply a remarkably just person, and I think we should commend her for being one, and perhaps reward her with the extra manna. Or even if we should not precisely *reward* her with the extra manna (since that *might* contradict the very principle of equality upon which *she* acted!), we might nevertheless let her have it. Justice can be mean and spiteful, but it's still justice even then: we shouldn't confuse different virtues. Portia was careful not to combine different virtues when she recommended that mercy season justice.[5]

In the foregoing scenario, Jane doesn't enjoy her initial surplus at anybody's expense, and that's why many think it would be foolish for her to

[4] Nozick himself said that equality might be the right distribution for manna from heaven, although he signally and consequentially failed to observe that the raw resources of the planet Earth *are* manna from heaven.

[5] [This example appears, with a bit of the color removed, in Cohen's *Rescuing Justice and Equality*, pp. 317–18.—Ed.]

throw it away. Note, further, that if she *does* throw it away, that will *also* not be at anybody else's expense.

Consider, now, a different example in which extra manna lands on everybody's plot, but 10 units of it on Jane's and only 5 on the plot of each other person. And suppose, further, that only Jane can do anything with respect to whether the manna stays or not, and that if she destroys her own, then everybody else's manna goes too.[6]

In this new example, Jane's having the surplus is once again at nobody's expense, but if she throws it away that *will* be at the expense of others. Now, nobody would deny that, in the *original* example, where she gets extra and nobody else does, Jane has the right to throw her surplus away, and I say that if she *does* throw it away, in that example, then she shows an admirable devotion to justice. But one may question whether she has the right to throw her surplus away in the second scenario, on the ground that Jane would thereby also rob others of something that *they* enjoy at nobody else's expense. Partly for that reason, I would say that if Jane does throw hers away in the second example, then she shows not an admirable but a fanatical devotion to justice. (Or, perhaps, her devotion to justice is admirable in that she is prepared to sacrifice her own interests to it but also fanatical in that she is prepared to sacrifice the interests of others to it.) People who don't agree with me may think that she is fanatical in both cases. But my own admirability/fanaticism judgments are, in my view, quite consistent with my judgment that the second and strongly Pareto-improving distribution is unfair.

Here is a further illustration. Among the reasons that Ronald Dworkin gives for opposing equality of welfare is that if we seek to make welfare as equal as possible then we must reserve an enormous quantity of resources for very handicapped people, such a large quantity of resources that servicing the needs of handicapped people might then exhaust the state's budget.[7] But this objection to equality of welfare, considered not as a policy but as a specification of the content of distributive justice, falsely supposes that it is a condition of justice that it should be able to be implemented through a reasonable state rule of regulation: there is, in that argument, a conflation of question (i) with question (ii).

It is pertinent to commend, here, a breathtakingly simple phrase that Derek Parfit has introduced for marking a distinction that is now, to the general profit, made more often in discussions about principles than it was before Derek introduced his felicitous phrase. And that is the distinction between desiderata of principle that are laid down as manda-

[6] This example is due to Valentina Urbanek.

[7] [See Dworkin, "Equality of Welfare," pp. 242–43, and "Equality of Resources," pp. 299–300.—Ed.]

tory and desiderata of principle that are overrideable but whose presence nevertheless makes a state of affairs, in Parfit's great phrase for that, "in one way better."[8] The challenge that the leveling-down objection presents against equality is that egalitarian principles mandate that in some circumstances some people should lose even if nobody gains. Yet the egalitarian can say that she would not level down, because equality isn't everything, but nevertheless maintain that equality, as such, is in one way better than its absence: something of value is lost, because there is an *unfairness*, and therefore a kind of injustice, when some have more than others through no relevant fault or choice of anyone. The leveling-down objection is not thereby eliminated, for some would deny that a world in which everyone is blind is in *any* way better than one in which some, but not all, can see. Some who would admire Jane for destroying her extra manna would think her a mere fool if she plucked her eyes out because others could not see. But, however that may be, it is important that those who think that the all-blind world is *in one way* better are not thereby committed to plucking out the eyes of the sighted in a world where some are blind and some are not.

The threefold distinction that I have latterly labored, between what the state should do, what justice is, and what's preferable to what, intersects with the two-by-two matrix introduced in Figure 1 above, and thereby things become *very* complicated: we now have a classificatory matrix with twelve cells in it. I think that's a big reason why people talk past one another in political philosophy. Often, people argue past one another because they don't realize that they're speaking within different cells of the matrix.

Yet, as before, it would be a mistake to be silent about a consideration that you believe bears upon competing principles unless you are absolutely *sure* which contest is in question (about justice, or about what the state should do, or about which social state is preferable), nor, *a fortiori*, need you be certain to which of the twelve cells your contribution belongs in order for that contribution to be worthwhile.

7. *Disquisition on obviousness.* Now, some remarks about obviousness. Some people are poor philosophers because, although they might be clever in other ways, they are wholly unable to conceive how people who disagree with them could see things differently from how they themselves see them. For many years I had a colleague who would greet unusual claims in undergraduate essays with the words "we *know* that's false" (as opposed to, for example, "Oh, that's an unusual thing to think. Why do you *think* it?"). His propensity to aggressive intellectual blindness

[8] [See sections V and XII of Parfit's *Equality or Priority?*—Ed.]

in the course of his pedagogy was matched by published work that was similarly blinkered.

(To be sure, there are highly inspired philosophers, of whom Ludwig Wittgenstein was perhaps one, who are blinded to alternative possibilities by their own deep insights.[9] If you're at that white-hot level, the present admonition may not apply.)

But why is it so important to understand the possibility of another point of view in philosophy, by contrast with physics, or, perhaps, literary theory? It is because so many philosophical problems are problems only because they arise on the ground of clashes of radically opposed points of view. And the significance and interest of at least many philosophical claims are discerned with particular clarity within a field of apparently inconsistent propositions among which we must choose, where the relevant claim is one contestable option.

Very often in philosophy, moreover, each of the partisans on the opposite sides of a question not only think those on the other side wrong, but think them *obviously* wrong. And each set of partisans, we can infer, is mistaken, because if the other point of view were *obviously* wrong, then it wouldn't have been occupied, as it in fact is, by many deeply reflective people, after a couple of thousand years of widespread reflection. Let me illustrate:

The problem of the freedom of the will
(1) We often have a real choice.
(2) All our behavior is scientifically explainable.
(3) If all our behavior is scientifically explainable, then we never have a real choice.

Not all of (1)–(3) can be true. But anyone who does not experience the strong pull of each is *pro tanto* not suited to philosophy.

Sometimes one simply has to settle for one obviousness against another. E.g., van Inwagen, finding it less hard to affirm the mystery of contra-causal freedom than the counterintuitivity of us lacking real choice.[10]

In really deep philosophical problems there are competing apparent obviousnesses. It seems obvious that we are not wrong when we describe the world commonsensically, yet it seems obvious that physics contradicts common sense. In less deep philosophical problems the clash is of plausibilities. I'll lay out some examples here. I won't try to say which propositions have a redolence of obviousness, as opposed to of mere plausibility. I start with a polyad which spells out the example to which I have already made reference.

[9] I owe this point to Alan Ryan.
[10] [See van Inwagen, *An Essay on Free Will*.—Ed.]

The leveling-down objection to egalitarianism

(1) Equality requires leveling down, when leveling up is impossible.
(2) Nobody benefits from leveling down (or, more generally, from relations between their own good and that of others).
(3) Something that benefits no one is in no way good.
(4) Equality is (at least in one way) good.

Temkin rejects (3),[11] and so do I. Some—for example, Thomas Christiano and Ingmar Persson—reject (1): they believe that a proper understanding of the nature of the case for equality excludes leveling down.[12] I believe that John Broome rejects (2), at least in its general form, because he speaks of an "individual good" which "depends on the relation between one person's position and other people's."[13] Many reject (4), as is shown by the fact that many press the leveling-down objection against egalitarianism.

The perfectionism controversy

(1) The state should ensure that people have good lives.
(2) The state should be neutral. It should not use as a consideration in favor of a policy that some lives are better than others.
(3) A state which is neutral cannot ensure that people have good lives.

Many antiperfectionist liberals challenge (1). So-called perfectionists challenge (2): how could it not favor a policy that it makes people's lives better? Dworkin's Tanner Lectures challenge (3).[14] In his view, the neutral policy *does* make people's lives better.

The sufficiency controversy

(1) No one who has enough has a right to complain about her share.
(2) Among all who have enough, some may have more than others.
(3) If some have more than others for no good reason, then those who have less have a right to complain.

Frankfurt, Roger Crisp, and Raz reject (3). Paula Casal rejects (1).[15]

The luck egalitarianism controversy

(1) It is unjust if some have more than others through no fault or choice of either those who have more or those who have less.

[11] [See Temkin, "Equality, Priority, and the Levelling-Down Objection."—Ed.]

[12] [See Christiano, "A Foundation for Egalitarianism," and Persson, "Why Levelling Down Could Be Worse."—Ed.]

[13] *Weighing Goods*, p. 181.

[14] [See Dworkin's "Equality and the Good Life," in his *Sovereign Virtue*.—Ed.]

[15] [See Frankfurt, "Equality as a Moral Ideal"; Crisp, "Egalitarianism and Compassion"; Raz, *The Morality of Freedom*, chapter 9; and Casal, "Why Sufficiency Is Not Enough."—Ed.]

(2) The implementation of principles of justice should lead to a morally attractive society.
(3) The implementation of the principle formulated in (1) would lead to a morally repugnant society.

Elizabeth Anderson rejects (1).[16] Cohen rejects (2).[17] *Perhaps* Richard Arneson rejects (3)—at the time of composition of this text, I haven't yet had the opportunity to check that out.[18]

The basic structure controversy
(1) Justice is the state's business only.
(2) Justice is concerned with the activities that shape people's lives.
(3) Individual choices, in aggregate, extensively shape people's lives.

Cohen and Liam Murphy reject (1). Rawls in effect rejected (3): he did not, at any rate, observe its truth. Andrew Williams rejects (2). (I don't affirm (2) in the writings in which I reject (1)).[19]

Are we obliged to help starving people?

Here are three related inconsistent polyads, which concern helping the starving:

Set A
(1) If a dying stranger is at your door, you have to save her, even if the sacrifice you thereby make is pretty big.
(2) *Either* (a) nearness makes no moral difference, *or* (b) whether I'm obliged to help someone depends on my capacity to help, not on his capacity to communicate with me.
(3) There are millions of dying strangers that you could help.
(4) You have a right to a good life.
(5) As it happens, you are not made like Mother Teresa, and you therefore can't have a good life if you're always helping strangers.

Set B
(1) We are not morally disgusting.
(2) Letting people die is morally disgusting.
(3) We regularly let people die.

[16] [See Anderson, "What Is the Point of Equality?"—Ed.]
[17] [See Section 2 of Chapter 1 of this volume and chapter 7 of *Rescuing Justice and Equality*.—Ed.]
[18] [Arneson reports in private correspondence that he would not reject (3).—Ed.]
[19] [See Cohen, chapter 3 of *Rescuing Justice and Equality*; Murphy, "Institutions and the Demands of Justice"; and Williams, "Incentives, Inequality, and Publicity."—Ed.]

Set C

(1) I think I ought to help the starving more than I do.
(2) If you really think you ought to do something that you don't do, then you feel guilty about that.
(3) I don't feel (particularly) guilty about not helping the starving more than I do.[20]

[20] With thanks to Alan Ryan for excellent criticisms of a forerunner draft.

Chapter Twelve

RESCUING JUSTICE FROM CONSTRUCTIVISM AND EQUALITY FROM THE BASIC STRUCTURE RESTRICTION

THE PRESENT PAPER concatenates excerpts from my book called *Rescuing Justice and Equality*.[1] The first two parts of the paper correspond to the distinct rescues indicated by that book title. Part One pursues the rescue of justice from constructivism. It is about the *identity* of justice. Part Two pursues the rescue of equality from the basic structure restriction. It is about the *scope* of justice. The identity question is at issue in an argument that I present against the Rawlsian identification of justice with the principles that constructivist selectors select. The scope question is at issue in an argument that I present against the Rawlsian restriction of the application of principles of distributive justice to the basic structure of society. The two Rawlsian positions (on identity and on scope) here under criticism are, as I shall explain, mainly in a very brief Part Three, substantially independent of each other, and so, too, as will be seen, are my arguments against them.

1. Rescuing Justice from Constructivism

In its most general description, constructivism is the view that a principle gains its normative credentials through being the product of a sound selection procedure. But I am not concerned in the present paper with constructivism in its entirely general form. I am concerned with, precisely, the constructivist approach to social justice in particular, which is constructivism, understood as characterized in general terms above, but with two differentiating features. First, social justice constructivism

Reprinted in part from *Rescuing Justice and Equality*, Cambridge, Mass.: Harvard University Press, 2008. By permission of Harvard University Press.

[1] [Roughly two thirds of this paper consists of such excerpts, which were seamlessly incorporated. In order of their appearance in this chapter, the excerpts are from pp. 274–77, 277–79, 282–84, 286, 313–15, 375–76, 8–10, 353, 357–58, and 279 of *Rescuing Justice and Equality*.—Ed.]

is applied to the identification of, in particular, fundamental (or "first")[2] principles of social justice, fundamental principles being ones that are not derived from other principles. Second, it proceeds by putting and answering the question "What rules of governance are to be adopted for our common social life?" Unless otherwise indicated, I shall mean all that by 'constructivism' here.

A leading example of the constructivist procedure, so understood, is John Rawls's use of the original position to determine the nature of justice, and that is the constructivism that I shall have centrally in view. But the broad outline of my critique of Rawlsian constructivism also applies, *mutatis mutandis*, to Scanlonian contractarianism, to Gauthier's contractarianism, and to Ideal Observer theory, where each is recommended as a procedure for identifying what justice, in particular, is.

I argue in what follows that the constructivist approach to social justice mischaracterizes justice *both* because it treats justice as sensitive to *certain sorts of fact and* because it fails to distinguish between justice and other virtues. The two errors reflect the single disfigurement by that constructivism from which I seek to rescue justice, and that is constructivism's identification of principles of justice with the optimal set of principles to live by, all things considered. My objection to that identification is that, simply because they *are* the *all*-things considered best principles to live by, optimal all-things-considered principles are not necessarily the best principles considered from the point of view of justice alone. I argue that the constructivist approach to social justice is, for that particular, and transparently simple, reason, misguided.

Social justice constructivism's misidentification of principles of justice with optimal principles of regulation is dictated by the question that it puts to its privileged selectors of principles. *They* are not asked to say what *justice* is: it is we who ask that question, and the constructivist doctrine is that the answer to *our* question is the answer to the different question that is put to constructivism's specially designed selectors, which is, what rules of social regulation would you choose? My generative criticism of constructivism is that the answer to that question need not, and could not, be the same as the answer to the question: what is justice?

I should acknowledge, here, a distinction among constructivisms that is of the first importance, philosophically, but which is not engaged within my proceedings. In one form of constructivist view, what it *is* for a principle to be valid is that it is the product of some favored constructivist procedure. In a contrasting but still constructivist view, the favored constructivist procedure merely (in some or other way) *makes* the principles it selects valid, but the view does not say that its-having-been-produced-

[2] That is Rawls's word for them.

by-the-favored-procedure is what it *is* for a principle to be valid.[3] The stated distinction is at the pinnacle of metaethics, a pinnacle that my discussion does not reach. My question is whether its being the product of a favored procedure for choosing the general rules for social existence establishes that a principle is one of justice, whether or not those who think so think it because they *also* think that they are describing what is, in a principle, the very property of validity itself, when they lay out what their favored procedure is.

Finally, let me point out, before I proceed, that the question of the primacy of the basic structure as a site of justice is not to the fore in the present critique of constructivism. My critique is of *how* constructivism selects principles of justice, and not, here, of what I conceive to be, and what I shall later argue is, an independent and unjustified restriction on the *scope* of principles of justice that Rawls and the Rawlsians enforce. If constructivists were to allow that the principles of justice that their procedure generates apply to government and citizens alike, if they imposed no restriction to the basic structure of the *scope* of social justice, then they would remain constructivists, and they would remain open to the challenge that I raise in Part One of this paper.

My critique of constructivism rests upon two distinctions. The first is the exclusive but not exhaustive distinction between (a) fundamental normative principles, that is, normative principles that are not derived from *other* normative principles, and (b) principles of regulation or, as I have preferred to say,[4] *rules* of regulation, whether they be those rules that obtain by order of the state or those that emerge within the milder order of social norm formation: income tax rules are state rules of regulation, and rules about what we owe to each other beyond the realm of state force, such as the rules that govern (or misgovern) the battle of the sexes, are nonstate rules of regulation. (The distinction is not exhaustive because there exist derivative normative principles[5] that are not rules of regulation.) We *create*, we *adopt*, rules of regulation, to order our affairs: we adopt them in the light of what we expect the effect of adopting them to be. But we do not in the same sense of 'adopt' adopt our fundamental principles, any more than we adopt our beliefs about matters of fact. (Or, indeed, our sentiments: my denial that we adopt our normative principles does not require a cognitivist view of ethics.)

Our fundamental principles represent our convictions. They are not things that we *decide* to have and that we consequently work to install

[3] Scanlon draws the stated distinction at p. 391, n. 21, of *What We Owe to Each Other*, and classifies his own theory as one that says "what it *is* for an act to be wrong" (emphasis added).

[4] See sections 13, 19, and 20 of chapter 6 of *Rescuing Justice and Equality*.

[5] Some fact-insensitive and some not.

or instill and sustain; we do not proceed with them as we do with rules of regulation. We do not decide what to believe, whether about fact or about value and principle, in the light of what we expect the effect of believing it to be. The adoption of rules of regulation is a practical task: the formation of conviction and attitude is not. It is our principled convictions that justify what we do, and that includes the doing that is adopting rules of regulation.

The question, "What are the rules of regulation that govern society?" is a sociological question, whereas the question, "What rules of regulation ought to govern society?" is a philosophical question, or, if you prefer, a question in political theory, because the answer to that second question depends strongly on general social facts. The question "What is justice?" is a philosophical question, and there is no coherent question of the form "What ought justice, or the principles of justice, to be?" The incoherence of that question reflects the status of justice as something that transcends rules of regulation.[6]

In further illustration of the confusion of levels that is to be avoided between fundamental principles and rules of regulation, consider an analogous, and, indeed, closely connected, possible confusion regarding rights. Some doctors who are educated at state expense take their services abroad. We may deplore that, but, on grounds of freedom, we may be loath to restrict their ability to do so. And we may grant that freedom consistently with thinking that the doctors behave unfairly and unjustly when they do what we believe they should be granted the freedom to do. But, and this is my key point here, we need not think that the doctors we educate should be free to go abroad *because* they have a *right* to go abroad. What we rather think is that they *should* have a right to go abroad *because* they should be free to go abroad. But the rights that doctors, or anybody else, *should have* are, transparently, not (necessarily) rights that they (just) have. The first are legal rights, the second not. The example shows that we cannot determine what rights people have, in the fundamental nonlegal sense, on the basis of what legal rights they *should* have. Deriving the content of justice from that of the optimal rules of regulation is, similarly, traveling in the wrong direction.

Let me now add to the distinction between fundamental principles and rules of regulation a simpler distinction, between justice and other values, and, therefore, between (c) principles that express or serve the value of justice and (d) principles that express or serve other values, such as human welfare, or human self-realization, or the promotion of knowledge. (In the senses that I intend here of the forthcoming emphasized

[6] Its incoherence also explains why I consider Andrew Williams's concepts of "constraints on" and "desiderata of" justice to be incoherent: see section 7 of chapter 8 of *Rescuing Justice and Equality*.

words, fundamental principles *express* values and rules of regulation *serve* them, by serving the principles that express them.)

Now, Rawlsians believe that the correct answer to the question, what is justice, is identical to the answer that specially designed choosers, the denizens of the Rawlsian original position, would give to the question "What general rules of regulation for society would you choose, in your particular condition of knowledge and ignorance?" Their answer to *that* question is supposed to give us the fundamental principles of justice. But in thus identifying justice with rules of regulation, Rawlsians breach *both* of the distinctions that were drawn above.

The present charge is not a criticism of the particular device, that is, the original position, that Rawls employs to *answer* the question, namely, what rules should we choose, that the denizens of the original position answer. Mine is not a criticism of the original position device *as* a device for answering *that* question. Instead, I protest against the identification of the answer to *that* question with the answer to the question "What is justice"? The said identification represents a double conflation, of fundamental principles with rules of regulation, and of principles of justice whether they be fundamental ones that express justice, or rules of regulation that serve to realize justice (as much as is possible and reasonable), with principles, whether, again, they be fundamental ones, or rules of regulation, that respectively express or serve other values. The upshot is a misidentification of fundamental principles of justice with optimal principles of regulation quite generally.

The two criticisms that I make of the Rawlsian procedure can be presented within a simple two-by-two matrix:

	(a) Fundamental principles	(b) Rules of regulation
(c) Justice	(1) Fundamental principles of justice	(2) that serves justice in particular
(d) Values in general	(3) Fundamental principles generally	(4) that serve fundamental principles generally

The effect of the original position procedure is to identify (1) and (4), and thereby to locate justice both in the wrong column and in the wrong row.[7]

[7]Editor's note: As Cohen explained in a draft of the material that constitutes this and the previous chapter, his questions (i)–(iii) on p. 227 of Chapter 11 of this volume relate as follows to the distinctions between (a), (b), (c), and (d) drawn in this matrix immediately above:

I argued in an article of 2003 called "Facts and Principles" that fundamental principles, principles, that is, which are not derived from other principles, do not rest on factual grounds. But I have not appealed to that premise in the foregoing presentation. The charge that justice cannot be identified with optimal rules of regulation does not require the claim that justice is wholly fact-insensitive: justice might, for all that the stated charge is sound, still depend (as I elsewhere argue that it does not) on the character of basic facts of human nature. So I have not here asked you to agree with my strong view, demonstrable though it is, that no facts control fundamental principles, but only with the weaker and overwhelmingly intuitive claim, that the sorts of facts about practicality and feasibility that control the content of sound rules of regulation do not affect the content of justice itself. The point will be illustrated later with respect to a property tax example.

• • •

Let me now summarize the foregoing critique of constructivism.

On the constructivist view of justice, fundamental principles of justice are the outcome of an idealized legislative procedure, whose task is to elect principles that will regulate our common life. In Rawls's version of constructivism, the legislators, the denizens of the original position, are prospective real-world citizens who are ignorant of how they in particular would fare under various candidate principles. In a Scanlonian version of constructivism about justice, the legislators are motivated to live by principles that no one could reasonably reject. But however the different versions of constructivist theories of social justice differ, whether in the nature of the selection procedure that they mandate, or in the principles that are the output of that procedure, they all assign to principles of justice the same *role*. That role is determined by the fact that constructivism's legislators are asked to elect *principles that will regulate their common life*: the principles they arrive at are said to qualify as principles of *justice* because of the special conditions of motivation and information under which principles that are to serve the role of regulating their common life are adopted.

The (a)/(b) distinction generalizes the (i) part of the (i)/(iii) distinction and provides an instantiation of the (iii) part of the (i)/(ii) distinction. (a) generalizes (i) beyond mere justice to all fundamental principles and (b) instantiates the (iii) question, which is what social states of affairs ought to be brought about: rules of regulation are instances of social states of affairs. And the (c)/(d) distinction is related to the original distinctions in that among the reasons why the (i) question is different from the (ii) and (iii) questions is that justice is not the only value to consider when we confront the (ii) and (iii) questions.

But, and here I restate the general ground of my disagreement with the constructivist metatheory, in any enterprise whose purpose is to select the principles that I have called "rules of regulation," *attention must be paid, either expressly or in effect, to considerations that do not affect the content of justice itself*: while justice (whatever it may be: the present point holds independently of who is right in disagreements about the *content* of justice) must of course influence the selection of regulating principles, factual contingencies that determine how justice is to be applied, or that make justice infeasible, *and* values and principles that call for a compromise with justice, also have a role to play in generating the principles that regulate social life, and legislators, whether flesh-and-blood or hypothetical, will go astray unless they are influenced, one way or another (that is directly, or by virtue of the structure of the constructivist device),[8] by those further considerations. It follows that any procedure that generates the right set of principles to regulate society fails thereby to identify a set of fundamental principles of justice, by virtue of its very success in the former, distinct, exercise. The influence of other values means that the principles in the output of the procedure are not principles of *justice*, and the influence of the factual contingencies means that they are not *fundamental* principles of anything.

The relevant nonjustice considerations do indeed affect the outcome of typically favored constructivist procedures. My complaint is not at all that constructivism fails to take them into account, but precisely that it *does* take them into account, inappropriately, when purporting to identify what justice is. For the influence of alien factors on the output of the constructivist procedure means that what it produces is not fundamental justice, and is, sometimes, not justice at all. Given its aspiration to produce fundamental principles of justice, constructivism sets its legislators the wrong task, although the precise character, and the size, of the discrepancy between fundamental justice and the output of a constructivist

[8] The denizens of Rawls's original position do not, of course, expressly distinguish between considerations of justice and other considerations. They simply choose whatever principle that, given their particular combination of knowledge and ignorance, they see (not as serving justice but) as serving their interests. But in order that they choose principles of regulation well, their choice must in *some* manner reflect both justice and nonjustice considerations.

In partly parallel fashion, the rules of criminal justice, which govern judgments of innocence and guilt, must take into account considerations other than what innocence and guilt *are*, and therefore cannot tell us what innocence and guilt are: they are, on the contrary, fashioned against the background of an antecedent understanding of what guilt and innocence are. See, further, the discussion of loyalty in section 7 of chapter 8 of *Rescuing Justice and Equality*.

procedure will, of course, vary across constructivism's variants. That it sets its idealized legislators the wrong task is my principal—and generative—complaint against constructivism, as a metatheory of fundamental justice.

If I am right that constructivists miscast fundamental principles of justice in the role of principles of social regulation, what, I may be asked, *is* the (contrasting and) proper role of fundamental principles of justice? The answer is that they have no proprietary role, apart from the obvious role of spelling out what justice is. Not everything in this world, not even every kind of principle, has the character that it does because of some role that it fulfills.[9]

Let me now make a point about placing justice in the wrong row of the matrix. If an institution is capable of more than one virtue, then you may properly have regard to each of the virtues of which it is capable in designing it. But the answer to the question, what is the right design of the institution?, could not, therefore, by itself, tell you the content in general of any one of the virtues, or even the particular distinctive contribution that that virtue makes to the design. You have to understand the content of any given virtue independently of knowing what the rules of the design are in order to identify the subset of rules that reflect *that* particular virtue.[10] And the point holds for the virtue of justice even if justice is, as I personally do not think it is,[11] the first virtue of social institutions, in the sense that Rawls said that it is. For that would not mean that justice is the *only* virtue that would be manifest in an acceptable design. Whether or not justice is the first virtue of institutions, they have, or lack, other virtues, too, and constructivist devices, whether or not they are capable of getting right all the principles that all the virtues of institutions require, cannot tell us which principles are ones of justice and which not. To discriminate principles of justice within the set of constructively selected principles, we need a contentful conception of justice that isn't constructed.[12]

[9] See, further, p. 267 of chapter 6 of *Rescuing Justice and Equality*.

[10] Note, further, that no particular subset need reflect exclusively any particular virtue, as opposed to the resultant of balancing several competing virtues.

[11] See section 4 of chapter 7 of *Rescuing Justice and Equality*.

[12] Rawls *in effect* recognizes the truth of what I say here when he writes as follows:

> A conception of social justice, then, is to be regarded as providing in the first instance a standard whereby the distributive aspects of the basic structure of society are to be assessed. This standard, however, is not to be confused with the principles defining the other virtues, for the basic structure, and social arrangements generally, may be efficient or inefficient, liberal or illiberal, and many other things as well as just or unjust. A complete conception defining principles for all the virtues of the basic structure, together with their respective weights when they conflict, is more than a conception

Let me now illustrate the distinction between fundamental principles of justice and rules of regulation. "Council tax," a British local property tax, works like this. Properties are divided into seven bands, according to their estimated market value. The tax rate varies from municipality to municipality, but, in any municipality, there are seven levels of tax, corresponding to the seven market value bands.

Council tax bands illustrate the proper influence of the nonjustice considerations of feasibility and Pareto optimality on rules of regulation. The bands are justified by a principle of justice that says that the broadest backs should bear the greatest burdens: so, the more valuable your dwelling is, the more tax you should pay. But the bands ensure that same-band people whose properties are of different value pay the same tax, and so the very principle of justice that inspires the banding scheme *also* condemns it of an *in*justice, because, for example, across a £90,000–99,999 band, the £90,000 person pays the same tax as the £99,999 person. Yet, although that is a flaw in the scheme from the point of view of the very principle of justice that inspires it, that flaw, from the point of view of justice, does not condemn the scheme *as* a rule of regulation. If Mr. 90,000 were to complain about the injustice of his paying as much as Mr. 99,999, the right thing to say to him would be that the only way to eliminate the injustice would be by designing a more fine-grained scheme which would impose so much extra administrative cost that everyone, including Mr. 90,000, would lose.[13]

I say that it is the very *concept* of justice that tells us that justice is not fully realized by a rule which embodies a step function of the sort that the council tax employs. You don't have to accept the principle that the broadest backs should bear the greatest burden to see that a step-functional rule of regulation like the council tax rule could not fully realize a principle of justice.

---

of justice; it is a social ideal. The principles of justice are but a part, though perhaps the most important part, of such a conception. (*A Theory of Justice*, rev. ed., pp. 8–9)

Rawls fails to see that justice cannot be *both* one virtue among several of institutions *and* the answer to the question the denizens of the original position answer, which is: how should institutions be organized? So, for example, those denizens are unquestionably moved by considerations of efficiency, but efficiency is contrasted with justice in the above passage. (It is independently curious that the value of being liberal is contrasted here with justice, since the First Principle of justice seems to confer what liberals require.)

[13] The very concept of the *precise* value of a piece of property is, moreover, obscure, unlike the concept of what it will *actually* command on the market, which is not quite the same thing. And that complicates the practical problem of identifying it. (By itself, without the practicality point, the conceptual point cuts no ice with respect to contrasting fundamental principles and rules of regulation. But it does so indirectly, by enriching the practicality problem.)

Someone has objected that, in those claims about property taxation, I am contentiously supposing that justice is a precisely specifiable relation (between, in this case, tax and wealth), whereas it is in fact only a rough relation. According to the objector, justice says that tax should correspond merely *roughly* to wealth: within an extreme form of the objection, it might be said to suffice for justice that tax be merely weakly monotonic with respect to wealth (which is to say that there is no injustice as long as wealthier folk don't pay less than *less* wealthy folk). The objector claims that justice *itself* can say no more than that about this sort of taxation: the rest is a matter of practical detail. Inspired by justice, we decide to adopt *some* such scheme, but we leave the domain of justice behind, and therefore institute no injustice, when we work out the practical details.

I have three responses to this objection. First, that while we can maybe just about tolerate the thought that it is not unjust, from the "broadest back" point of view, that Mr. 90,000 pays the *same* as Mr. 99,999, it is much harder to accept that such justice smiles on the circumstance that Mr. 90,000 pays significantly more than Mr. 89,999 does. More generally, the strongest objection to the property taxation scheme from the point of view of the justice that it is intended to deliver is not to the spread within the band, a spread that such justice might well be thought to permit, but to the step-functional character of workable bands.

Second, consider how the proposed supposedly "postjustice" purely practical discussion of exactly what divisions we should have would go. Suppose someone says that there should be twenty-five bands. The reply will be: that would be impracticable. But suppose someone says: let's have two. The objection could not now be that *that* would be impracticable: two bands are more practicable than any larger number of bands. So the objection to the two-bands proposal would be . . . what? What conceivably other than: that two bands would be *too* unjust? So the idea that justice, being rough, is left behind when we discuss how *many* rungs we should have is false.

Third, suppose, perhaps impossibly, that a supercomputer could calculate, cheaply, all property values with precision (within the limits of the conceptual barrier that was explained in n. 13). The function from dwelling price to property tax would then approximate to a straight line. Who could deny that the distribution of tax burden would then be *more* just than the distribution that we are actually able to achieve?

I conclude that, as I said, the example shows that rules of regulation can run counter to the very principle of justice by which they are inspired, because of the legitimate influence on the formation of rules of regulation of considerations other than justice, such as, in the present case, efficiency.

2. Rescuing Equality from the Basic Structure Objection

I said earlier that my case against constructivism is neutral with respect to the question whether the basic structure of society is the sole site at which justice applies. Whether or not that restriction on the *scope* of principles of justice is sound, their *derivation* by constructivist means is flawed for the two reasons that I have labored. Let us now pass from the question what justice is to the question of its *scope*: is Rawls right to restrict its purview to the basic structure of society?

The basic structure restriction is pressed against a train of argument that I develop in challenge to the Rawlsian claim that the difference principle justifies unequalizing incentive payments to productive people, since the surplus production that those incentives induce is necessary to render the worst off as well off as they can be made to be. My objection to that justificatory claim does not challenge the difference principle itself (objections to which compose chapter 4 of *Rescuing Justice and Equality*), but, rather, the credentials of the incentives argument *as* an application of the difference principle. I claim that, properly understood, the difference principle does not justify unequalizing incentives.

My challenge to that supposed application of the principle asks *why* the inequality in question should be thought *necessary* to benefit the worst off. And the answer has to be that, if the inequality is indeed necessary, then it's necessary because and only because productive people would be unwilling to be as productive as they are if they did not prosper better than others do. That's pretty obvious, but it has two important consequences.

The first thing that follows is that the inequality isn't *really* or strictly necessary to make the worst off better off: it is not necessary independently of human will—it is necessary only because and insofar as the productive are unwilling to act otherwise: it is *their choices* that *make* the inequality necessary. But how could *the better off* justify the inequality by saying that it is *necessary*, when they themselves *make* it necessary? If I make it necessary for you to pay the toll to go through the gate, and there is good reason for you to go through the gate, and you ask me to justify the toll, can I say: well, the toll is necessary for you to be able to go through the gate? My reply presents an offer that you would be unwise to refuse, but it does not justify the demand that I was asked to justify.

And the second thing that follows from the fact that the inequality is necessary only because productive people would be unwilling to be as productive as they are without it is that the productive people act as they do only because they *themselves* reject the principle that an inequality is justified only if it benefits the worst off. They couldn't act as they do if they *themselves* accepted the difference principle, and acted in conformity with the conception of justice that it states. So the incentive justification of inequality works only in a society which by Rawlsian criteria is unjust because not everybody in it observes the right principle of justice. How, then, could the result be justice?

It follows from my case against the Rawlsian endorsement of incentives that a full implementation of the difference principle requires it to be observed not only by the state but also by citizens at large: potential high earners must forbear from seizing the advantages that their bargaining power puts within their reach and that the state cannot efficiently prevent them from seizing. It follows, in a word, that a full implementation of the difference principle requires the presence across society of an *ethos* of egalitarian justice, a set of attitudes and dispositions whose effect is to assign a certain priority to the interests of the worst off people in society. I'll explain why I say (only) a *certain* priority a little later.

Now, the basic structure objection to my position on incentives says that principles of justice apply to the basic structure of society alone, and not to the choices of citizens *within that structure*. Because they endorse the difference principle, conscientious citizens comply with the rules of the structure, but, so the objection to my position runs, they are not only free as a matter of fact but also *morally* free, and free as far as justice is concerned, to choose as they wish within those rules. It is only public decisions, the decisions of the state and of institutions allied to it, which are up for assessment at the bar of justice, and not the decisions, within the law, of agents acting in their private capacity.

I do not claim, in response, on absolutely general grounds, that people *must* have the same obligations as states, and that the difference principle must *therefore* apply to individual choice. I do not say, with Liam Murphy, that "all fundamental normative principles that apply to the design of institutions apply also to the conduct of people."[14] I eschew that Murphyan premise because there are plenty of cases where the point of a set of rules should *not* be directly pursued by those who operate within them, even when they themselves endorse the rules *because* of that point. As I have said elsewhere, it is not "*in general* true that the point of the rules [that govern] an activity must be aimed at when agents pursue that activity in good faith. Every competitive sport represents a counterexample to that generalization."[15] And even if Murphy's position is too sophisticated to be falsified by that simple counterexample, the example nevertheless suffices to show that one cannot require that citizens apply the difference principle in their daily lives on absolutely *general* grounds.

[14] "Institutions and the Demands of Justice," p. 251.

[15] *If You're an Egalitarian*, p. 128.

Without, then, embracing Murphy, who is a hedgehog, I simply ask, in my contrastingly foxlike way,[16] *why* the difference principle should *not* apply to individuals, and I argue against three reasons that are given in answer to that question, which we can call the impact reason, the moral division of labor reason, and the publicity reason.

The chief reason for the basic structure restriction that is offered in Rawls's *A Theory of Justice* is that the impact of the basic structure on our lives is profound and present from the start. But that is a feeble argument for restricting the purview of justice to the basic structure, because it is certainly not in *general* true that coercive structure has more impact than social ethos on how much inequality there will be. Ethos has a huge impact, on, for example, how *progressive* taxation can safely be, without becoming counterproductive.

Suppose that a country called "Swedeland" once had a strong welfare state that greatly benefited the worst off, but that the Swedeland state taxed its financially more successful people at rates against which the upper and middle classes in time rebelled, through various forms of literal and "internal" emigration, to the detriment, of, principally, the worst off, as tax revenue, and, therefore, the welfare state, sagged. Some think that that story is true of Swed*en*, but I say "Swede*land*" to cater for possible dissidence on that score. Whether or not the story is true of some actual state, it is not only coherent but credible, and its credibility suffices to demonstrate the extreme importance of the presence or the absence of the ethos for which I contend.

A second reason that may be derived from *A Theory of Justice* for resisting the extension of the difference principle into the personal domain pleads the propriety of a moral division of labor, under which the state sees to justice, and the individual, having herself willingly seen to justice insofar as the state requires her to do so, sees, then, to the imperatives and values of her own personal life. That moral division of labor is justified, so it is thought, by the presence in morality of two standpoints, an impersonal standpoint on the one hand, to which the state responds, and a personal standpoint on the other, to which the individual, other than in her capacity as a law-abiding citizen, may rightly be dedicated. Those who in this fashion criticize my extension of the reach of distributive justice into personal choice might be disposed to cite on behalf of their view the pregnant observation by Thomas Nagel that "Institutions," such as the state, "unlike individuals, don't have their own lives to lead."[17]

[16] Cf. Berlin, *The Hedgehog and the Fox*.

[17] *Equality and Partiality*, p. 59. Typical of many, Julius ("Basic Structure and the Value of Equality," p. 327) describes the stated position as the "Rawls/Nagel ideal of a division of labor."

I accept both the thesis of the duality of standpoints, personal and impersonal, that animates this objection, and also Nagel's point that the state contrasts with individuals in not having its own life to lead. But I reject the conclusion that impersonal justice is a matter for the state only, a conclusion that neither Nagel himself nor Rawls actually draws.

Chapters 6 and 9 of Nagel's *Equality and Partiality* articulate a more nuanced view of the matter under inspection than the one described above, but it is not relevant, here, to go into the Nagel details. What matters here is that the view described above is not that of Rawls: so much is evident from Rawls's assignment to individuals of a set of "natural duties," duties, that is, that lie on individuals rather than on the state, and that include the duties to respect others, to uphold and foster just institutions, to do a great good when the cost of doing so is not excessive, and so forth. These Rawlsian duties respond to utterances of the impersonal standpoint, but they apply at the heart of personal life: they are, expressly, principles for individuals rather than for institutions. So Rawls can affirm at most a *reduced* version of the moral division of labor thesis, one that restricts it to the domain of distributive justice: and in *this* domain Rawls *indeed* divides the task of the state, which is to set the just framework, from the nontask of the individual, which is to do as she pleases within that framework. The real opposition between Rawls and me, on the present issue, is not, therefore, whether the impersonal standpoint reaches personal decision but whether the demands of distributive justice in particular do so. And while it is quite consistent for Rawls to think both that *they* do not but that other deliverances of the impersonal standpoint do, the Rawlsian position about distributive justice cannot be *based* on a general bar to impersonal justice entering individual decision: it diminishes the plausibility of the division of labor thesis with respect to distributive justice in particular that it cannot be said to reflect something more general.

The profound truth that there exist Nagel's two standpoints, and the further truth that the state, unlike individuals, has no life of its own to lead, do not justify a moral division of labor between a justice-seeking state and justice-indifferent (save insofar as they are willingly obedient citizens) individuals. The Nagelian premises provide no warrant for the asserted division of labor, nor, therefore, for extruding the demands of impersonal justice from personal choice.

We can, in fact, distinguish three possible views, with respect to who must see to distributive justice in particular, that are consistent with the Nagelian premises of the argument, each of which contradicts the view, often misattributed to me, that the individual must be as dedicated to such justice as the state is. There is, first, the Rawlsian view that distributive justice is a task for the state alone. A second view would say that the individual must show some regard to what the state is fully dedicated to in this domain. Finally, there is my own view, which is that both the state, with no life of its own, and the individual, who is indeed thus endowed, must, in appropriately different fashions, show regard in economic matters both to impersonal justice and to the legitimate demands of the individual.

To elaborate. There are many forms of motivation along the continuum between unrestrained market maximizing at one end and full self-sacrificing restraint in favor of the worst off on the other. The first extreme is permitted by Rawls (and I regard that as absurd), but the second extreme isn't required by me. Requiring the second extreme is, in my view, excluded by a legitimate personal prerogative. The prerogative grants each person the right to be something other than an engine for the welfare of other people: we are not nothing but slaves to social justice. But the individual who affirms the difference principle must have some regard to it in her economic choices, whatever regard, that is, which starts where her personal prerogative stops.

The final argument for exempting individual choice from the writ of distributive justice to be reviewed today is due to the Welsh philosopher Andrew Williams. According to Williams, principles of social justice are principles that we fulfill collectively: a given individual person is not obliged to observe them unless others are doing so too. Accordingly, the individual cannot be expected to observe them, she cannot be *obliged* to observe them, unless she can be *assured* that others, too, are observing them. But she cannot be assured of that unless she can *tell* whether others are observing them, and she cannot tell whether others are appropriately observant unless the principle in question issues precise and unambiguous instructions. But the egalitarian ethos, properly tempered by a personal prerogative, is, as I would amply concede, vague and general in its directive, and not at all precise. It requires people to have appropriate regard to the worst off in their economic decisions, but within the limits of a reasonable personal prerogative. And that prescription, Williams urges, is too vague to count as a demand of justice. The implications of the difference principle for personal choice are too vague, partly because it is vague where the line is to be drawn that acknowledges our personal prerogative, and partly because it is unclear what we should do, in the service of the difference principle, beyond that line.

The Williams argument has four premises:

(1) Obligations of social justice are collective.
(2) You are obliged to fulfill a collective obligation only if you can be assured that others, too, will comply with it.
(3) You can be assured that others are complying with an obligation only if you know precisely what it means to comply with

that obligation, so that you can check whether others are indeed complying with it.

(4) You cannot know precisely what would fulfill the obligations of an egalitarian ethos.

∴ (5) The egalitarian ethos is not required by justice.

I argue against each of Williams's four premises in chapter 7 of *Rescuing Justice and Equality*, but I shall restrict myself, in the present paper, to some remarks about the third premise of the argument.

Contrary to that third premise, we *can* know that good faith effort on behalf of a principle obtains, broadly, in a society even when people's obligations under that principle are *not* precisely defined. During the Second World War in Britain, a social ethos induced people to sacrifice personal interests for the sake of the war effort, and everyone was expected, as a matter of justice, to "do his bit," to shoulder his just share. But no one could have stated precisely what amount of sacrifice that injunction required, and it is true, therefore, that, with respect to many people, one couldn't tell, and, with respect to some, they couldn't even themselves tell, whether they were sacrificing on the required scale. There are too many details in each person's life that affect what the required sacrifice should be: Max has a bad back, Sally has a difficult child, George has just inherited £20,000, etc. "Yes, Jack goes out only once a week, not, like most us, twice, on guard duty, but then Jack has to take care of his mother." But "the extent to which individuals conform[ed] to"[18] the requirements of sacrifice could certainly be known, in rough-and-ready terms. The sacrifice ethos *was* amenable to sufficient sub-Williamsian rough-and-ready public checkability for social assurance, and "do your bit," despite its vagueness, was understood and applied as a principle of justice. It would have been crazy to have asked for it to be carefully defined, but it would also be crazy to deny that "do your bit" performed a task of social regulation, in the interest of justice. And all of that can be said, *mutatis mutandis*, about the egalitarian ethos that I claim to be required for justice.

I would add that Williams's views of this matter is demonstrably at variance with that of Rawls himself. For Rawls lays duties on individuals whose characterization is vague in the extreme. So, for example, the Rawlsian "duty of justice" "requires us to support and to comply with just institutions that exist and apply to us. It also constrains us to further just arrangements not yet established, at least when this can be done *without too much cost to ourselves*."[19] Rawls does not say how much cost is too much, and Aristotle and I don't think he has to. But Williams,

[18] [This is a quotation from Williams, "Incentives, Inequality, and Publicity," p. 233.—Ed.]

[19] *A Theory of Justice*, p. 115 (rev. ed., p. 99), emphases added.

who purports to be Rawls's champion, must tell us why the duty of justice, with its reference to the vague "without too much cost to ourselves," is not, despite its vagueness, defeated by a publicity constraint, when a duty to forgo economic benefit "without too much cost to ourselves," is, according to Williams, defeated by that same constraint.

Or consider the "natural duty to bring about a great good." Although we are under that duty if we can discharge it "relatively easily, we are released from [it] when *the cost to ourselves is considerable.*"[20] But what constitutes a "considerable" cost, and how can we know how considerable the cost is that someone would have to incur to discharge the duty? The Williams questions apply as much here as they do to the egalitarian ethos. And I say that they have no bite in either case. Speaking of the natural duties in general, Rawls allows that "their definition and systematic arrangement are untidy"[21] but he does not therefore set them aside. I propose the same conceptually and epistemically relaxed attitude to the claims of egalitarian duty in everyday life.

3. Rescuing Justice and Rescuing Equality

My attempt to rescue equality from the basic structure restriction is part of a wider campaign in defense of the claim that, very roughly speaking, equality constitutes distributive justice. I want to indicate, in closing, how my case against constructivism's mismanagement of the concept of justice helps to sustain that egalitarian campaign. It does so because each of the two errors in the Rawlsian identification of principles of justice with optimal rules of regulation induces us to disidentify justice and equality. The first error, the placing of justice in the wrong column of the matrix (see p. 240), induces that disidentification because difficulties of obtaining relevant information and other practical problems make equality an infeasible policy goal: one can only approach it, but that is not a reason for someone of an initially egalitarian persuasion to identify justice with whatever workable rule comes closest to equality, as opposed to with what she is trying to approach, that is, equality itself. And the second error, the placing of justice in the wrong row, introduces principles other than that of justice which may rightly compete with equality in various contexts. Accordingly, the rescue of the *concept* of justice serves the end of rescuing an egalitarian view of the *content* of distributive justice.

Although the two rescues are in that way connected, it remains true that, as I said on p. 238 above, the constructivism issue and the basic

[20] Ibid., p. 117 (rev. ed., p. 100), emphases added.

[21] Ibid., p. 339 (rev. ed., p. 298).

structure restriction issue are substantially independent of each other. You can be a constructivist without imposing the basic structure restriction on the scope of principles of justice, and you can impose that restriction without being a constructivist. Constructivism divorces justice from equality by conflating justice with other values, but that conflation supports no basic structure restriction on the scope of justice. Constructivism also divorces justice from equality by conflating questions about justice with questions about what sorts of rules can and cannot be implemented. That second antiegalitarian element in constructivism would support a basic structure restriction only if the difficulties of obtaining relevant information, of the sort that rules of regulation might be thought to demand, disqualify egalitarian rules from consideration, because, for example, those rules are too *vague* to be implemented. But my reply to Williams shows that vagueness is no bar to implementation. So constructivism doesn't support the basic structure restriction in that way, and perhaps also not in any other way, and, in my view, or conjecture, they are indeed independent threats to equality.

Afterword One

In the wake of the recent financial ructions in the United States, two sets of agents were criticized. Government was criticized for having deregulated, and bankers were criticized for having behaved greedily and riskily in the new, deregulated, environment. And there is, among the various ways of specifying those criticisms, an inverse relationship between how strongly the government is to be criticized and how strongly the bankers are to be criticized. For the government is criticized in two styles: (a) The deregulation was foolish, because *any* normally self-seeking marketer would act in the way the bankers did one it had been introduced. (b) The deregulation was foolish, not because (a) is true, but because it *enabled* the greedy and selfish action on the part of at least some bankers that ensued, and government should have realized that some bankers would be bastards. My "inverse relationship" claim is that the more severe the criticism of the bankers—it is more severe in (b)—the less severe is the criticism of government.

Clearly, in one way or another, both what the government did and what the bankers did substantially produced the result, including the injustice in the result.

You might think that not too much must be made of this, in support of my aim of breaking the barrier between the basic structure and individual choice, since the context was not a Rawlsian one in which government had legislated optimally. But it is not realistic to expect that government could find rules that are so well honed that greed could not pervert their intent. So whatever is optimal in practice requires an ethos, for principle to be properly served. Rawls supposes that the basic structure can be rendered optimal, with respect, for example, to fulfilling the difference principle, but that would probably require intolerably directive directives. Absent same, you *have* to rely on private virtue.

Contrast Rawls's early attitude to people and institutions:

> There is also the temptation to blame objective institutions for the evil in the world. It was an 18th-century idea that bad institutions were one of the great barriers to a fully good mankind. Individuals cannot, however, be separated from institutions. Institutions are merely the objective rules and methods which men set up to deal with social problems. Bad institutions are a sure sign of sinful men. There would be no oppressive institutions were there not greed and malice to reinforce them.[22]

Afterword Two

It has been suggested that the principles that the original position is designed to produce are not rules of regulation but principles for judging rules of regulation. I need not disagree. For any such principles, if defensible, must have regard both to values other than justice and to practical constraints. Accordingly, such principles cannot be ones of justice, nor can they be ones for the assessment of the *justice* of rules of regulation.

[22] Rawls, *A Brief Inquiry into the Meaning of Sin and Faith*, p. 190.

WORKS CITED

Note: Unless otherwise indicated, all above page references in this volume are to the first version listed below of writings that have been reprinted.

Alexander, Larry, and Maimon Schwarzschild. "Liberalism, Neutrality, and Equality of Welfare versus Equality of Resources." *Philosophy and Public Affairs* 16 (1987): 85–110.

Anderson, Elizabeth. "What Is the Point of Equality?" *Ethics* 109 (1999): 287–337.

Arneson, Richard. "Equality and Equal Opportunity for Welfare." *Philosophical Studies* 56 (1989): 77–93.

———. "Liberalism, Distributive Subjectivism, and Equal Opportunity for Welfare." *Philosophy and Public Affairs* 19 (1990): 158–94.

———. "Property Rights in Persons." *Social Philosophy and Policy* 9 (1992): 201–30.

Arrow, Kenneth. "Some Ordinalist-Utilitarian Notes on Rawls' Theory of Justice." In his *Collected Papers*. Vol. 1. Cambridge, Mass.: Harvard University Press, 1983.

Ashcraft, Richard. "Class Conflict and Constitutionalism in J. S. Mill's Thought." In Nancy Rosenblum, ed. *Liberalism and the Moral Life*. Cambridge, Mass.: Harvard University Press, 1989.

Berlin, Isaiah. *The Hedgehog and the Fox*. London: Weidenfeld & Nicolson, 1953.

———. *Four Essays on Liberty*. London: Oxford University Press, 1969.

———. "Political Ideas in the Twentieth Century." In Berlin, *Four Essays on Liberty*.

———. "Two Concepts of Liberty." In Berlin, *Four Essays on Liberty*.

———. *The First and the Last*. London: Granta Books, 1999.

Black, Max. "Inductive Support of Inductive Rules." In Black, *Problems of Analysis*. London: Routledge & Kegan Paul, 1954.

Brenkert, George. "Self-Ownership, Freedom, and Autonomy." *Journal of Ethics* 2 (1998): 27–55.

Broome, John. *Weighing Goods*. Oxford: Blackwell, 1991.

Casal, Paula. "Why Sufficiency Is Not Enough." *Ethics* 117 (2007): 296–326.

Christiano, Thomas. "A Foundation for Egalitarianism." In Nils Holtug and Kasper Lippert-Rasmussen, eds. *Egalitarianism*. Oxford: Oxford University Press, 2007.

Clayton, Matthew. "The Resources of Liberal Equality." *Imprints* 5 (2000): 63–84.

Cohen, G. A. "Robert Nozick and Wilt Chamberlain: How Patterns Preserve Liberty." *Erkenntnis* 11 (1977): 5–23. Reprinted with revisions in Cohen, *Self-Ownership, Freedom, and Equality*.

———. *Karl Marx's Theory of History*. Princeton: Princeton University Press, 1978; revised edition, 2000.

———. "Capitalism, Freedom, and the Proletariat." In Alan Ryan, ed. *The Idea of Freedom*. Oxford: Oxford University Press, 1979. Reprinted in extensively revised form in David Miller, ed. *Liberty*. Oxford: Oxford University Press, 1991; in David Miller, ed. *The Liberty Reader*. Edinburgh: Edinburgh University Press, 2006; and as Chapter 7 of this volume.

———. "Illusions about Private Property and Freedom." In John Mepham and David-Hillel Ruben, eds. *Issues in Marxist Philosophy*. Vol. 4. Brighton: Harvester Press, 1981. Reprinted in Steven Cahn, ed. *Philosophy for the 21st Century: A Comprehensive Reader*. Oxford: Oxford University Press, 2002. Reprinted in part in Chapter 7 of this volume.

———. "The Structure of Proletarian Unfreedom." *Philosophy and Public Affairs* 12 (1983): 3–34. Reprinted with revisions in Cohen, *History, Labour, and Freedom*.

———. *History, Labour, and Freedom*. Oxford: Oxford University Press, 1988.

———. "Are Disadvantaged Workers Who Take Hazardous Jobs Forced to Take Hazardous Jobs?" In Cohen, *History, Labour, and Freedom*.

———. "Are Freedom and Equality Compatible?" In Jon Elster and Karl O. Moene, eds. *Alternatives to Capitalism*. Cambridge: Cambridge University Press, 1989.

———. "On the Currency of Egalitarian Justice." *Ethics* 99 (1989): 906–44. Reprinted as Chapter 1 of this volume.

———. "Equality of What? On Welfare, Goods, and Capabilities." *Recherches Economiques de Louvain* 56 (1990): 357–82. Reprinted in Martha C. Nussbaum and Amartya Sen, eds. *The Quality of Life*. Oxford: Oxford University Press, 1993. Reprinted in part as Chapter 2 of this volume.

———. "Isaiah's Marx and Mine." In Avishai Margalit and Edna Ullmann-Margalit, eds. *Isaiah Berlin: A Celebration*. London: Hogarth Press, 1991.

———. "Incentives, Inequality, and Community." In Grethe B. Peterson, ed. *The Tanner Lectures on Human Values*. Vol. 13. Salt Lake City: University of Utah Press, 1992.

———. "Mind the Gap." *London Review of Books*, Vol. 14, No. 9, May 14, 1992, pp. 15–17. Reprinted in part as Chapter 9 of this volume.

———. "Amartya Sen's Unequal World." *New Left Review*, No. 203, January–February 1994, pp. 117–29. Reprinted in part as Chapter 3 of this volume.

———. "Back to Socialist Basics." *New Left Review*, No. 207, September–October 1994, pp. 3–16. Reprinted in Jane Franklin, ed. *Equality*. London: Institute for Public Policy Research, 1997. Reprinted in part as Chapter 10 of this volume.

———. *Self-Ownership, Freedom, and Equality*. Cambridge: Cambridge University Press, 1995.

———. "Once More into the Breach of Self-Ownership: Reply to Narveson and Brenkert." *Journal of Ethics* 2 (1998): 57–96.

———. "Expensive Tastes and Multiculturalism." In R. Bhargava, A. K. Bagchi, and R. Sudarshan, eds. *Multiculturalism, Liberalism, and Democracy*. New Delhi: Oxford University Press, 1999.

———. *If You're an Egalitarian, How Come You're So Rich?* Cambridge, Mass.: Harvard University Press, 2000.

———. "Freedom and Money." *Revista Argentina de Teoria Juridica* 2 (2001): 1–32. Reprinted as Chapter 8 of this volume.

———. "Why Not Socialism?" In Edward Broadbent, ed. *Democratic Equality.* Toronto: University of Toronto Press, 2001. Reprinted in revised and expanded form as Cohen, *Why Not Socialism?*

———. "Facts and Principles." *Philosophy and Public Affairs* 31 (2003): 211–45. Reprinted with revisions as chapter 6 of Cohen, *Rescuing Justice and Equality.*

———. *Between Marx and Nozick.* Nanjing: Jiangsu People's Publishing House, 2007.

———. *Rescuing Justice and Equality.* Cambridge, Mass.: Harvard University Press, 2008. Reprinted in part as Chapter 12 of this volume.

———. *Why Not Socialism?* Princeton: Princeton University Press, 2009.

Commission on Social Justice. *The Justice Gap.* London: Institute for Public Policy Research, 1993.

———. *Social Justice in a Changing World.* London: Institute for Public Policy Research, 1993.

Crisp, Roger. "Egalitarianism and Compassion." *Ethics* 114 (2003): 119–26.

Daniels, Norman. "Equality of What: Welfare, Resources, or Capabilities?" *Philosophy and Phenomenological Research.* Supplementary volume. 50 (1990): 273–96.

Dworkin, Ronald. "Is There a Right to Pornography?" *Oxford Journal of Legal Studies* 1 (1981): 177–212. Reprinted in Dworkin, *A Matter of Principle.*

———. "What is Equality? Part I: Equality of Welfare." *Philosophy and Public Affairs* 10 (1981): 185–246. Reprinted in Dworkin, *Sovereign Virtue.*

———. "What is Equality? Part II: Equality of Resources." *Philosophy and Public Affairs* 10 (1981): 283–345. Reprinted in Dworkin, *Sovereign Virtue.*

———. *A Matter of Principle.* Oxford: Oxford University Press, 1985.

———. "Liberalism." In Dworkin, *A Matter of Principle.*

———. "Why Liberals Should Care about Equality." In Dworkin, *A Matter of Principle.*

———. *Sovereign Virtue.* Cambridge, Mass.: Harvard University Press, 2000.

———. "Equality and the Good Life." In Dworkin, *Sovereign Virtue.*

———. "Sovereign Virtue Revisited." *Ethics* 113 (2002): 106–43.

Flew, Antony. *A Dictionary of Philosophy.* London: Macmillan, 1979.

Frankfurt, Harry. "Equality as a Moral Ideal." *Ethics* 98 (1987): 21–43. Reprinted in Frankfurt, *The Importance of What We Care About.*

———. *The Importance of What We Care About.* Cambridge: Cambridge University Press, 1988.

Gray, John. "Marxian Freedom, Individual Liberty, and the End of Alienation." In Ellen Frankel Paul et al., eds. *Marxism and Liberalism.* Oxford: Blackwell, 1986.

———. "Against Cohen on Proletarian Unfreedom." In Ellen Frankel Paul et al., eds. *Capitalism.* Oxford: Blackwell, 1989.

Griffin, James. "Modern Utilitarianism." *Revue Internationale de Philosophie* 36 (1982): 331–75.
Hart, H.L.A. "Are There Any Natural Rights?" In Jeremy Waldron, ed. *Theories of Rights*. Oxford: Oxford University Press, 1984.
Hurley, Susan. *Justice, Luck, and Knowledge*. Cambridge, Mass.: Harvard University Press, 2003.
Husami, Ziyad. "Marx on Distributive Justice." *Philosophy and Public Affairs* 8 (1978): 27–64.
Julius, A. J. "Basic Structure and the Value of Equality." *Philosophy and Public Affairs* 31 (2003): 321–55.
Kymlicka, Will. "Subsidizing People's Choices." Subsection of section on Rawls of unpublished Princeton lecture notes on Contemporary Political Philosophy, 1987.
———. *Multicultural Citizenship*. Oxford: Oxford University Press, 1995.
Landesman, Bruce. "Egalitarianism." *Canadian Journal of Philosophy* 13 (1983): 27–56.
Larkin, Marilynn. "Eating Passion Unleashed by Brain Lesions." *Lancet* 349 (1997): 1607.
Lippert-Rasmussen, Kasper. "Arneson on Equality of Opportunity for Welfare." *Journal of Political Philosophy* 7 (1999): 478–87.
———. "Egalitarianism, Option Luck, and Responsibility." *Ethics* 111 (2001): 548–79.
Mackie, J. L. *The Cement of the Universe*. Oxford: Oxford University Press, 1974.
Marx, Karl. *The Grundrisse*. Harmondsworth: Penguin, 1973.
———. *Capital*. Vol. 1. Harmondsworth: Penguin, 1976.
———. *Capital*. Vol. 3. Harmondsworth: Penguin, 1981.
Mill, John Stuart. *Principles of Political Economy*. In John M. Robson, ed. *The Collected Works of John Stuart Mill*. Vol. 2. Toronto: University of Toronto Press, 1965.
———. *Considerations on Representative Government*. In John M. Robson, ed. *The Collected Works of John Stuart Mill*. Vol. 19. Toronto: University of Toronto Press, 1977.
Miller, David. *Principles of Social Justice*. Cambridge, Mass.: Harvard University Press, 1999.
Morrison, Toni. *Beloved*. London: Picador, 1987.
Murphy, Liam. "Institutions and the Demands of Justice." *Philosophy and Public Affairs* 27 (1998): 251–91.
Nagel, Thomas. "Libertarianism without Foundations." In Jeffrey Paul, ed. *Reading Nozick*. Totowa, N.J.: Rowman and Allanheld, 1981.
———. *Equality and Partiality*. New York: Oxford University Press, 1991.
Narveson, Jan. "Libertarianism vs. Marxism: Reflections on G. A. Cohen's *Self-Ownership, Freedom and Equality*." *Journal of Ethics* 2 (1998): 1–26.
Nozick, Robert. "Coercion." In Peter Laslett, W. G. Runciman, and Quentin Skinner, eds. *Philosophy, Politics and Society*. 4th series. Oxford: Blackwell, 1972.
———. *Anarchy, State, and Utopia*. New York: Basic Books, 1974.

———. *The Examined Life*. New York: Simon and Schuster, 1989.
Otsuka, Michael. "Justice and Alienation." Oxford University B.Phil. thesis, 1988.
———. "Luck, Insurance, and Equality." *Ethics* 113 (2002): 40–54.
———. "Equality, Ambition, and Insurance." *Proceedings of the Aristotelian Society*. Supplementary volume. 78 (2004): 151–66.
Parfit, Derek. *Reasons and Persons*. Oxford: Oxford University Press, 1984.
———. *Equality or Priority?* The Lindley Lecture. Department of Philosophy, University of Kansas, 1995.
Persson, Ingmar. "Why Levelling Down Could Be Worse for Prioritarianism Than for Egalitarianism." *Ethical Theory and Moral Practice* 11 (2008): 295–303.
Plekhanov, George. *The Development of the Monist View of History*. Moscow: Foreign Languages Publishing House, 1956.
Pogge, Thomas. *World Poverty and Human Rights*. Cambridge: Polity Press, 2002.
Price, Terry. "Egalitarian Justice, Luck, and the Costs of Chosen Ends." *American Philosophical Quarterly* 36 (1999): 267–78.
Rakowski, Eric. *Equal Justice*. Oxford: Oxford University Press, 1991.
Rawls, John. *A Theory of Justice*. Cambridge, Mass.: Harvard University Press, 1971; revised edition, 1999.
———. "Fairness to Goodness." *Philosophical Review* 84 (1975): 536–54.
———. "A Kantian Conception of Equality." *Cambridge Review* 96 (1975): 94–99.
———. "Social Unity and Primary Goods." In Amartya Sen and Bernard Williams, eds. *Utilitarianism and Beyond*. Cambridge: Cambridge University Press, 1982. Reprinted in Rawls, *Collected Papers*.
———. "Justice as Fairness: Political Not Metaphysical." *Philosophy and Public Affairs* 14 (1985): 223–51.
———. "Citizens' Needs and Primary Goods." Unpublished manuscript, 1986.
———. *Political Liberalism*. New York: Columbia University Press, 1993.
———. *Collected Papers*. Samuel Freeman, ed. Cambridge, Mass.: Harvard University Press, 1999.
———. *A Brief Inquiry into the Meaning of Sin and Faith*. Thomas Nagel, ed. Cambridge, Mass.: Harvard University Press, 2009.
Raz, Joseph. *The Morality of Freedom*. Oxford: Oxford University Press, 1986.
Reeve, Andrew. *Property*. London: Macmillan, 1986.
Scanlon, T. M. "Preference and Urgency." *Journal of Philosophy* 72 (1975): 655–69.
———. "Equality of Resources and Equality of Welfare: A Forced Marriage?" *Ethics* 97 (1986): 111–18.
———. "The Significance of Choice." In Sterling McMurrin, ed. *The Tanner Lectures on Human Values*. Vol. 8. Salt Lake City: University of Utah Press, 1988.
———. "Value, Desire, and the Quality of Life." In Martha C. Nussbaum and Amartya Sen, eds. *The Quality of Life*. Oxford: Oxford University Press, 1993.
———. *What We Owe to Each Other*. Cambridge, Mass.: Harvard University Press, 1998.

Searle, John. *The Construction of Social Reality*. London: Penguin, 1995.
Sen, Amartya. *On Economic Inequality*. Oxford: Oxford University Press, 1973.
———. "Equality of What?" In Sterling McMurrin, ed. *The Tanner Lectures on Human Values*. Vol. 1. Cambridge: Cambridge University Press, 1980.
———. *Choice, Welfare and Measurement*. Oxford: Blackwell 1982.
———. "Liberty as Control: An Appraisal." *Midwest Studies in Philosophy* 7 (1982): 207–21.
———. "The Living Standard." *Oxford Economic Papers*. Supplementary volume. 36 (1984): 74–90.
———. *Resources, Values and Development*. Oxford: Blackwell, 1984.
———. "Development: Which Way Now?" In Sen, *Resources, Values and Development*.
———. "Economics and the Family." In Sen, *Resources, Values and Development*.
———. "Ethical Issues in Income Distribution: National and International." In Sen, *Resources, Values and Development*.
———. "Goods and People." In Sen, *Resources, Values and Development*.
———. "Rights and Capabilities." In Sen, *Resources, Values and Development*.
———. *Commodities and Capabilities*. Amsterdam: North-Holland, 1985.
———. "Well-Being, Agency and Freedom: The Dewey Lectures 1984." *Journal of Philosophy* 82 (1985): 169–221.
———. *The Standard of Living*. Geoffrey Hawthorn, ed. Cambridge: Cambridge University Press, 1987.
———. "Well-Being and Agency." Unpublished manuscript, 1987.
———. "Capability and Well-Being." Unpublished 1988 draft of the paper published in Martha C. Nussbaum and Amartya Sen, eds. *The Quality of Life*. Oxford: Oxford University Press, 1993.
———. *Inequality Reexamined*. Oxford: Oxford University Press, 1992.
Steiner, Hillel. "The Natural Right to Equal Freedom." *Mind* 83 (1974): 194–210.
———. "The Natural Right to the Means of Production." *Philosophical Quarterly* 27 (1977): 41–49.
———. "The Structure of a Set of Compossible Rights." *Journal of Philosophy* 74 (1977): 767–75.
———. *An Essay on Rights*. Oxford: Blackwell, 1994.
Tawney, R. H. *Equality*. London: Allen and Unwin, 1964.
Temkin, Larry. "Inequality." *Philosophy and Public Affairs* 15 (1986): 99–121.
———. *Inequality*. Oxford: Oxford University Press, 1993.
———. "Equality, Priority, and the Levelling-Down Objection." In Matthew Clayton and Andrew Williams, eds. *The Ideal of Equality*. Basingstoke: Palgrave Macmillan, 2002.
Vandenbroucke, Frank. "Responsibility: Rule-Currency." Unpublished manuscript, 1998.
van der Veen, Robert, and Philippe Van Parijs. "Entitlement Theories of Justice: Nozick and Beyond." *Economics and Philosophy* 1 (1985): 69–81.
van Inwagen, Peter. *An Essay on Free Will*. Oxford: Oxford University Press, 1983.

Walzer, Michael. *Spheres of Justice*. New York: Basic Books, 1983.
Williams, Andrew. "Incentives, Inequality, and Publicity." *Philosophy and Public Affairs* 27 (1998): 225–47.
———. "Equality for the Ambitious." *Philosophical Quarterly* 53 (2002): 377–89.
Williams, Bernard. "Forward to Basics." In Jane Franklin, ed. *Equality*. London: Institute for Public Policy Research, 1997.
Wittgenstein, Ludwig. *Philosophical Investigations*. 2nd edition. G.E.M. Anscombe and Rush Rhees, eds. Oxford: Blackwell, 1958.
Wolff, Jonathan. "Freedom, Liberty, and Property." *Critical Review* 11 (1997): 345–57.

INDEX